HOME PLUMBING MADE EASY
AN ILLUSTRATED MANUAL

To my three sons, Steve, Rex, and Blake, who can fix things that I cannot. "To each his own."

HOME PLUMBING MADE EASY

AN ILLUSTRATED MANUAL

JAMES L. KITTLE

Some illustrations by Gary McKinney

TAB BOOKS Inc.

Blue Ridge Summit, PA 17214

Notices

Channellock® Channellock Co.
Laco Self-Cleaning Flux® Lake Chemical Co.
Liquid Wrench®
No-Korode®
Ridgid® Ridge Tool Co.
Teflon®
The Culligan Man® Culligan Co.
Uncopper® Genova Plastics
Wrot® Mueller Brass Co.
Con-aire® Sta-Rite

FIRST EDITION
FIRST PRINTING

Copyright © 1987 by TAB BOOKS Inc.
Printed in the United States of America

Library of Congress Cataloging in Publication Data

Kittle, James L., 1913-
Home plumbing made easy.

Includes index.
1. Plumbing—Amateurs' manuals. I. McKinney,
Gary. II. Title.
TH6124.K55 1987   696'.1   87-1920
ISBN 0-8306-0397-2
ISBN 0-8306-2797-9 (pbk.)

Questions regarding the content of this book should be addressed to:

Reader Inquiry Branch
Editorial Department
TAB BOOKS Inc.
P.O. Box 40
Blue Ridge Summit, PA 17214

Contents

Acknowledgments

The following companies provided illustrations and text for this book. Their cooperation and courtesy are greatly appreciated:

Building Officials & Code Administration International, Inc., Country Club Hills, Illinois.

Genova Company, Davison, Michigan.

Kohler Company, Kohler, Wisconsin.

Macomb County, Michigan Health Department, Mt. Clemens, Michigan.

Mueller Brass Company, Port Huron, Michigan.

Nibco Inc., Elkhart, Indiana.

Plumb Shop, Smith-Winchester, Southfield, Michigan.

Ridge Tool Company, Elyria, Ohio.

Stockham Valves & Fittings, Birmingham, Alabama.

Universal-Rundle, New Castle, Pennsylvania.

U. S. Brass/Wallace Murray Corp. Abilene, Texas.

Watts Regulator, Lawrence, Massachusetts.

Many thanks to Vi Stancell for typing and retyping parts of my manuscript, and correcting my punctuation.

Introduction

Nearly everyone, if they persevere, can work on the plumbing system of a dwelling. Sometimes the work is hard and dirty; often the pipes and fittings are stubborn and cannot be loosened. With the proper tools and a book to guide you, the repair or replacement project can be completed easily.

Specialized tools such as pipe dies, flaring tools, tubing benders, and others might be necessary. Often these tools can be rented. Perhaps the most common tools are already in your workshop, or you might like to buy those you will use again.

This book will try to show you how to do nearly every type of repair, replacement, or extension of your plumbing system. Tools that you will need are listed and their uses described in Chapter 6. Plumbing materials described in Chapter 5 range from iron pipe, to plastic and copper tubing, to soil pipe.

Major projects, such as tapping into the water and sewer mains (lines in the street) and trenching from the street to your dwelling, are described so that you will be familiar with these procedures. The actual work should be done by a plumbing contractor. This is required by the governing body having jurisdiction.

All work inside the dwelling can be done by you. Follow directions in this book and you will find ideas and hints from an "old timer" in the plumbing and pipefitting business. I hope my 40 years plus of experience will help your work go smoother and even be enjoyable.

When you buy tools, buy the best of the major brands. American-made tools *are* the best, and if treated well will last literally forever. For example, my Yankee push drill (the nickel plated tool that all telephone repair persons carry in their tool pouches) is over 50 years old. I am on my third set of drill bits and just replaced the chuck. The original price of perhaps $8 is now $35, but the tool's design has not changed.

It is best to buy the highest quality that you can afford. Some plumbing fixtures can be very elaborate and extremely expensive. These super deluxe fixtures work no better and last no longer than the standard top-quality fixtures, and cost up to three times as much. Always buy fixtures from a reputable place to assure yourself of good quality, and the option of returning the fixture if need be.

Follow all safety rules, work carefully, take your time and use this book as a guide to methods and procedures. You *will* save money and have the satisfaction of a job well done.

Domestic
Water Supplies

Sources of water for domestic use are restricted, generally, to the following: municipal water systems, private wells, and the cistern or "catchment" system.

THE MUNICIPAL SUPPLY SYSTEM

Most cities and villages maintain a constant supply of potable (clean and safe to drink) water for their residents. At present, most small towns and suburban cities buy their water from a large nearby municipality. In this case, the small city will either have installed its own distribution system, or will contract with a large contractor to install such a system.

Large cities such as New York, Chicago, and Detroit each supply whole areas surrounding them. These areas can supply as many as 20 to 30 suburbs.

In addition to supplying water to these satellite cities, the large city accepts the sewage from them. Sewer rates are charged as a percentage of the water rate since sewage flow is not metered. This is possible because larger cities are able to finance such a project. The raw water source in such instances is either a large inland lake or a mountain stream, depending on the area and the proximity of a source.

Charges to each satellite city are determined by reading a master meter at that city's water department distribution station. This is also the method of charging the homeowner for water and sewer service.

Fees are charged for tapping into the water main in the street in front of the homeowner's house. Tapping into the sewer also requires payment of a stiff fee. These fees, of course, help pay for inspectors and—in the case of sewers—sometimes pay for a portion of the cost of extending the lines. These water and sewer lines are usually under the street proper. Sometimes water and gas utility lines are installed in the area between the curb and public sidewalk, which makes the distance to the opposite side of the street greater. Methods are now available to bore holes underneath the pavement or roadway and push these small pipes through, eliminating excavating across the roadway. Nowadays it is usually required that at least the sewer lines be extended beyond the right-of-way so that opening future pavement will not be required. Figure 1-1 shows a partial map of city mains.

Normally there will be a "corporation stop" (water shutoff valve) near the public sidewalk area and a gas shutoff nearby. These are the property of their respective utilities, and are opened and closed using a long-handled wrench which reaches down to the valve at the bottom of a long tube that is topped by a cover.

PRIVATE WELLS

Small rural communities have many dwellings that have their own private wells. This is quite satisfactory until the number of wells drawing on an *acquifer* (an underground vein of water) deplete or lower the water table during long dry spells. If the dry spell lasts too long, there will be many dry wells and homes that have no water. This could also result in the contamination of flowing wells from industrial chemicals and raw sewage, which could cause serious health problems.

Deep wells have a better chance of weathering long dry spells than shallow wells because of the depth and size of their acquifers. Deep wells also tend to have better, purer water than the shallow wells. Wells, especially deep wells, are expensive to drill, build, and maintain. Certain sanitary precautions are necessary to prevent surface water and other liquid contaminants from entering the well.

The equipment used to drill a well system is similar to an oil drilling rig, only smaller. As the drilling progresses a casing is lowered into the hole; this seals the hole from ground water and other contaminants. Additional sections of the well casing are connected to the previous section using couplings. This continues until a satisfactory water supply is located. This well casing will be from 4 to 6 inches in diameter. These submersible, high-speed pumps need to produce pressure rather than suction because they are immersed in water and do not need to "suck" except to get the water inside the pump housing. The pump motor, directly connected to the pump itself is also submerged. It is sealed so that water cannot damage the motor wind-

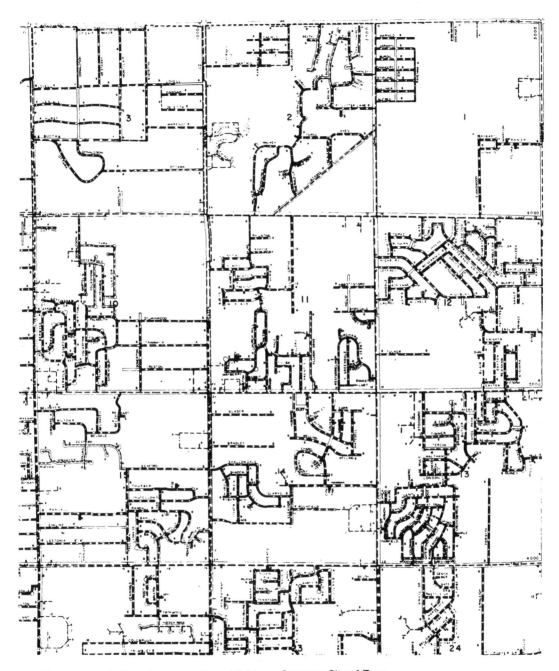

Fig. 1-1. Partial map of city water mains, Troy, Michigan, Courtesy City of Troy.

ings. Complete working well systems can cost up to $2000, depending on the depth and pumping equipment needed.

These systems, properly installed, maintained and operated, function very well. Note that all piping between the well head and the house (the top of the well proper) *must* be protected from freezing. The well head must be accessible at all times because the pump might need to be pulled up for repairs. A hoist will need to be positioned over the well to accomplish this. *Caution:* Do not build your house over the well head.

Figures 1-2 through 1-13 illustrate various types of pumps available for use on private well systems. Tables 1-1 and 1-2 give performance data and ordering information on Sta-Rite brand pumps. Table 1-3 gives composite performance curves for the Series 25EL 25 GPM Goulds Submersible Pump.

Well Pumps

Pumps for use in deep wells are more expensive than shallow well pumps. These pumps are designed to operate under extreme conditions; they must pump to greater heads (heights), and their operation is different.

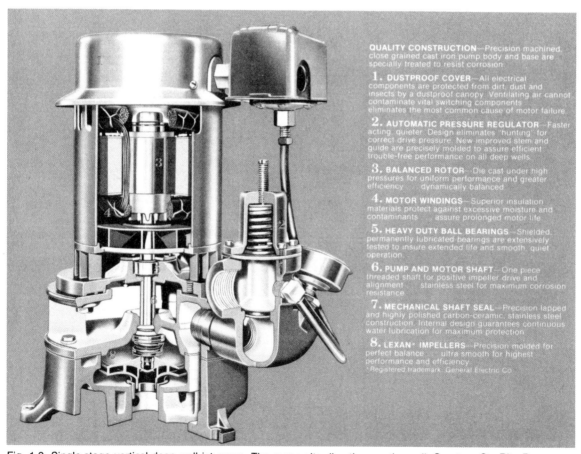

QUALITY CONSTRUCTION—Precision machined, close grained cast iron pump body and base are specially treated to resist corrosion.

1. **DUSTPROOF COVER**—All electrical components are protected from dirt, dust and insects by a dustproof canopy. Ventilating air cannot contaminate vital switching components eliminates the most common cause of motor failure.

2. **AUTOMATIC PRESSURE REGULATOR**—Faster acting, quieter. Design eliminates "hunting" for correct drive pressure. New improved stem and guide are precisely molded to assure efficient trouble-free performance on all deep wells.

3. **BALANCED ROTOR**—Die cast under high pressures for uniform performance and greater efficiency . . . dynamically balanced.

4. **MOTOR WINDINGS**—Superior insulation materials protect against excessive moisture and contaminants . . . assure prolonged motor life.

5. **HEAVY DUTY BALL BEARINGS**—Shielded, permanently lubricated bearings are extensively tested to insure extended life and smooth, quiet operation.

6. **PUMP AND MOTOR SHAFT**—One piece threaded shaft for positive impeller drive and alignment . . . stainless steel for maximum corrosion resistance.

7. **MECHANICAL SHAFT SEAL**—Precision lapped and highly polished carbon-ceramic, stainless steel construction. Internal design guarantees continuous water lubrication for maximum protection.

8. **LEXAN* IMPELLERS**—Precision molded for perfect balance . . . ultra smooth for highest performance and efficiency.
*Registered trademark: General Electric Co.

Fig. 1-2. Single-stage vertical deep well jet pump. The pump sits directly over the well. Courtesy Sta-Rite Pumps.

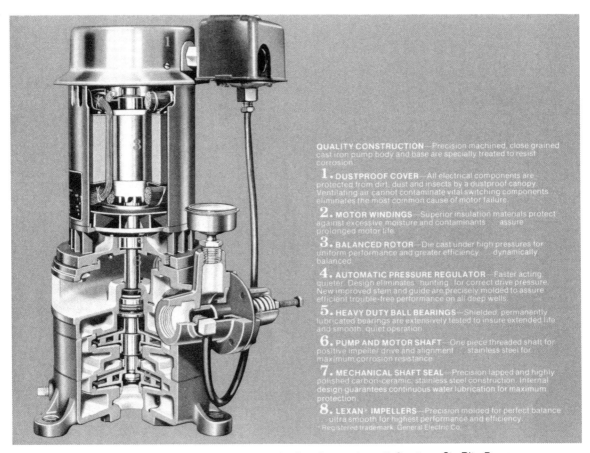

QUALITY CONSTRUCTION—Precision machined, close grained cast iron pump body and base are specially treated to resist corrosion.

1. DUSTPROOF COVER—All electrical components are protected from dirt, dust and insects by a dustproof canopy. Ventilating air cannot contaminate vital switching components eliminates the most common cause of motor failure.

2. MOTOR WINDINGS—Superior insulation materials protect against excessive moisture and contaminants . . . assure prolonged motor life.

3. BALANCED ROTOR—Die cast under high pressures for uniform performance and greater efficiency . . . dynamically balanced.

4. AUTOMATIC PRESSURE REGULATOR—Faster acting, quieter. Design eliminates "hunting" for correct drive pressure. New improved stem and guide are precisely molded to assure efficient trouble-free performance on all deep wells.

5. HEAVY DUTY BALL BEARINGS—Shielded, permanently lubricated bearings are extensively tested to insure extended life and smooth, quiet operation.

6. PUMP AND MOTOR SHAFT—One piece threaded shaft for positive impeller drive and alignment . . . stainless steel for maximum corrosion resistance.

7. MECHANICAL SHAFT SEAL—Precision lapped and highly polished carbon-ceramic, stainless steel construction. Internal design guarantees continuous water lubrication for maximum protection.

8. LEXAN* IMPELLERS—Precision molded for perfect balance . . . ultra smooth for highest performance and efficiency.
* Registered trademark, General Electric Co.

Fig. 1-3. Multi-stage vertical deep well pump. The pump sits directly over the well. Courtesy Sta-Rite Pumps.

To properly select a pump for a well consider:

● The size of the well. Well casings (the pipe extending down to the water level) are various diameters from 3-inch to 6-inch. The 4-inch size is most common. The casing size determines the size and type of pump that will fit into the well casing.

● The level of the water in the well when the pump is running. Wells "draw down" when the pump is running, which makes the effective water level lower than the standing level. If the pump is some distance from the well head and/or at a higher elevation than the wall head, this distance must be added to the draw-down level in order to get the effective water level.

● The pressure at the plumbing fixtures—this is the determining factor, not the pressure at the pump and tank. Many times the house is on higher ground, and has a second or even a third story with plumbing fixtures. Water pressure should be at least 15 pounds per square inch gauge (psig), preferably higher. Common pump pres-

SPQ
STA-RITE PREMIUM
QUALITY PUMPS

Rugged Non-Corrosive
Submersibles built with
uncompromising quality.

EXCLUSIVE UL LISTING. All SPQ submersibles are listed with Underwriters Laboratory, assuring the highest level of product safety.

SPQ MOTOR BEARING HOUSINGS feature a combination of high fiberglass content thermoplastic with a cast iron core to provide maximum strength and alignment with complete rust and corrosion resistance.

ENERGY EFFICIENT CONTROL BOX. Capacitor-run controls are available from 1/3 through 5 horsepower. They significantly reduce power consumption, so important in today's energy conscious world. Saving electrical usage translates directly to cooler motor temperatures, resulting in longer motor life. Only Sta-Rite offers the option of conventional or capacitor-run designs throughout all horsepower ranges.

Fig. 1-4. Rust-proof, premium-quality, 4-inch submersible pump. Courtesy Sta-Rite Pumps.

Fig. 1-5. Well pump and storage tank system. Courtesy Sta-Rite Pumps.

sure at the pump is 40 psig. The pressure switch (usually mounted on the pump housing or on the tank) is set to start the pump at 30 psig and stop the pump when the pressure in the system reaches 50 psig.

● The capacity of the system in gallons per hour (gph). The pump should have the capacity to deliver the total water requirements for two hours of continuous operation. One method of calculating the water requirements is to count the fixtures and outlets in the home

Fig. 1-6. Well pump and storage system, vertical tank. Courtesy Sta-Rite Pumps.

Fig. 1-7. HMS Series convertible jet pump. Courtesy Sta-Rite Pumps.

and multiply this figure by 60 gph, as in this example:

Kitchen sink	1
dishwasher	1
Bath lavatory	1
tub	1
toilet	1
1/2 bath lavatory	1
toilet	1
Laundry washer	1
tubs	1
Faucets	2
TOTAL	11
	× 60
TOTAL GPH	660

Fig. 1-8. SPQ Submersible pump. Courtesy Sta-Rite Pumps.

The well system must be able to provide 660 gph at 40 psig. This calculation provides for nearly all contingencies except a drop in the water table. There are times when a shallow or medium deep well will run dry, and a new well must be drilled. This is expensive, but in certain locations the only way to have a reliable supply of water.

Shallow well pump prices in the Midwest start at $170 for 20 to 40 psig; $219 for 30 to 50 psig, and $240 for 40 to 60 psig. The convertible jet pump (for depths of up to 110 feet) costs $170. The deep

Fig. 1-9. Goulds shallow well jet pump. Courtesy Goulds Pumps.

well jet pump is $330. The submersible deep well pumps start at $400. A captive air tank is available with a neoprene diaphragm that effectively separates the air from the water in the tank. The air pressure can be renewed by using an air valve (similar to a tire valve) and connecting to a tire pump to increase the pressure in the air chamber.

It must be remembered that water pressure is reduced when passing through pipes and fittings on its way to faucets. Table 1-4 gives the number of feet of 1-inch pipe equivalent to elbows (el's), tees, globe valves, reducing fittings, and any other devices that restrict liquid flow. These figures must be taken into consideration in determining loss of pressure at the far end of the water system, and also at the highest point in the system.

Fig. 1-10. Goulds pump on an ''Aqua-Air'' tank, vertical. Courtesy Goulds Pumps.

Fig. 1-11. Goulds submersible pump for deep wells. Courtesy Goulds Pumps.

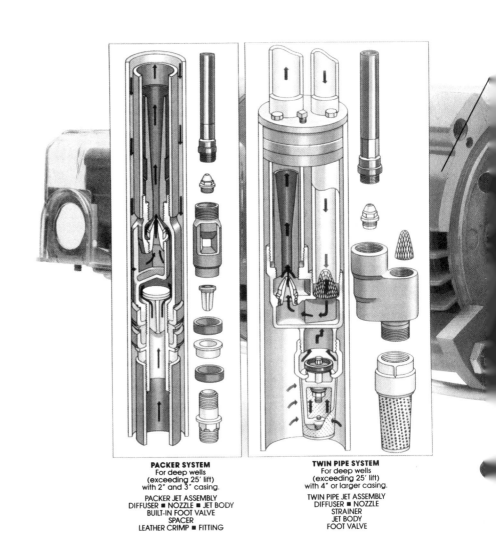

PACKER SYSTEM
For deep wells
(exceeding 25′ lift)
with 2″ and 3″ casing.

PACKER JET ASSEMBLY
DIFFUSER ■ NOZZLE ■ JET BODY
BUILT-IN FOOT VALVE
SPACER
LEATHER CRIMP ■ FITTING

TWIN PIPE SYSTEM
For deep wells
(exceeding 25′ lift)
with 4″ or larger casing.

TWIN PIPE JET ASSEMBLY
DIFFUSER ■ NOZZLE
STRAINER
JET BODY
FOOT VALVE

Fig. 1-12. Cutaway of a centrifugal pump and illustrations of jet pump construction. Courtesy Goulds Pumps.

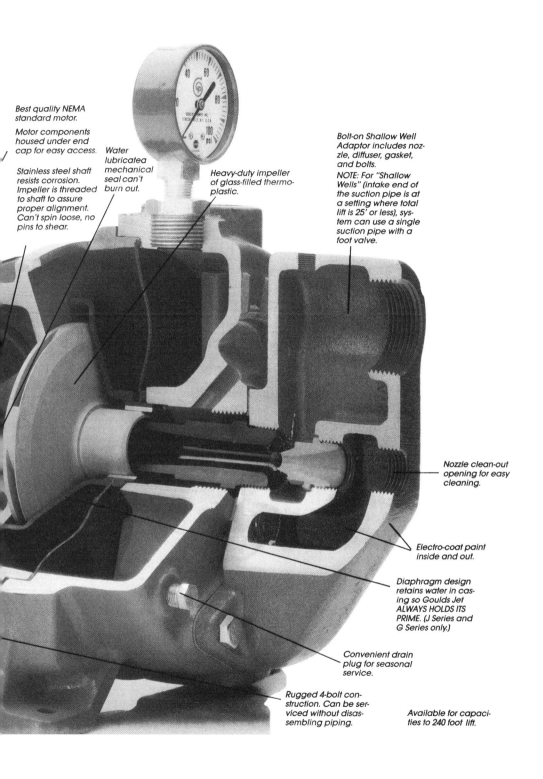

Best quality NEMA standard motor.

Motor components housed under end cap for easy access.

Stainless steel shaft resists corrosion. Impeller is threaded to shaft to assure proper alignment. Can't spin loose, no pins to shear.

Water lubricated mechanical seal can't burn out.

Heavy-duty impeller of glass-filled thermoplastic.

Bolt-on Shallow Well Adaptor includes nozzle, diffuser, gasket, and bolts.
NOTE: For "Shallow Wells" (intake end of the suction pipe is at a setting where total lift is 25' or less), system can use a single suction pipe with a foot valve.

Nozzle clean-out opening for easy cleaning.

Electro-coat paint inside and out.

Diaphragm design retains water in casing so Goulds Jet ALWAYS HOLDS ITS PRIME. (J Series and G Series only.)

Convenient drain plug for seasonal service.

Rugged 4-bolt construction. Can be serviced without disassembling piping.

Available for capacities to 240 foot lift.

15

Table 1-1. Performance Data of Sta-Rite Brand Pumps.

Deep Well 3″ Single Pipe (CP) & 4″ Double Pipe (EP)

H.P.	CAT. NO.	3″	4″ JET NO.	SUCT.	DRIVE	DISCH. PRESS.	20	30	40	50	60	70	80	90	100	110	120	130	140	150	160
1/2	HMSC	30CP	46EP	1 1/4	1	20	690	615	530	430	350	250									
						30	570	510	450	390	330	240									
						40	445	390	325	255	205	135									
						50	305	260	190	130	72										
						60	180	120	60												
						D.P.	25	25	26	26	26	26									
						S.O.	73	69	65	60	55	50									
1/2	HMSC	22CP	22EP	1 1/4	1	20					360	310	270	225	180						
						30					360	310	270	225	180						
						40					285	250	210	175	140						
						50					210	175	135	105	70						
						60					135	105	60	39							
						D.P.					28	29	29	30	32						
						S.O.					82	77	72	67	62						
3/4	HMSD	17CP	16EP	1 1/4	1	20	990	890	770	625	540	420									
						30	910	830	745	625	540	420									
						40	765	690	610	535	455	365									
						50	610	540	470	390	320	235									
						60	460	390	325	240	165	84									
						D.P.	28	30	32	33	34	36									
						S.O.	89	85	81	76	71	65									
3/4	HMSD	18CP	17EP	1 1/4	1	20					510	450	385	320	270	215					
						30					510	450	385	320	270	215					
						40					470	415	360	320	270	215					
						50					375	325	275	225	175	120					
						60					280	225	180	135	90	35					
						D.P.					37	37	37	37	38	38					
						S.O.					91	85	80	75	70	65					
3/4	HMSD	16CP	15EP	1 1/4	1	20											235	205	180	150	120
						30											235	205	180	150	120
						40											235	205	180	150	120
						50											200	175	150	125	105
						60											150	125	100	80	60
						D.P.											45	46	46	47	47
						S.O.											97	91	85	80	75

PUMPING DEPTH IN FEET

HMSE 7CP 6EP — pipe sizes 1 1/4, 1 1/4, 1 (HP: 1)

	Col 1	Col 2	Col 3	Col 4	Col 5	Col 6	Col 7
20	1225	1080	960	830	710	575	460
30	1200	1080	960	830	710	575	460
40	1070	970	875	780	685	575	460
50	900	815	730	635	545	460	375
60	745	655	565	480	385	295	210
D.P.	32	35	38	41	43	44	45
S.O.	99	94	89	84	79	75	70

HMSE 9CP 8EP — pipe sizes 1 1/4, 1 1/4, 1 (HP: 1)

	Col 1	Col 2	Col 3	Col 4	Col 5	Col 6	Col 7	Col 8
20	655	600	540	475	400	350	300	245
30	655	600	540	475	400	350	300	245
40	640	590	540	475	400	350	300	245
50	555	510	530	405	360	310	270	210
60	460	415	370	310	260	220	175	120
D.P.	42	43	44	45	45	46	46	47
S.O.	111	106	101	95	89	84	80	74

HMSE 29CP 42EP — pipe sizes 1 1/4, 1 1/4, 1 (HP: 1)

	Col 1	Col 2	Col 3	Col 4	Col 5
20	300	270	235	210	180
30	300	270	235	210	180
40	300	270	235	210	180
50	290	260	230	205	175
60	245	220	195	170	145
D.P.	45	46	47	50	53
S.O.	117	111	106	101	95

1 1/2 HMSF 10CP 9EP — pipe sizes 1 1/4

	Col 1	Col 2	Col 3	Col 4	Col 5	Col 6	Col 7
20	1560	1380	1200	1020	860	660	480
30	1450	1320	1200	1020	855	660	480
40	1300	1180	1075	955	840	660	480
50	1120	1020	915	795	690	545	425
60	930	815	720	610	485	365	245
D.P.	39	41	43	46	48	49	50
S.O.	100	95	90	85	80	75	70

1 1/2 HMSF 9CP 8EP — pipe sizes 1 1/4

	Col 1	Col 2	Col 3	Col 4	Col 5	Col 6	Col 7	Col 8
20	675	660	640	585	535	450	390	330
30	670	660	640	585	535	450	390	330
40	665	660	635	580	535	450	390	330
50	660	645	630	580	535	450	390	330
60	655	625	560	510	460	400	345	280
D.P.	51	54	56	57	58	58	58	58
S.O.	131	126	120	115	109	104	99	92

1 1/2 HMSF 19CP 4EP — pipe sizes 1 1/4

	Col 1	Col 2	Col 3	Col 4	Col 5
20	415	365	315	275	245
30	415	365	315	275	245
40	415	365	315	275	245
50	415	365	315	275	245
60	360	315	280	240	195
D.P.	55	55	56	56	53
S.O.	114	107	102	96	90

D.P. = Minimum Drive Pressure   S.O. = Shut Off Pressure in lbs.
Capacities shown in Gallons Per Hour. Tested and rated in accordance with Water Systems Council standards.

Courtesy of Sta-Rite Pumps.

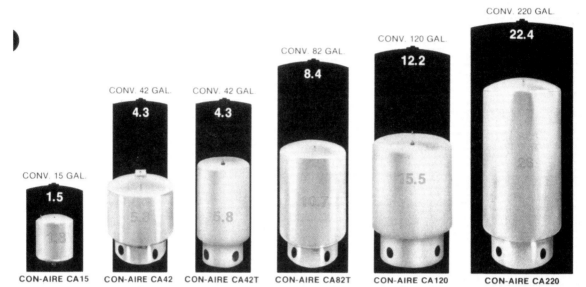

CONV. 15 GAL. 1.5	CONV. 42 GAL. 4.3	CONV. 42 GAL. 4.3	CONV. 82 GAL. 8.4	CONV. 120 GAL. 12.2	CONV. 220 GAL. 22.4
CON-AIRE CA15	CON-AIRE CA42	CON-AIRE CA42T	CON-AIRE CA82T	CON-AIRE CA120	CON-AIRE CA220

The draw-down figures reflected in the illustration above are based on a pressure switch setting of 30-50 PSI.

Water yield between the start and stop cycle of a pump is the absolute measure of tank efficiency. The draw-down comparison chart below, and accompanying illustration, show that the CON-AIRE is more efficient than a conventional tank twice its size. Pump life is extended due to the ability of the CON-AIRE tank to provide maximum draw-down consistently on every cycle.

Pressure Switch Setting		15 GAL.	42 GAL.	82 GAL.	120 GAL.	220 GAL.
20-40	Conv.	2.3	6.5	12.7	18.6	34.1
	Con-Aire	2.2	6.9	12.7	18.3	30.0
30-50	Conv.	1.5	4.3	8.4	12.2	22.4
	Con-Aire	1.8	5.8	10.7	15.5	26.0
40-60	Conv.	1.1	3.0	5.9	8.8	16.1
	Con-Aire	1.6	5.0	9.3	13.4	22.0

Ordering Information

Catalog No.	Maximum Capacity U.S. Gallons	Tank Diameter	Tank Height	Tank Discharge Tapping	Approx. Ship. Wt. Lbs.
CA15	6	12"	16-1/8"	3/4"	20
CA42	19	20"	23-1/32"	1"	57
CA42T	19	16"	30-11/32"	1"	52
CA82T	35	20"	34"	1"	72
CA120	50	24"	36-5/16"	1-1/2"	110
CA220	85	24"	54"	1-1/2"	135

See Page 22 for Jet Pump Tank Fitting Packages and Pages 33-37 for Submersible Pump Packages.

Fig. 1-13. Different sizes of storage tanks. The "Con-Aire" uses a smaller tank by having a diaphragm to separate the air from the water. Courtesy Sta-Rite Pumps.

Table 1-2. Performance Data and Ordering Information of Sta-Rite Brand Pumps.

Pump Performance

Cat. No.	H.P.	Jet No.	PUMP SIZES Suct.	Press.	30	40	50	60	70	80	90	100	110	120	130	140	180	200	220	240	260	280	300	320
4" Double Pipe Jets																								
MSC	½	16EP	1¼"	1"	890	770	600	400	210															
MSC	½	23EP	1¼"	1"	730	650	600	460	360	270														
MSC	½	15EP	1¼"	1"	330	330	320	315	310	270	250	210	190	160	130									
MSD	¾	16EP	1¼"	1"	1030	880	710	540	400	270														
MSD	¾	23EP	1¼"	1"	730	670	630	540	435	330	225	150												
MSD	¾	15EP	1¼"	1"	330	330	330	330	330	300	280	240	210	200	170	150								
MSE	1	23EP	1¼"	1¼"	730	730	730	730	690	580	510	400	320	250	190									
MSE	1	15EP	1¼"	1¼"	330	330	330	330	330	320	310	305	300	290	270	230	190	150	115	80				
MSF	1½	23EP	1¼"	1¼"	730	730	730	730	700	680	660	620	570	510	420	240	80							
MSF	1½	22EP	1¼"	1¼"	460	460	460	450	450	440	430	420	410	400	390	260	240	190	130					
MSF	1½	15EP	1¼"	1¼"	330	330	330	330	330	330	320	310	305	300	300	295	280	240	225	190	155	120		
MSG	2	23EP	1¼"	1¼"	730	730	730	730	710	680	670	665	660	600	520	410	240	120						
MSG	2	22EP	1¼"	1¼"	460	460	460	450	450	445	440	440	430	430	420	420	320	300	280	240	180	130		
MSG	2	15EP	1¼"	1¼"	330	330	330	330	330	330	320	320	310	305	305	300	300	290	280	270	260	240	200	160
2" Single Pipe Jets																								
MSC	½	12AP	1¼"	1"	700	560	500	400	300	160														
MSC	½	8AP	1¼"	1"	300	300	300	300	300	260	240	210	140	120										
MSD	¾	12AP	1¼"	1"	720	660	560	430	360	210	150													
MSD	¾	8AP	1¼"	1"	330	330	320	310	300	290	240	210	180	150	110									
MSE	1	12AP	1¼"	1"	730	710	705	660	600	480	430	350	210	110										
MSE	1	8AP	1¼"	1"	360	360	360	360	360	360	360	350	320	290	270	250	140							
MSF	1½	12AP	1¼"	1"	880	880	880	870	770	690	600	520	430	340	250	200								
MSF	1½	8AP	1¼"	1"	360	360	360	360	360	360	360	355	350	340	320	260	210	160	100					
MSG	2	12AP	1¼"	1"	900	900	900	900	850	770	700	615	500	450	380	320								
MSG	2	8AP	1¼"	1"	360	360	360	360	360	360	360	360	360	360	350	330	280	260	220	190	150			
3" Single Pipe Jets																								
MSC	½	17CP	1¼"	1"	890	770	600	400	210															
MSC	½	23CP	1¼"	1"	730	650	600	460	360	270														
MSC	½	16CP	1¼"	1"	330	330	320	315	310	270	250	210	190	160	130									
MSD	¾	17CP	1¼"	1"	1030	880	710	540	400	270														
MSD	¾	23CP	1¼"	1"	730	670	630	540	435	330	225	150												
MSD	¾	16CP	1¼"	1"	330	330	330	330	330	300	280	240	210	200	170	150								
MSE	1	23CP	1¼"	1"	730	730	730	730	690	580	510	400	320	250	190									
MSE	1	16CP	1¼"	1"	330	330	330	330	330	320	310	305	305	300	290	270	230	190	150	115	80			
MSF	1½	23CP	1¼"	1"	730	730	730	730	700	680	660	620	570	510	420	240	80							
MSF	1½	22CP	1¼"	1"	460	460	460	450	450	440	430	420	410	400	390	260	240	190	130					
MSF	1½	16CP	1¼"	1"	330	330	330	330	330	330	330	310	310	305	300	300	295	280	240	225	190	155	120	
MSG	2	23CP	1¼"	1"	730	730	730	730	710	680	670	665	660	600	520	410	240	120						
MSG	2	22CP	1¼"	1"	460	460	460	450	450	445	440	440	430	430	420	420	320	300	280	240	180	130		
MSG	2	16CP	1¼"	1"	330	330	330	330	330	330	320	320	320	310	305	300	300	290	280	270	260	240	200	160

Capacities are shown in gallons per hour at 20 PSI. All models tapped for 1" discharge.

Ordering Information

Cat. No.	H.P.	Max. Press. Reg. Setting	Stages	Motor Voltage	Approx. Ship. Wt. Lbs.
MSC	½	30 p.s.i.	2	115/230	65
MSD	¾	40 p.s.i.	2	115/230	67
MSE	1	60 p.s.i.	2	115/230	73
MSF	1½	85 p.s.i.	3	115/230	120
MSG	2	95 p.s.i.	3	230	125

Order pump from ordering information table on left. A JET PACKAGE ON PAGE 22 SHOULD BE ORDERED WITH EVERY Design Series "MS" PUMP. All installations require an appropriate size adapter flange. See Page 23 for Well Seal, Foot Valve or other accessory ordering information.

Adapter Flange

Cat. No.	Description	Used With
J216-26	1¼" x 1"	Offset Single Pipe, 4" Double Pipe through ¾ H.P.
J216-27	1¼" x 1¼"	4" Double Pipe 1, 1½ and 2 H.P.

Courtesy of Sta-Rite Pump.

Table 1-3. Composite Performance Curves of Goulds Submersible Pump.

Series
25EL
25 GPM

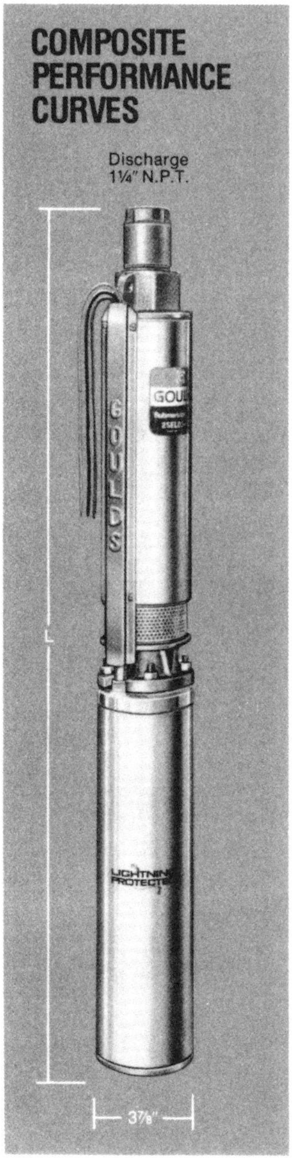
COMPOSITE PERFORMANCE CURVES
Discharge 1¼" N.P.T.
3⅞"

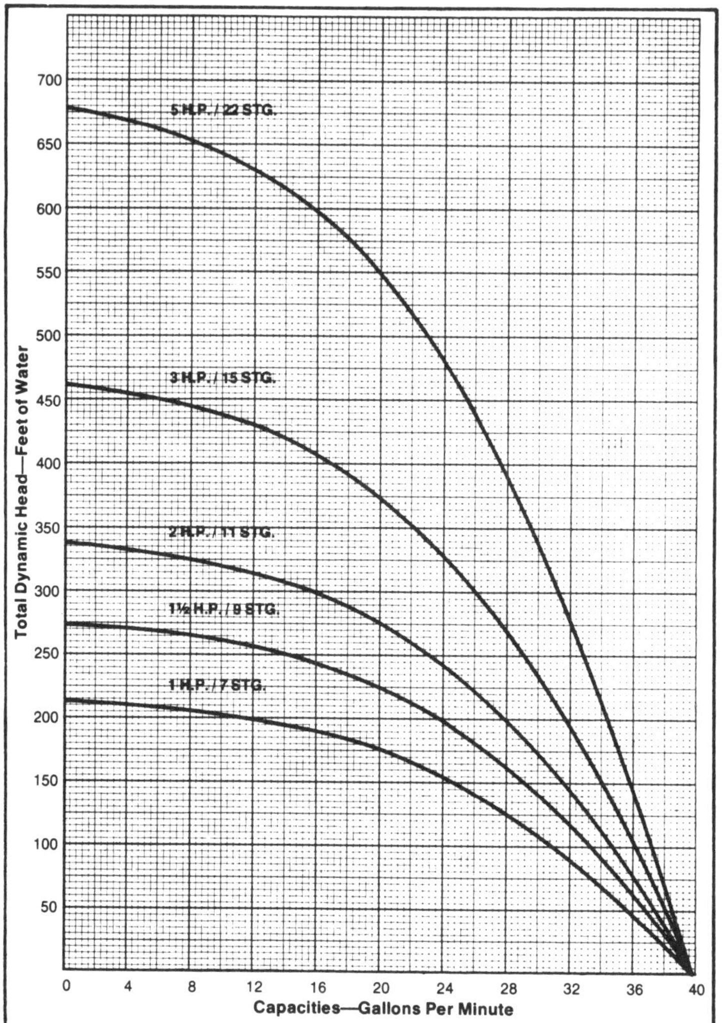
Total Dynamic Head—Feet of Water
700
650
600
550
500
450
400
350
300
250
200
150
100
50
5 H.P. / 22 STG.
3 H.P. / 15 STG.
2 H.P. / 11 STG.
1½ H.P. / 9 STG.
1 H.P. / 7 STG.
0
4
8
12
16
20
24
28
32
36
40
Capacities—Gallons Per Minute

DIMENSIONS AND WEIGHTS

Horse-Power	Stages	3-WIRE Model No.	3-WIRE Length	2-WIRE Model No.	2-WIRE Length	Approx. Unit Weight (lbs.)
1	7	25EL10412	27⅛"	25EL10422	27⅝"	36
1½	9	25EL15412	33"	25EL15422	32¼"	48
1½	9	25EL15432	31⅝"	—	—	43
2	11	25EL20412	41½"	—	—	71
2	11	25EL20432	39"	—	—	67
3	15	25EL30412	51⅜"	—	—	81
3	15	25EL30432	45⅜"	—	—	83
5	22	25EL50412	59⅛"	—	—	107
5	22	25EL50432-34	58"	—	—	107

Courtesy Gould Pumps.

90° std. ell		3.0
45° std. ell		1.8
90° side tee		5.0
Coupling or run of tee		0.9
Gate valve		0.6
Globe valve		25.0
Angle valve		15.0

Table 1-4. One-Inch Pipe Fittings and Equivalents in Feet of Straight Pipe.

Pressure loss of water in pounds per square inch gauge (psig) per 100 feet of smooth pipe
10 GPM through 1-inch pipe = 3.5 psig pressure drop

Construction and Maintenance of Private Wells

In rural areas, private wells are necessary for the domestic water in isolated farm homes and outbuildings. Information in this book does not pertain to digging or drilling a well. It covers the operation of pumps and their maintenance, and includes precautions to prevent contamination by ground water from the surface and upper soil layers seeping into the well around the well casing (the large pipe leading down to the water table).

The well casing must extend 6 inches above the ground and 1 inch above the well platform. The well platform, of concrete, must slope in all directions, and extend 2 feet in all directions. The well casing must be watertight, durable, and extend to a depth of 10 feet. The connection between the well casing and pump must also be watertight. The well must be above any high water flood level to prevent contamination. All septic tanks, fields, and sewers must be at least 50 feet from the well location.

This information is provided so that if you are buying a used home or farm having its own well system, you will know what to look for. Corrections to a well and pump system to provide for pure water might cost more than you want to spend on the system. It is also advisable to have the water from the well tested for purity and contamination, in addition to checking the above cautions, concerning the location and construction of the well.

The well proper can take many forms. It can be a shallow well, having a piston pump or a centrifugal pump. Newer wells might have a shallow well jet pump or a convertible jet pump.

Shallow well pumps that "suck" can only pump from a water table (height of water in the ground) less than 22 feet below ground level. Modern pumps can pump up to 540 gallons per hour with a lift of 5 feet. A lift of 20 feet reduces the discharge to 340 gph. Both capacities are delivered at 40 pounds per square inch gauge (psig), using a 1/2-hp motor, a 1 1/4-inch suction, and 1-inch discharge pipes. This refers to a convertible jet pump. All pumps can be easily repaired.

For use in deep wells, you will need the 4-inch submersible pump. Capacities are listed for water tables as deep as 900 feet. At that depth, capacities are greatly reduced or else the horsepower has to be increased to perhaps 5 hp. Because three-phase power is usually not available, most rural well systems have only 240-volt, single-phase motors. Single-phase motors of 1/3-, 1/2-, and 3/4-hp are always available for replacement and can be repaired almost everywhere.

Also available are repair or replacement parts such as: submersible well (casing) seals, fitting packages for tanks, tanks, check valves, relief valves, etc.

Shallow wells are usually driven using a well point/screen combination. The tapered point is on the bottom end and the screen is above it to filter out the sand or other unwanted particles. Usually of brass or bronze, the point and section above it (which is cut away to allow water to enter) are one piece and take the driving force. The brass screen wraps around the cut-out section to complete the well point. The point is driven by hand or power to the depth needed to reach the water table.

Deep well casing is usually 4-inch, larger for commercial wells. The 4-inch casing will accommodate the submersible pump. These submersible pumps are entirely satisfactory. Because these pumps weigh up to 75 pounds, equipment for hoisting the pump/motor assembly out of the casing for repairs or replacement will be necessary. A tripod can be easily built from wood 2-x-4s or metal pipes, either material tied together to form a tripod. Either a block and tackle or a "comealong" (a ratcheting hoist using chain and a handle to be operated in a pumping action) can be used, suspended from the tripod. Sections of the discharge pipe from the pump must be disconnected as the pump is raised. Because this is a complicated procedure, it is best to test to determine if the pump or motor is bad.

Electrical testing equipment can determine if the motor is in good condition and if the cable from the power source is perfect. You might want to call an electrician to make these tests before hoisting the pump. Most well pumps can be furnished in 120 or 240 volts. The higher voltage is better because the ampere draw is about half that of a motor running on 240 volts. This will allow the use of smaller wire for the submersible cable. Single-phase motors require an induction control box, which must be ordered separately. Other accessories that might have to be ordered are storage tanks and pressure controls to operate the pump to maintain an average pressure of 40 to 50 psig.

Newly completed wells must be disinfected with a 5 percent solution of sodium hypochlorite—a common household bleach such as Clorox. Pour about 1 pint of the solution into the well for each 100 gallons of water in the well, pump, and piping. Afterwards, the pump should be operated while all the faucets are opened. When the strong smell of chlorine is obvious, close the faucets and allow the chlorine to work, then open the faucets again until *no* chlorine odor is noticed.

As mentioned previously, the top of the casing of all wells, shallow and deep, must be sealed. These seals incorporate a type of **O** ring between two metal castings. The top casting has a flange that prevents the seal assembly from dropping into the well casing. The bottom casting is connected to the top casting by four bolts. Tightening the bolts squeezes the **O** ring, pressing it against the inside of the well casing and making a tight seal, thus keeping the well in a sanitary condition.

Many county health agencies will test the well water for bacteria, chemicals, or other contaminants. Contact your county health department if you are having problems.

THE CATCHMENT SYSTEM

This special water supply arrangement is reminiscent of the old cistern and hand pump in the kitchen which provided soft rainwater for washing and bathing. Rain falling on the roof flowed to gutters and down to a stone or concrete tank in the cellar. The hand pump in the kitchen brought the water up to be available at the kitchen sink.

Fig. 1-14. Main tank for catchment system, 25,000 gallons. Note roof gutters connected by pipes leading into tank.

Fig. 1-15. Full view of catchment tank, 25,000 gallons.

Many isolated homes that have no municipal water supply or a suitable well use this system. Because it is modern, with a pump and pressure tank, and operates similar to a well system, this is a very satisfactory system. Water is obtained from the roof surfaces of the dwelling and is led into one or more storage tanks close to the dwelling. The roof surface is either corrugated galvanized steel or specially formulated roofs used for catchment purposes. The pump has no lift to speak of because the storage tank is on the same level as the house.

With this arrangement, the system becomes, in effect, a shallow well system. The pump and accessories will cost $300 to $500. The catchment tanks sometimes hold up to 40,000 gallons. The tanks are covered and have the necessary filters and strainers; the tanks will cost $2000 to $3000 each. It is best to have a tank of adequate size to carry over any long dry spells. Because Hawaii uses the catchment system, Figs. 1-15 through 1-18 illustrate such a system.

The catchment system is simple in construction. A special roofing material is required, which will eliminate any contamination of the water draining into the catchment tank from the roof. Catchment tanks

24

Fig. 1-16. Storage tank. Right-hand pipe is for filling tank, left-hand pipe is vent to prevent airlock.

need to be sized for: the number of persons living in the residence, water usage (such as irrigation), and annual rainfall. Tanks come in various sizes and materials; sizes range from 10,000 to 100,000 gallons. Covers are provided to protect the water from contamination.

The lines from the roof to the catchment tank are connected together and enter the top of the tank as one line. This line is similar to gutter downspout. The flow to the tank is by gravity. The lines are large, 2- to 3-inch size, just as downspouts are.

The suction line is usually 1 inch from the tank to the pump. This line is laid in a trench or on top of the ground, rises vertically alongside the storage (catchment) tank, then descends inside to about 12 inches from the bottom of the tank. This prevents the accidental draining of the tank due to a leak in the suction line.

On the house side of the pump/pressure tank assembly, the water system resembles a standard house plumbing installation. System pressure is 40 psig, plus or minus 10 pounds. A pressure switch is mounted on the pump or tank for "on 30 pounds, off 50 pounds" or other settings. A standard high-pressure pump will generally be in-

Fig. 1-17. Pump and pressure tank for catchment system. System operates at 40 psig.

stalled. The shallow well jet pump shown in Fig. 1-18 includes a "controlled air water system tank." This special tank has a vinyl diaphragm that separates the air charge from the water. The air space is on top of the tank, and has an air valve for reducing or increasing the air pressure to meet the pressure switch setting. The setting is usually 30 to 50 psig. This averages out to 40 psig, plus or minus 10 pounds, as mentioned previously. The purpose of the diaphragm is to prevent the air volume of the tank from being absorbed into the water, thus losing the advantage of the pressure of the air.

Goulds Pumps also makes a captive air system. These are both excellent for use on these catchment systems. Figure 1-10 illustrates this water system.

All manufacturers of pumps provide adequate stocks of repair/replacement parts at plumbing wholesalers throughout the coun-

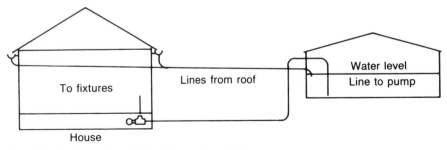

Fig. 1-18. Typical piping diagram for a catchment system.

26

try. Many hardware stores and home centers also carry pumps, accessories, and repair parts.

You will need a filter/strainer ahead of the pump. This should have a removable cartridge so that a new cartridge may be installed as necessary, to provide clear water to the pump and system. Chlorination is usually not required. It is especially important to make certain the roofing material is compatible with a catchment system, and that it does not contaminate the rain water flowing over it.

2

Disposal
Sewage Systems

As with sources of water supplies, there are only three approved types of disposal systems: The public sewer system, the septic tank system, and the cesspool.

PUBLIC SEWER SYSTEMS

Public sewer systems are very expensive and costly to install and maintain. In large metropolitan areas, the central large city has established and built its own sewer system, perhaps 100 years ago. As the suburban areas began to develop, these suburbs asked and were given permission to tie into the system of the central city. This then became an area system, serving communities within a radius of 10 to 20 miles. The suburban cities usually connect to both the water and sewer lines, although some suburbs have built their own sewer systems. The central city might pressure the suburb having its own sewer to connect up immediately. In other cases, the suburb might feel its system disposal plant is too old or too small and decide to tie in as soon as possible.

Sewer lines run down all streets, and perhaps alleys. You need permission to connect to the city sewer lines. A permit can be obtained at the inspection department, and the fee is paid before the work can be started. The fee can be as much as $500. If you are planning to do your own plumbing in a new house, it is advisable to contract for

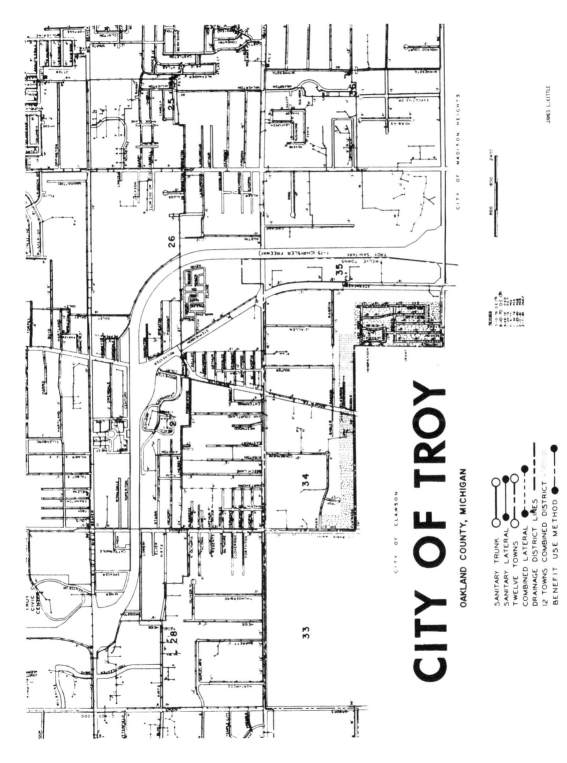

CITY OF TROY

OAKLAND COUNTY, MICHIGAN

SANITARY TRUNK
SANITARY LATERAL
TWELVE TOWNS
COMBINED LATERAL
DRAINAGE DISTRICT LINES
12 TOWNS COMBINED DISTRICT
BENEFIT USE METHOD

JAMES L. KITTLE

Fig. 2-1. Partial map of city sewer lines, City of Troy, Michigan. Courtesy City of Troy.

the trenching, the laying of the sewer line, and the connections to the city sewer line in the street, with a plumbing contractor. A city system is shown in Fig. 2-1.

It is possible to do this work yourself, but the heavy labor involved and the necessity of obtaining the correct pitch (slope) for the line and the connection to the city line might discourage you. The city could also prohibit you from doing this work because it involves opening up the street, perhaps tearing up paving, all on city property. This involves legal considerations, and is best left to a plumbing contractor. The point at which the sewer line is extended beyond the front property line and is on your property is the best time to begin doing work yourself.

If the sewer and water lines have been extended past the city property previously, check with the city inspection department and they can tell you where the lines end. *Caution:* Be advised that trenching is hard, heavy work and that the sides of the trench must be braced to prevent cave-ins, which are very dangerous!

The sewer line can be either cast iron or vitreous clay tile, 6-inch size. Cast iron is best because clay tile is apt to be invaded at the joints by tree roots, which could cause much trouble over the years. The cast-iron pipe is available in the "hubless" style. Because the joints are connected by stainless steel bands with an internal rubber sleeve; this does away with caulking using lead and oakum. As the band is tightened, the joint is made watertight. This type of installation must be supported in the trench and inside a building because the joints are somewhat flexible. There can be no sags in the line; this will cause possible clogging.

Municipal Sewer Systems

A municipal sewer system is very expensive and complicated. It consists of many miles of sewer lines, all arranged to slope to the sewage treatment plant. If necessary, lift pumps are installed to raise the sewage over hills and to connect to sections on higher ground, or to start a new "high end" of a sewer section. Long runs of line—a mile or more—might need a lift pump at the low end because a continuous drop will eventually lead to a very deep sewer. Excavating equipment is often unable to dig a trench beyond a 20-foot depth, therefore the sewer system is divided up so that pumps are provided at low ends to lift the sewage up again. An elevation would present a sawtooth design of ups (by pumps) and slopes using gravity to induce flow (Fig. 2-2).

There are many instances in which it is necessary to lift sewage: if the topography is such that a continuation of the present slope would make the sewer so deep that the construction cost would be excessive (more than the installation of a pumping station); if sewage must be carried over a hill; or if the discharge is into a body of

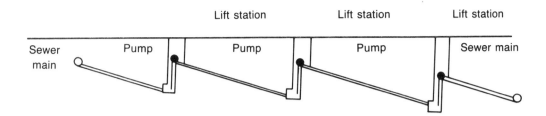

Fig. 2-2. Diagram of lift pumps on long city sewer lines.

water or into a sewage treatment plant that is higher than the sewer line discharge level.

Specially designed pumps known as sewage pumps are used to pump solids. These are easily opened for removing larger solids that the pump cannot handle. At times, the sewage must be raised by the pump as much as 15 feet. Many of these pumps operate automatically, with no attention except periodic maintenance. Some are underground and have a manhole and ladder for easy access.

Sump pumps are also used to lift sewage, but are used mostly by private buildings that have low basements and sewer lines that are below the street sewer. Many older buildings in downtown sections of large cities might have as many as three basements, each above the one below it. This can leave the drain from the third basement as much as 30 feet below the street sewer. In this case, sump pumps will be privately owned by the building management.

The layout of sewer lines in city streets is determined by the topography of the area, zoning laws, present needs, and future projected needs (see Fig. 2-1). One or two main trunks will run through the city with sub-trunks that run at right angles to the main trunks. Sometimes the sub-trunks will be higher and at junctions (usually manholes) the discharge of the sub will drop 1 or 2 feet to the level of the main trunk. This will prevent any backup into the subs if the main is overloaded.

If the city or village is not a suburb of a large city, and is isolated, it will have its own sewage treatment plant and be self-sufficient, both for its sewage disposal and water supply facilities. In the case of a city or village adjacent to a large central city, generally the large city will furnish both sewage disposal and water supply services to these suburbs. The central city will bill the suburbs for water used and for sewage treatment, based on a percentage of the water usage. Water use is metered while sewage use is not. This method of billing is used also for individual homeowners.

Sewer maintenance is required on a regular basis because stoppages occur frequently. Many of the sewer cleaning tools used in municipal sewers are larger versions of those used by homeowners. These consist of gouges, scoops, claws, screws, a root cutter, wire brush, and a scraper. All of these can be attached to a flexible cable, which in turn is rotated on the surface by power equipment. Cleanouts are placed at nearly every intersection, which allows the use of shorter cables and ease of operation.

Many times the sewer lines of clay tile become broken, and the street must be dug up to make these repairs. Large sewers constructed of brick need repairs, including brick replacement or pointing of mortar joints. Sometimes a finish of cement and sand called Gunite is sprayed on these brick sewer mains to give a smoother surface. All this is hazardous and hard work, but it is necessary for proper maintenance.

Sewage is not just waste from private homes, but a mixture of home, apartment, public and private buildings, factories, laboratories, and hospitals. Many of the waste materials entering the sewer lines need very special treatment even before entering the main sewage treatment facility of the city. At the present time, with more concerns about pollution being voiced, many manufacturing facilities are being forced to provide extensive treatment for their own wastes, or are being taxed by the city to have it done for them. These companies discharge sewage having oil, grease, chemicals, and other pollutants that push the treatment plant to its limit.

The by-product of the sewage treatment plants of large metropolitan areas (sludge) can be used as fertilizer, and is either sold to farmers or fertilizer manufacturing companies. Chicago, Milwaukee, and Houston do this and recover nearly the complete cost of disposing of the sludge. Milwaukee makes and sells its treated sludge as Milorganite, a lawn fertilizer distributed throughout the Midwest.

Storm water is usually carried away in "storm sewers," as distinguished from sanitary sewers. In certain areas, it is feasible to combine both types of sewers into one.

It is a known fact that large paved areas such as parking lots and freeways greatly increase the load on storm sewers and combination sewers serving these areas because they have a slower absorption rate. The coefficient of runoff for parks, gardens, lawns, and meadows is 0.05 to 0.25, while that for asphalt pavement in good condition is 0.85 to 0.90.

Open areas that previously had absorbed the rainfall now send it to the storm sewer system, which becomes greatly overloaded. Many residential areas are now protected by holding ponds. These "retention" ponds collect the water and release it slowly through a drain line, thereby reducing the almost instant overload on the storm sewer system. Retention ponds, constructed at relatively small cost, eliminate the enormous expense of increasing the size of the storm sewers.

Many new subdivisions have trouble with the storm drains becoming stopped up with sand and other types of debris from the construction sites. These areas must be monitored by inspection authorities to prevent such stoppage.

SEPTIC TANKS

Small towns and remote areas such as farms, will use the septic tank system. This system, a miniature of that used in large cities, consists of the line from the house, the septic tank, the distribution box, and the absorption field. On such premises, the septic system must be separated from a private well by certain distances. These same distances must also be maintained from any neighbor's well. The septic tank itself must be no less than 50 feet from any well and the absorption field must be no less than 100 feet from any well. These are *minimum* distances. Figure 2-3 shows the layout of a septic system for

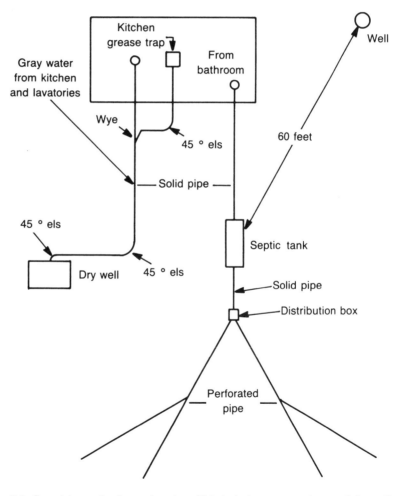

Fig. 2-3. Complete septic disposal system. This includes a grease trap and dry well and reduces the load on the septic system.

Fig. 2-4. Septic tanks ready for delivery to job site.

the home. Notice the grease trap inside the house. If grease enters the septic system, it will prevent it from operating properly, if at all.

The septic tank itself must be pumped out periodically to get rid of solids still in the tank. If this is not done, the system will not operate properly and might require extensive and costly repairs. The tank should be inspected yearly. Typical septic tanks are shown in Figs. 2-4 through 2-10. In Figs. 2-11 and 2-12 the capacity of the tank is cast in the concrete of the tank. The 1000- and 1250-gallon labels are shown.

Before installing a septic system for a new residence, a percolation or "perc" test must be made. This is done by digging a 12-inch deep by 4-inch diameter hole in the soil at the location proposed for the field. This is filled with water and allowed to stand overnight, and next morning, 6 inches of water is poured into the hole. The rate the water drains away depends on the porosity of the soil. A fall of 1 inch per minute is excellent, and a fall of 1 inch in 5 is poor. The rate of absorption governs the size of the field needed for the residence, depending on the number of bedrooms. The field should be installed oversize, to allow for any increases that might be needed in the fu-

Fig. 2-5. Septic tank stored inverted for curing.

Fig. 2-6. Septic tank, 1000-gallon size.

ture. Also, the septic tank size starts at 750 gallons for two bedrooms and 1000 gallons for four bedrooms.

Septic systems require constant maintenance if they are to operate in a satisfactory manner. Pamphlets are available from County Extension Services in your area, giving very detailed installation and maintenance instructions. Examples of this information is included in Figs. 2-13 through 2-16.

Septic tanks act as settling basins and prevent solid materials from entering the drainfield. These solids clog the drain holes in the pipes and also clog the soil of the field. This causes the effluent to rise to the surface or back up into the basement. Therefore these conditions make it imperative that the tank be pumped out and cleaned at least every 2 years by a licensed septic tank maintenance company.

A septic tank should be cleaned when the bottom side of the scum layer is within 3 inches of the submereged inlet pipe, or when the sludge accumulated depth equals one third or more of the liquid depth.

It is strongly recommended that only human waste and liquids be allowed to flow into the septic tank and field. The garbage disposal puts a very great load on the septic system and should be used sparingly. While some cities require the installation of disposals, restrict

Fig. 2-7. Interior of distribution box.

Fig. 2-8. Manhole in distribution box.

their use to a minimum. Another device, the water softener, puts a very large quantity of sodium into the septic system. Recharging the water softener adds hundreds of gallons of water to the system each week. This water can safely be discharged to some other disposal location, thus taking that load off the septic system.

The septic system consists of the septic tank itself, the distribution box, and the soil absorption field. In addition, there must be a grease trap in the line inside the house, since grease in the septic tank greatly reduces its efficiency. Be aware that any chemicals flushed into the septic system—including garbage disposal waste and water softener washdown, which includes sodium salts—will interfere greatly with the action of the bacteria in the tank. Because of the vulnerability of this system, water usage habits and the disposal of all types of materials must be changed. Many households never pour grease down the kitchen drain, instead they pour it into a container for disposal with solid wastes.

Because the septic system is a bacteriological process, anything that kills or interferes with the reproduction of the bacteria or their action in digesting the waste will reduce the efficiency of the system. Only human waste, liquids free of harmful materials, and toilet paper

Fig. 2-9. Cover for septic tank. Note lifting rings.

Fig. 2-10. Access covers for large septic tank.

Fig. 2-11. Septic tank by Advance Concrete, 1000-gallon size.

Fig. 2-12. Septic tank by Advance Concrete, 1250-gallon size

should be disposed of in the system. The septic system is not a garbage can. By eliminating solids other than human waste as much as possible, the frequency of pumping the septic tank is reduced. Again, the tank should be pumped out every two years or the disposal field may be destroyed. The removal and replacement of the field is accomplished only at great expense, $1500 to $4000, while pumping costs at most $150.

Introduction

A septic tank system is an underground private sewage disposal system. It is the best method of sewage disposal in areas where community sewage disposal facilities are not available, and where soil drainage is acceptable.

What is a Septic Tank System?

A septic tank system usually is made up of two parts -

1. **Septic Tank** - a water tight container (made of concrete) receives the untreated household waste.
2. **Tile Field** - consists of a series of pipes with holes in them (perforated) which distribute the liquid from the septic tank to the surrounding below ground soil.

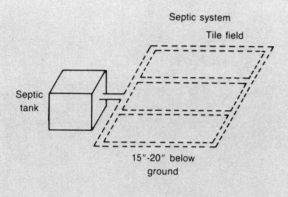

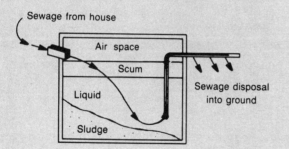

How does the Septic System Work?

Waste material from the house enters the septic tank slowly so that solids can:

(1) settle to the bottom and form a sludge layer
(2) raise to the top and form a scum layer

In between these two layers is a liquid waste center.

When waste enters the tank, bacteria begins to breakdown the solid materials. This process is called "decomposition." As a result of decomposition, solids are reduced, leaving a residue behind in the tank. As time passes, the remaining residue builds up, and must be removed to prevent it from entering the tile field and clogging the system.

The center liquid layer flows slowly from the tank into the tile field. Because the pipes in the tile field are perforated, this allows the liquid to be distributed equally in specially prepared gravel filled trenches. Once the liquid reaches the trenches, it soaks into the soil. The soil then acts as the final filter in the treatment of waste receives by the septic system.

Why is it important to maintain my Septic System?

1. A failing Septic System can be very costly. Often times failing systems are impossible to repair, and must be replaced. Even when the system can be repaired, the expense is much greater than that of a simple cleaning. A failing septic system can also cause your property value to go down. In other words, "An ounce of prevention is worth a pound of cure."
2. A failing Septic System is a real health hazard. Sewage may contain harmful disease causing bacteria and viruses. When a system fails, sewage may back up into the house and also may raise to the above ground surface over the tile field. Therefore, people and pets may be exposed to these harmful bacteria and viruses.

Continued from page 38.

3. A failing Septic System is a real nuisance. When a system fails, there is the possibility that it will cause damage to your property. Offensive odors in the house and outside area are also results of a failing system.

Do's and Don'ts

DO'S

- **DO** have the septic tank pumped out by a licensed operator every 2 years.
- **DO** know where it is located, have an easy way to reach it and make sure it can be pumped out.
- **DO** try to limit the amount of kitchen wastes you put into the system through a garbage disposal.
- **DO** make normal use of bleaches, detergents, soaps, bowl cleaners or drain cleaners.

DON'TS

- **DO NOT** allow heavy vehicles to drive over the tile field, the drain tiles will be damaged.
- **DO NOT** allow trees and shrubs to grow over the septic field.
- **DO NOT** allow large amounts of water to be drained into the septic tank at the same time. For example, do not run the dishwasher and take a shower at the same time if possible.

- **DO NOT** connect downspouts, sump pumps or water softener backwash to the septic system.
- **DO NOT** put harmful materials down your drains, such as fats, oils, solvents, or solids like plastic, paper towels, sanitary napkins, or disposable diapers.
- **DO NOT** use additives that claim to help septic systems work better.

SEPTIC TANK CARE

Fill in with periodic maintenance information and store with important household documents:

DATE: _____

_____
_____
_____
_____
_____
_____
_____
_____
_____
_____
_____

Contractor _____
Phone #_____
* *

Diagram of your Septic Tank and Tile Field

Fig. 2-13. Septic tank information. Courtesy Macomb County, Michigan, Dept. of Health.

SUBSURFACE SEWAGE DISPOSAL SYSTEM ISOLATION DISTANCES

1. Water wells must be located at least 50', if residential, and 75', in all other cases, from any septic tank and tile field system (your own or your neighbor's).
2. Water supply pressure lines must be located at least ten feet (10') from any part of your sewage disposal system. If the water supply line from your well to your house is a suction lime, it must meet the isolation distances required for wells.
3. Other isolation distances are as follows:

Septic Tank and Tile Field to Foundations. . . . . .5'
Septic Tank and Tile Field to Property Lines. . . . . .5'
Septic Tank and Tile Field to Roadside Ditches. . . . . .10'
Septic Tank and Tile Field to Lakes and Rivers. . . . . .100'

4. Septic Tank and Tile Field Systems are not to be installed in rights-of-way or easements.

SUBSURFACE SEWAGE DISPOSAL SYSTEM PRECAUTIONS

1. Construction of any type over the top of a septic tank or tile field is prohibited, as is also the driving or parking of vehicles.
2. Septic tanks must be cleaned approximately once every two years (2) for average 4-5 member household, to prevent the buildup of excess sludge, and resultant shortened tile field life.
3. Excessive water use in the house should be avoided.
4. Grass watering devices and rain water downspouts should be directed away from the tile field area.
5. Sump pump and water softener effluent must not go into the septic tank and tile field system.
6. Grease, oil and caustic drain cleaners may be harmful to a septic tank-tile field system.

Fig. 2-14. Sub-surface sewage disposal system, isolation distances. Courtesy Macomb County, Michigan Dept. of Health.

Simple tests can be performed to determine when or if the tank must be pumped. To test the scum thickness (scum is the lightweight material, grease and oil, that floats on top of the liquid), make a stick having a hinged flap on the end. This flap must be mounted so that when it is pushed *down* through the scum, it folds up against the side of the stick. When the stick is pulled up, the flap drops down at right angles to the stick, and looks somewhat like a garden hoe. The flap must not fall down completely, but must stay at 90 degrees to the stick. With the flap in this position, it will catch on the underside of the scum and you will feel resistance. At this point, mark the handle from a reference point such as the manhole edge. Lower the stick again to the top of the scum layer; mark the handle again. This will give you the thickness of the scum layer as the distance between the two marks. If the bottom of the scum layer is closer than 3 inches to the bottom of the baffle (measured with the stick with the flap), the tank needs to be pumped out.

The sludge at the bottom of the tank is measured using another stick with an old towel tied around the bottom end for about 18 inches. Lower this stick down through the baffle (the T-shaped tile at the exit of the tank) and push it down to the tank bottom. Pull the stick out; the towel will be black part way up. This is the depth of the sludge. Also use the stick with the flap to measure the distance to the top of the sludge from the reference point. If the top of the sludge is less than 12 inches from the bottom of the baffle, the tank should be pumped out.

Caution: It is extremely dangerous to enter a septic tank. There are always toxic fumes present, and a person inside the tank may be overcome. Any work of this nature should be left to a professional. In an emergency such that you must enter the tank, be sure to have one, or better still, two persons standing by. Tie a rope around your chest so that you can be pulled out if you pass out. Also have as much ventilation as possible.

In pumping out the tank, the contents must be completely removed, not just the liquid. Do not use any chemicals or additives; sewage contains all the necessary bacteria for proper digestion of the sewage.

Design and Construction of a Septic System

The septic system is a method of disposing of raw sewage and household waste water in a safe and sanitary way in areas where there is no public sewer system available for connection. In most cases, soil conditions permit septic system installation. In rare cases, the soil will not be able to absorb the effluent liquid because it is nearly pure clay, and clay is not porous. To determine if the soil on your property is suitable for a septic drainfield, you must perform a percolation test. When locating the drainfield remember that it must be as far away as possible from all wells, your own and those on neighboring farms or cottages. The area should be lower than the nearby wells, and rain water should not stand on the area. Avoid nearby trees; their roots will clog the drainfield.

The percolation test is the only sure method of locating the field in the ideal place for efficient operation. To make this test, dig a number of holes in the proposed field. Five to eight test holes are needed, depending on the size of the field needed, because the soil can vary in its composition—from all sand to all clay. You might ask the county agent for advice as to the location and shape of the field. Locate holes to give an average over the proposed area.

The test holes should be at least 24 inches deep and 12 inches in diameter. Dig straight down to make the sides vertical. Do not com-

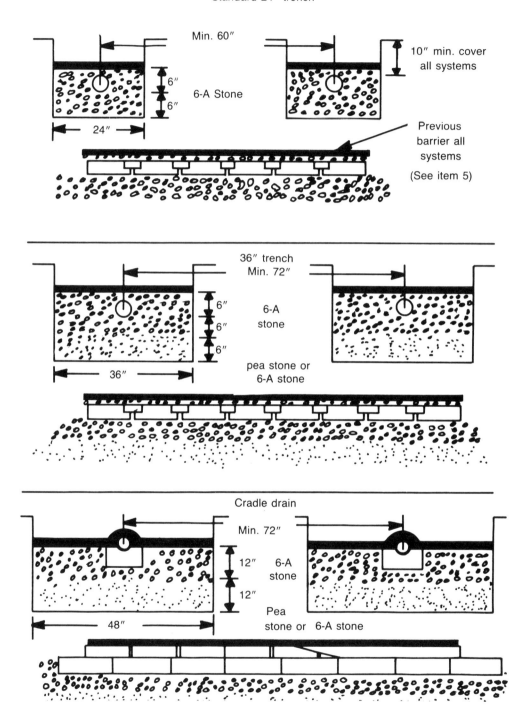

Fig. 2-15. Tile field design. Courtesy Macomb County, Michigan Dept. of Health.

TILE FIELD DESIGN

1. Tile trenches shall be constructed as indicated in figures 1, 2, and 3. Contact the Macomb County Health Department for information regarding deep trenches, completely excavated tile field areas, and tile fields laid in a bed of stone.
2. Clay or concrete drain pipe (4" × 12") laid with a 1/8" or 1/4" gap or certain types plastic pipe are used in the tile field. Contact the Macomb County Health Department for the list of approved plastic pipe.
3. Washed, clean 6-A stone or in specific instances pea stone are the filter medias used in tile field construction. (See requirements for type of system proposed)
4. The top one-half of clay or concrete drain pipe shall be covered with tar paper or plastic.
5. The top of the stone in a tile trench or bed shall be covered with *untreated* building paper or two-inch layer of hay or straw to prevent the stone from becoming clogged by the earth backfill.
6. The tile disposal field shall be installed as near to level as possible with a maximum grade towards the footer of 3" per 100'.
7. Provide a minimum of 12" of stone beneath the tile in sections of the tile field which are within 10' of trees or dense shrubbery.
8. Frozen material shall not be used for backfilling and/or covering tile fields.
9. Be certain that the septic tank-tile field system complies with all of the conditions of the permit. (See reverse side of permit)
10. Cover over tile laterals to be a minimum of 10" and a maximum of 24".

APPLICATION IS HEREBY MADE FOR:
( ) EVALUATION OF SOILS
( ) RE-EVALUATION OF SOILS
( ) PERMIT TO CONSTRUCT AN ONSITE WASTEWATER DISPOSAL SYSTEM
( ) PERMIT TO REPAIR, MODIFY, OR REPLACE AN EXISTING ONSITE WASTEWATER DISPOSAL SYSTEM

HAS AN APPLICATION BEEN PREVIOUSLY SUBMITTED?   ( ) YES   ( ) NO

XXXXXXXXXXXXXXXXXXXXXXXXXXXXXXXXXXXXXXXXXXXXXXXXXXXXXXXXXXXXXXXXXXXXXXXXXXXXXXX

SITE BEING APPLIED FOR / PROPERTY DESCRIPTION

( ) MORE THAN ONE ACRE   ( ) LESS THAN ONE ACRE   LOT/PARCEL NO. _____   SECTION NO. _____
STREET/ROAD (ADDRESS) _____ SUBDIVISION _____
MUNICIPALITY _____ OTHER MEANS OF IDENTIFICATION: _____
_____

XXXXXXXXXXXXXXXXXXXXXXXXXXXXXXXXXXXXXXXXXXXXXXXXXXXXXXXXXXXXXXXXXXXXXXXXXXXXXXX

PLOT PLAN

TO BE COMPLETED BY APPLICANT

1. INDICATE DIRECTION OF NORTH.
2. INDICATE ON PLOT PLAN LOCATION OF EXISTING AND/OR PROPOSED BUILDINGS, DRIVEWAYS, WATER COURSES, BOATWELLS, ETC.
3. INDICATE ON PLOT PLAN THE LOCATION PROPOSED FOR INSTALLATION OF THE SEPTIC TANK AND TILE FIELD. THIS DESCRIBED AREA WILL BE EVALUATED FOR SOIL SUITABILITY.

SERVICE REQUEST

I/WE REQUEST THE FOLLOWING ON THE ABOVE DESCRIBED PROPERTY:

( ) ONSITE SOIL EVALUATION TO A DEPTH OF 5.5 FEET AS INDICATED.
( ) OBSERVATION OF DEEP SOIL PROFILE STUDIES AS INDICATED.

I/WE UNDERSTAND THAT I/WE WILL BE BILLED AT THE CURRENT HOURLY SERVICE FEE RATE FOR TIME IN EXCESS OF AMOUNT DEPOSITED. I/WE FURTHER UNDERSTAND THAT ANY PERMIT ISSUED AS A RESULT OF THIS APPLICATION WILL BE ONLY FOR THE LAND USE WHICH I HAVE DESIGNATED.

_____ FT.

_____ FT.

_____ FT.

_____ FT.

_____ STREET

_____ TOWNSHIP

_____ SIGNATURE OF APPLICANT

XXXXXXXXXXXXXXXXXXXXXXXXXXXXXXXXXXXXXXXXXXXXXXXXXXXXXXXXXXXXXXXXXXXXXXXXXXXXXXX

PROPOSED PERMIT DATA

NO. OF BEDROOMS	_____	NO. OF LAVATORIES	_____	NO. OF APTS./MOTEL UNITS	_____
GARBAGE GRINDER	_____	NO. OF EMPLOYEES	_____	CENTRAL LAUNDRY FACILITY	_____
NO. OF WATER CLOSETS	_____	NO. PER SHIFT	_____	NO. OF BOOTHS	_____
NO. OF BATHS/SHOWERS	_____	SEATING CAPACITY	_____	NO. OF STUDENTS	_____
AUTO. LAUNDRY	_____	OPERATING PERIOD	_____	NO. OF PATIENTS	_____
AUTO. DISHWASHER	_____	PUBLIC TOILETS	_____	NO. OF ROOMS	_____
SEWAGE EJECTOR PUMP	_____	URINALS	_____	NO. OF BERTHS	_____
WATER SUPPLY	_____			NO. OF STORES	_____

SINGLE FAMILY DWELLING ( )   DUPLEX ( )   APT. ( )   CONDO. ( )   INDUSTRIAL ( )
SHOPPING CENTER ( )   COMMERCIAL - TYPE ( ) _____

_____
REMARKS: _____

XXXXXXXXXXXXXXXXXXXXXXXXXXXXXXXXXXXXXXXXXXXXXXXXXXXXXXXXXXXXXXXXXXXXXXXXXXXXXXX

PLEASE COMPLETE THE FOLLOWING   (PRINT OR TYPE)

NAME OF APPLICANT	ADDRESS	POST OFFICE	ZIP	PHONE
NAME OF OWNER	ADDRESS	POST OFFICE	ZIP	PHONE

XXXXXXXXXXXXXXXXXXXXXXXXXXXXXXXXXXXXXXXXXXXXXXXXXXXXXXXXXXXXXXXXXXXXXXXXXXXXXXX

DATE: _____ APPLICATION NO. _____ PERSON TAKING APPLICATION _____

Fig. 2-16. Septic system Application Permit. Courtesy Macomb County, Michigan Dept. of Health.

pact the sides of the hole because this will change the test results. Pour fine gravel (pea gravel) into the test hole to about 2 to 3 inches in depth. Set a yardstick vertically on the gravel bed, and support it against a board laid horizontally across the hole. The yardstick must be supported vertically against the board by tying it to the board with wire or twine. Pour water into the hole to a level parallel to the center of the proposed drain pipe. Make a mark on the yardstick, or select an inch mark to coincide with the level of the water.

Start timing before the water has started to drain. If you plan to make this test in more than one hole at the same time, be sure to write down the starting time for each hole. Keep careful check on each hole to accurately time the moment when each is empty. Refill and repeat the test at each hole at least three times, especially if the results vary widely.

Refer to Table 2-1. As an example, assume the trench for the drain tile is 24 inches deep and the drain center line is 12 inches, multiply:

$$12 \times 12 \times 2 = 288 \text{ square inches}$$
$$288 \div 144 = 2.0 \text{ square feet/lineal foot}$$

If the effluent flow is 600 gallons/day, to find out the number of square feet of wall area needed, divide:

$$600 \div 4.0 = 150 \text{ (area for 10 minute rate)}$$

To find out the length of trench needed, divide:

$$150 \div 20 = 75 \text{ lineal feet of trench needed}$$

If the trench is made deeper, say 36 inches, and the drain line is kept at 12 inches, the effective trench wall area is doubled and the length of trench is halved. Do not take the length of trench from your calculations as ideal. The amount of rainfall, the variation in perme-

Table 2-1. Percolation Test Data.

Rate	Recommended minimum drain pipe wall area
1 minute or less	1.0 sq. ft./gal/day
2	1.5
3	2.0
4	2.5
5	3.0
10	4.0
20	4.6
30	5.2
40/60	7.0/9.-

ability of the soil, and the composition of the sewage all affect the operation of the drainfield and the septic tank itself. It is therefore wise to add perhaps 20 percent to the size of the field specified to take care of increases in usage of the system from extra persons and added appliances (a dishwasher or an automatic clothes washer).

Septic tanks are manufactured of concrete and come in many sizes to suit the use to which they are put. Common sizes for individual dwellings are: 1000-gallon regular tank, 1000- and 1250-gallon double compartment tank, and the 1500-gallon double compartment tank. The double compartment tanks (called a "Double Protection System") are recommended for use with garbage disposals. They also increase the life of the drainfield by reducing the chance of sludge entering the field.

The complete septic system can become overloaded, both the tank and the drainfield. This is apparent if effluent backs up and surfaces. Sometimes the effluent is black, and it always has a very unpleasant odor. The most common reason for overloading is that the discharge of liquids and solids into the system is in excess of its rated capacity. The standard of water use by an individual is 95 gallons/day. This breaks down as:

10 gallons cooking, etc.
6 gallons, lavatory
30 gallons, tub
15 gallons, dishwasher, every other day
24 gallons, toilet
10 gallons, automatic clothes washer, twice a week

The sewage from the normal dwelling is roughly 99 percent water and 1 percent solids. Of the solids, 80 percent is organic (feces, detergents, soaps, urine, food particles from disposals, and food pieces that fall into the sink drains accidentally). The remainder, the inorganic solids, are water softeners, borax, paint, photographic chemicals, household cleaners, and others. Nearly half the water in the sewer line is only slightly contaminated and is called *gray water*. Water used to flush the toilet is called *black water*.

Because gray water is relatively clean, (bathwater, shower water, and lavatory water) it does not need to go through the septic system. It may be diverted to a *dry well*. A dry well is similar in action to a section of the drainfield in that the draining action occurs on the sides of the well (also through the bottom). The well is in the form of a manhole. The difference is that the walls are laid up of block or brick, spaced an inch or so apart, and the bottom is soil. Thus the gray water is able to drain out and be carried away into the surrounding soil. Another type of dry well is a circular excavation filled with all sizes and shapes of rock piled loosely in the hole and covered with flat stones and tar paper. The gray water line enters the area of either type of dry well through the side wall.

Kitchen water has much grease in it, therefore a grease trap must be installed in this line before this water can be sent on to the dry well for disposal. In this case, if the gray water *is* diverted from the septic tank and field, the septic tank and field size can be reduced by one third. Using the 33 1/3 percent reduction allows some excess capacity in the septic system above the calculations, which is good. An even further increase might be advisable if the number in the household is expected to increase, or if large water-using appliances are purchased—such as automatic clothes washers and dishwashers.

Take the example of 4 people in the dwelling under consideration. Each person generates 95 gallons of waste water and solids:

$$4 \times 95 = 380 \text{ gallons}$$
Five days discharge shows
$$5 \times 380 = 1900 \text{ gallons}$$

Now allowing the 33 1/3 percent deduction for gray water, a five-day capacity septic tank would need to have a capacity of 1265 gallons, rounded off to 1500 gallons. This size of tank supposes that a dry well will be constructed. Even though this entails additional expense and labor, money is saved on the tank and field expense. At this point, it is wise to consult with the county agent as to conditions and the common construction methods used in the area of your property.

In the rare case that the soil in the area of the proposed drainfield is pure clay, you can do one of two things: find another site for the field (the septic tank should be fairly close to the field but can be some distance from the dwelling), or call in an expert and have your problem diagnosed and hopefully solved. It is rare that a satisfactory disposal field cannot be found, but in these cases professional help is needed.

When you have decided on the locations of the field, septic tank, dry well, and grease trap, make a complete layout to scale, with all dimensions and distances noted. Use a pencil because it might be necessary to make changes. Take this layout to the county agent or to the county health department. Apply for a permit to build this system. The personnel can answer all of your questions and even go out to look over your land and make suggestions. These people are very experienced and know the area and soil conditions. Take their advice. For layout see Fig. 2-3.

The Tile Field

Lay out the tile field carefully. The straighter the lines, the easier it will be for the effluent to flow through them. You might need some

90-degree turns, but avoid them. Use long sweep elbows, or 45-degree elbows. Wye fittings work well. If your field is extensive, it is best to hire a *trencher*. This machine is power operated. Trenches are 18 to 24 inches wide. Because the bottom of the trench is not included in the absorption surface, 24 inches is preferable. Many layouts include a *distribution box*. The line from the septic tank leads to this box (solid pipe up to this point). Two or more perforated lines leave this box to make up the drainfield in whatever layout pattern you have selected.

Plastic pipe or clay tile is used for the field. Plastic pipe has perforations down both sides. These holes should be positioned on each side, not on the top or bottom. Clay tile is laid, with 1/4-inch separation of each length from the next one. This opening is covered with a piece of tar paper on top to prevent soil from falling into the pipe. Plastic pipe makes it easier to maintain proper pitch (1/4 inch to 10 feet). Clay tile requires more care because the individual tiles can point "up hill" if you are not careful to maintain a downward pitch. As a guide to maintaining proper pitch, use a 10-foot 2 × 4 with a nail pounded on the bottom near the end, so that 1/4 inch protrudes. A level set on top of this will show level when the guide board is placed on the tile line. This gives the 1/4-inch to 10-foot pitch. The maximum pitch allowed is 3 inches per 100 feet. This is about 1/4 inch to 9 feet. The effluent must not run fast in the drain line because it must have time to trickle out and through the small holes in the sides of the plastic tube or out between the clay tile sections.

Fine stone is laid in the trench to a depth of 6 inches. This should be 6-A stone or pea stone. The drain line is then laid on this stone bed and 6 inches more of the same stone is put in, covering the drain line (see Figs 2-16 and 2-17). *Untreated* building paper, hay, or straw must be put over the stone to prevent soil from clogging the stone. Backfill is put in with a minimum of 10 inches and a maximum of 24 inches. The earth can be mounded to allow for settling. All these requirements might vary in different sections of the country, due to local regulations.

A good method of maintaining correct pitch when using clay drain tile is to use a *gradeboard*, a 2 × 4 about 10 feet long, with four short pointed stakes 8 inches long, nailed at right angles to the board length, flush with the top of the board. This is positioned in the bottom of the trench and leveled, using the guideboard and the level. Also available is a plumber's level, having a stud at one end which is adjusted down from the lower edge of the level to set the "pitch" or "grade" desired, then locked in place with the jamb nut on the other end of the stud. The level is then set on the gradeboard. When the level reads "level," the pitch of the gradeboard is correct.

When the gradeboard is in place, pour pea stone or 6-A stone in the trench to the top of the board (the gradeboard stays in the trench).

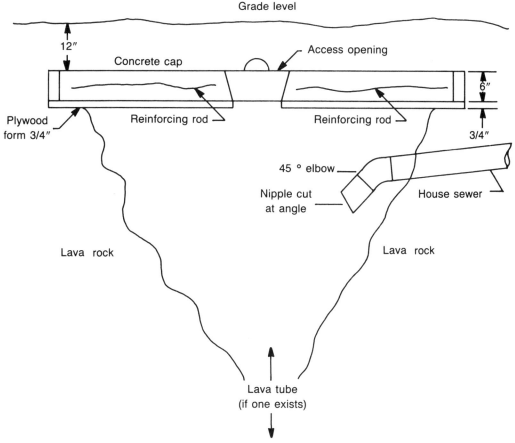

Fig. 2-17. Cesspool construction in the Hawaiian Islands.

After the drain tile is positioned on top of the gradeboard, more stone is poured. *Caution:* Be sure to cover the tile joints with tar paper pieces, covering only the top half of the tile joint before adding the remainder of the stone. This layer of stone should be 6 inches deep, measuring from the top of the gradeboard. Plastic drain pipe does not need the tar paper, just be sure the holes are on each side of the pipe, not on the top and bottom. You *can* do without using the guideboard (the one you set the level on), if you make sure the stone bed has the proper pitch (grade).

After the drainfield has been laid out and excavated, the gravel and drain lines have been installed, and the field excavations have been backfilled (note that the backfill should be mounded to allow for settling over time), you should proceed with the excavation for the septic tank and lines from the house to the tank, and from the tank to a distribution box (if used) and to the drainfield. All the ex-cavating can be done at one time if you use power equipment. Remem-ber that the deep pit for the tank and the open trenches invite accidents and liability on your part; cover them with plywood or boards.

It is best if you excavate the drainfield and install the tile and back-fill the trench promptly, to prevent heavy rains and other elements from damaging the open trench, stone, and tile. If you have one or two helpers, you might be able to complete the drainfield and instal-lation of the tank sewer lines, and distribution box in two or three days.

I recommend buying a precast septic tank. The tank manufactur-ing company will deliver the tank and place it in the excavation for you for a fixed price, depending on the size tank you need. A garbage disposal increases the size of the septic tank by one third or one half. Bear this in mind when doing your calculations for the size of the tank needed.

The excavation for the septic tank should be large enough to per-mit the tank to be lowered into the pit with at least 18 inches clear-ance all around. The tank must be level and the top must be 24 inches below ground level. Trenches leading from the house to the tank and from the tank to the field must be at least 36 inches below the sur-face and have a pitch (slant) of 1/4 inch per foot of length. This line must be solid pipe *not* having perforations on the side. If these lines must turn to make connections, use "long sweep" elbows. These el-bows, 90- and 45-degree bends, have a more gradual curve (radius is larger) which imposes less restriction to the flow of the sewage and effluent, thus tending to prevent clogging of these lines.

It is advisable to mark the location of the septic tank and distri-bution box (if used) with some sort of permanent marker. Steel pipes driven in the ground are a good choice. The trap door in the septic tank top should also be marked, because this tank must be pumped out at regular intervals (1 to 2 years). The tank truck that does the pumping out must not be allowed to drive over the tank, lines, or drainfield. Take this into consideration when laying out the system. Prompt and proper cleaning of the tank, a dry well for the gray water, and a grease trap will help create a nearly trouble-free system.

Consider what you put into the toilet and other plumbing fixtures that the septic system cannot handle and that will eventually clog the tank or drainfield. Items that are *not* disposable are baby diapers, sani-tary napkins, and anything that cannot dissolve in water. This includes rubber, plastic, bones, metal, wood, and chemicals. This is your dis-posal system. When it clogs or breaks down, you must fix it. People living in cities do not have these concerns because repairs to the sewer and water systems are not their responsibility, even though major repairs can cause an increase in taxes to pay for these repairs. Even then, the service continues to operate. If your septic disposal system or water supply fails, you are on your own. This makes it very impor-tant that both systems must be maintained and repaired periodically.

Troubleshooting

If the system is maintained properly it will operate with no attention for at least 10 to 20 years. As stated before, septic tank and field capacity must be increased by 1/3 to 1/2 to process the discharge from a garbage disposal, so reduce the use of the disposal if possible. Small bones, such as chicken and chop bones, even though ground into small pieces cannot be processed by the septic system and remain as sludge to be pumped out regularly. Be aware of the following symptoms of trouble:

1. Odors at the tank or at the field. The system, when operating correctly, will have no odor whatsoever. When the tank is opened for servicing, however, there is an odor. This is normal. Stoppage or clogging at the tank or in the field will be evident by a foul odor. You must take action at once to prevent permanent damage to the drainfield and pipe in the trenches.

2. Black or gray liquid oozing from the drainfield. This indicates a stoppage is plugging the drainfield. Have the tank pumped out as soon as possible. This also means permanent damage if not taken care of very soon.

3. Faulty operation. Sewage is broken down and digested in the septic tank by anaerobic bacteria which do not need oxygen. (The tank is airtight). This action is inhibited by paint solvents, bleaches, detergents, soaps and bowl or drain cleaners, and chemicals used in photo processing and other hobbies. Aerobic bacteria, which need oxygen to do their work, are in the drainfield. (The soil is porous and oxygen is present). Normal amounts of water are required for proper operation, but downspouts, sump pump discharge, and water softener backwash are all very hard on the septic system. Also, remember to refrain from using additives sold to make your system "work better." They do not help and might harm your system!

THE CESSPOOL

This type of disposal system is usually not approved because it can cause unsanitary conditions, and can result in the contamination of nearby wells. In the Hawaiian Islands, however, the cesspool is approved because the ground is composed of very porous lava rock, and the sewage will be absorbed readily and cause no problems. The cesspool might also be approved for temporary use if a municipal sewer system is to be installed in the near future.

The cesspool is excavated using dynamite and power equipment. A concrete cover is built, having an access opening for pumping the cesspool out, if necessary. The same companies that are in business pumping out septic tanks service cesspools.

The following regulations for cesspool construction are furnished courtesy of the State of Hawaii:

A. Cesspools

(1) Each cesspool shall be at least six (6) feet in diameter, clear opening, and should have a minimum sidewall of at least ten (10) feet below the inlet pipe, provided, however, that when a stratum of gravel or equally pervious material of at least four (4) feet thickness is found, or a lava tube is encountered which provides adequate drainage, the depth of such sidewall may be reduced. The ultimate depth required shall be determined by the Director based on actual soil materials encountered on the site and on the record of experience with the performance of cesspools in the area. Multiple cesspools, three (3) diameters apart from outer edges, may be used. Sidewall depth reduction may be allowed when multiple cesspools are utilized.

(2) Cesspool sidewalls shall be properly protected against cave-in by means of approved types of concrete rings, hollow tile blocks, or other approved materials. Where natural geological formations are encountered which are sufficiently stable to prevent caving of sidewalls, such as rock, white coral, clay or other similar composition, the stable material may be used as sidewall lining.

(3) A structurally sound concrete cover protruding at least six (6) inches beyond the perimeter of the cesspool and resting on firm ground shall be provided. The top of such cover shall be at least twelve (12) inches below the finished ground surface. At least one (1) covered manhole twelve (12) inches in minimum dimension must be provided in the cesspool cover for inspection, rodding or the emptying of the contents when required.

Layout and Construction of a Cesspool System

The cesspool system used in Hawaii is quite simple. In most areas of that state, a hole about 20 or more feet deep and 10 to 15 feet in diameter is blasted in the ground, using dynamite. A suitable location should be at least 50 feet from a well, and at least 10 feet from any property line (Table 2-2).

Most houses have a crawl space underneath, therefore the main sewer line will be constructed toward the cesspool opening rim. The portion leaving the crawlspace should be underground from that point to its discharge into the cesspool pit. Usually a 45-degree elbow is used to direct the sewage downward. (All drainlines should use *only* 45-degree elbows so as not to restrict the flow of sewage.) The pitch of the main sewer line should be 1/4 to 1/2 inch to the foot. More pitch will cause the liquid to flow over the solids, and not carry them along with the liquid. Less pitch will make both the liquids and solids clog the line. Maintain the pitch between these limits.

Table 2-2. Sewage Disposal Distances (State of Hawaii).

Minimum Horizontal Distance From	Cesspool (ft)	Septic Tank (ft)	Seepage Pit (ft)	Sub-Surface Disposal Field (ft)	Household Aerobic Unit (ft)	Injection Well (ft)
Wall line of any roof structure or building	10	5	5	5	5	
Property line	9	5	9	5	5	
Stream, the ocean at mean sea level, pond, lake	50	50	50	50	50	50
Large trees	10	5	10	10	5	
Seepage pit	18		12	5		
Cesspool	18		18	5		

Courtesy of State of Hawaii.

While the cesspool is under construction, the pit must be covered with plywood. A form of 3/4-inch plywood must then be constructed, with an overlap on solid ground of at least 12 inches. A 12-inch square hole must be cut near the center of the pit, and a form made 6 inches high, with sloping sides. This is an access opening for pumping and inspection. In addition, a form can be made around the edges of the plywood to contain the concrete. It is important to have reinforcing rods in the concrete so that it does not collapse. This will also give great strength to the concrete. Figure 2-17 shows the construction.

With luck, the pit will connect to a "lava tube," a tube or opening extending a great distance down into the earth. In this case, the cesspool will probably never fill up, because the tube may go down as much as 100 feet.

It is recommended that the top of the concrete be 12 inches below the finished grade, so that the top soil or other materials can be used as a covering for the concrete. This cesspool installation can only be used with suitable soil conditions or lava rock formations. Approval must be given by the county health authorities before starting construction. This system works very well when properly constructed and maintenance is almost nil. The access cover should be opened every two years for inspection.

3

Water System Components

This chapter gives the arrangement of the various components of the water system in a dwelling.

ENTRANCE INTO THE DWELLING

The water supply usually enters the dwelling from the street directly into the house basement. Sometimes it is necessary to have the line enter on the side of the house. If there is a well and a septic system in use, both these lines might already come in through the side or the back of the house. In this case, the new lines from the street can be brought in through the side. It is necessary to keep the sewer line at least 5 feet away from the house foundation. This is a requirement of the Plumbing Code.

THE METER

From a municipal supply, the water meter will be either in the basement (in cold climates) or in a meter box near the curb (in warm climate). All water pipes *must* be protected from freezing at all times. Protect the sewer line also. To accomplish this, both lines must be buried 4 to 5 feet deep. The line will come up out of the floor in the basement and the meter will be close to that point. A gate valve will be ahead of the meter, to shut off the water from the street in case the meter has to be removed for any reason. Usually a copper jumper

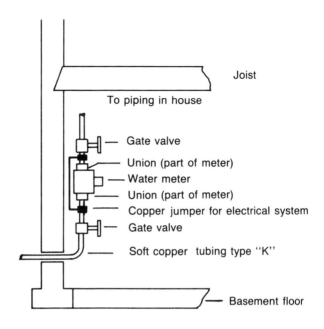

Joist

To piping in house

— Gate valve

— Union (part of meter)
— Water meter
— Union (part of meter)
— Copper jumper for electrical system
— Gate valve

— Soft copper tubing type "K"

— Basement floor

Fig. 3-1. Location of gate valves to isolate water meter from system and city water main. Note electrical jumper—this is required for electrical system grounding.

cable is connected to the pipes on each side of the meter. This is a part of the electrical wiring system for grounding purposes. On the other side of the meter is another gate valve. This prevents the water in the house pipes from running on the floor if the meter is removed (Fig. 3-1).

THE WATER SOFTENER

Water softeners are often necessary if very hard water is supplied by the well or the municipality. Nearby will be the water heater. Both are connected to the cold water line. Figure 3-2 is a typical line diagram showing how different lines are connected. It is customary to branch off from the main cold water line to feed the water softener first, because the water heater is to be supplied with softened water. The cold softened water continues on and supplies—as does the hot softened water—the following fixtures and appliances: dishwasher, shower, lavatories (wash basins), laundry tub, and automatic clothes washer faucets. Because the kitchen cold water faucet is used for drinking and cooking, it is *not* connected to the softened water supply. All toilets should be connected to a non-softened cold water supply because they use large amounts of water.

Many areas do not need water softeners because the water supply is very soft. Note that hard water is more healthful than soft water.

Water softeners can either be installed by the homeowner, or a

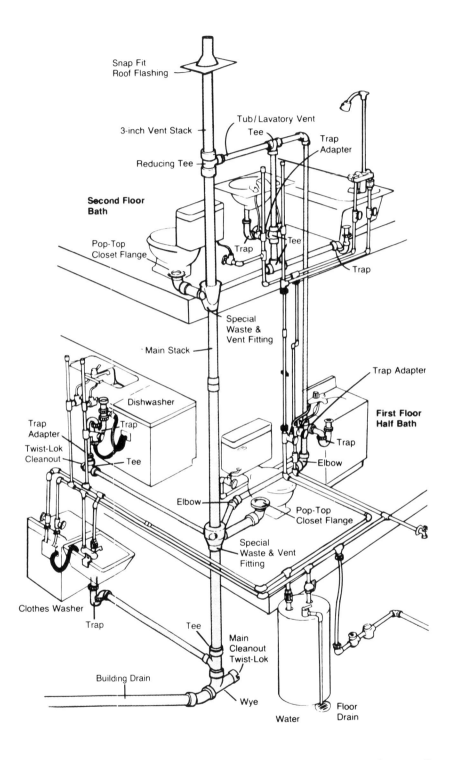

Snap Fit
Roof Flashing

3-inch Vent Stack

Tub/Lavatory Vent
Tee

Trap
Adapter

Reducing Tee

**Second Floor
Bath**

Pop-Top
Closet Flange

Tee

Trap

Trap

Special
Waste &
Vent Fitting

Main Stack

Trap Adapter

Dishwasher

First Floor
Half Bath

Trap
Adapter

Trap

Twist-Lok
Cleanout

Tee

Trap

Elbow

Elbow

Pop-Top
Closet Flange

Special
Waste & Vent
Fitting

Clothes Washer

Trap

Tee

Main
Cleanout
Twist-Lok

Building Drain

Wye

Water

Floor
Drain

Fig. 3-2. Piping layout showing hot and cold water lines and drainage systems. Courtesy Genova.

periodic service can be provided by a softener service company. The home-owned system takes some maintenance and time, but is probably cheaper than the service company.

THE WATER HEATER

There are three fuel sources for the water heater to use: natural or bottled gas, electricity, and fuel oil. The use of fuel oil is very rare now because these heaters are difficult to maintain and do not operate efficiently. Natural gas is cheapest. Bottled gas is somewhat higher but costs less than electricity, which is very high. If you have a choice, install natural gas. As far as installation costs, electric water heaters are the cheapest but recovery is slow, and power to the heater can be shut off at any time by the utility by means of a radio signal. There is a special lower rate for this usage or a much higher rate for "anytime usage" without interruption. Gas *is* best.

INSULATION

Water pipes should be insulated, not only to save energy but to prevent cold water pipes from sweating in basements and dripping. Do-it-yourself insulation is available at home improvement centers and hardware stores. The semi-rigid foam type is the best even though more expensive. Note that insulation will not prevent freeze-ups. Extreme cold will penetrate any insulation. The best protection is to use electric heat cables. Even those areas that are usually warm can experience rare freezing temperatures.

PLUMBING MATERIALS

Plumbing materials and fittings take many forms. The underground piping uses clay tile or cast iron soil pipe for sewer lines. Water lines underground are copper tubing Type K, a flexible form of copper tubing. Materials used inside the building are galvanized iron pipe with threaded fittings, or copper tubing either hard (rigid) or soft (able to be bent easily), which is soldered into different copper fittings such as elbows, tees, and many others. Plastic tubing and fittings are now being used extensively for both hot and cold water lines and sewer lines in houses. Some of this tubing is soft and can be fished into areas that hard plastic tubing could not fit easily.

Various supporting and clamping items are used to anchor each type of tubing, both metal and plastic. Plastic tubing is made in many chemical formulations such as PVC, polybutylene, polyethylene, ABS, and CPVC. Each type of plastic *must* be joined with the proper primer and cement for the type of plastic pipe being used.

Note: The use of plastic pipe and fittings of whatever composition is restricted or prohibited in certain areas by local plumbing codes. Contact your building inspection department before buying or using any plastic materials.

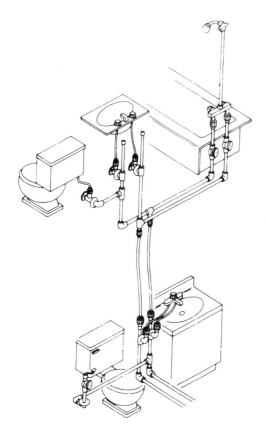

Fig. 3-3. Shutoff valves for easy repair or replacement of individual faucet assemblies. Courtesy Genova.

SIZING THE WATER SUPPLY SYSTEM

The water system in a dwelling must be sized so as to supply sufficient water at normal pressure (about 40 pounds). This is necessary to enable appliances such as the clothes washer and dishwasher to operate properly.

In the average one-family dwelling, the pipe size of the supply from a public source to the meter will be 1 inch nominal. After the meter and feeding the water heater and water softener, the size is 3/4 inch nominal. Branches from the main supply, after the softener and heater, are reduced to 1/2 inch to feed sinks, lavatories, toilets, bathtubs, dishwashers, and clothes washers.

All lines directly attached to each fixture are 3/8-inch OD (outside diameter) flexible copper, chrome-plated copper, or plastic tubing. This is a reduction from the 1/2-inch supply line. Attached to the end of the supply line is a stop valve, 1/2- x -3/8-inch compression. This valve reduces the line and also is a means to shut off the water supply when making repairs or replacing the fixture or faucet assembly (Fig. 3-3). Many years ago stop valves were not used, and the complete water system had to be shut down to make repairs of any kind.

These sizes and designs are accepted by most inspection departments, but it is wise to check with the department before installing pipe sizes or materials that might not be approved locally. An approved pressure-reducing valve is needed if the water pressure exceeds 80 pounds per square inch (psi). High water pressure will cause water hammer and can damage valves and appliances. Low water pressure will cause appliances such as dishwashers and clothes washers to fail to operate properly.

4

Sizing Sanitary
Drainage Lines

All drain lines must be sized, so as to provide capacity for fixtures connected to them. Tests revealed that the standard lavatory (washbowl) would discharge, through its drain, 7 1/2 gallons of water in one minute. This was established as one drainage fixture unit (dfu). One cubic foot equals 7 1/2 gallons. A listing of the common dwelling fixtures is shown in Table 4-1.

The minimum size of a stack or vent must not be smaller than 3 inches. Note also that only two water closets (toilets) are allowed to drain into a 3-inch line. No water closet shall discharge into a line smaller than 3 inches. There are other factors to take into consideration when sizing the drain lines. A horizontal drain of the proper size should be 1/3 full of sewage. This amount of sewage flow assures a "scouring action" in the drain. Too large a drain will inhibit this action; in this case larger is not better. The flow will be sluggish and solid material will settle to the bottom of the pipe and remain there while the liquid flows around it. Too small a drain will produce back pressure, basement flooding, and may siphon water out of traps connected to this drain.

Horizontal lines must slope (1/4 inch to the foot) uniformly. Sags in the line can cause stoppage, and at least, the sag will be filled with water and so block sewer gas from going out the vent stack. No soil (sewer) stack is permitted to be smaller than the largest horizontal branch connected to it. Every dwelling must have at least one vent

60

Table 4-1. Drainage Fixture Unit Values for Various Plumbing Fixtures.

BOCA TABLE P-601.1*		
Type of Fixture	Drainage Fixture Unit Value (dfu)	Minimum Fixture Trap and Drain Size
Clothes washer	3	1 1/2
Bathtub	2	1 1/2
Dishwasher	2	1 1/2
Floor drain, 2-inch waste	2	1 1/2
Lavatory	1	1 1/4
Laundry tray	2	1 1/2
Shower	2	1 1/2
Sink with disposer	2	1 1/2
Sink with two traps	3	1 1/2
Water closet (toilet)	6	3 or 4
*Partial table as applies to dwelling units only.		

stack extended full size through the roof using 3-inch pipe or larger. Also most plumbing codes require that the main building sewer be at least 4-inch.

SIZING SOIL AND WASTE STACKS

The waste stack (Table 4-2) shows that two kitchen sinks emptying into a single stack require the stack be 2-inch. A stack, which will have an offset of 45 degrees or less, is sized as though it was a totally ver-

Table 4-2. Building Drains and Sewers.

BOCA TABLE P-601.2a*	
Diameter of pipe in inches	Fall per foot
2	21
2 1/2	24
3	42#
4	216
5	480
6	840
*Partial table as applies to drains up through 6-inch. #Not over two water closets or two bathroom groups.	

tical stack. A stack that has the offset more then 45 degrees shall have the offset sized as a horizontal drain. Refer back to Table 4-1 for the dfu.

INSTALLING DRAINAGE PIPING

As stated before, there commended pitch is 1/4 inch to the foot. Sometimes, when the run from the dwelling to the street sewer is very long, the pitch must be made less so that the elevation at the street end does not end up below the street sewer elevation. This should be determined with a surveyor's instrument. The pitch might end up as 1/8- or 1/16-inch to the foot. In a dwelling without a basement, there might be sufficient drop to use the 1/4 inch to the foot pitch. Also previously noted, too great a pitch will cause problems, such as pulling the water seal from traps. Additional information is given in Tables 4-3 through 4-8.

To insure proper drainage action, fittings that change direction of the line should be of a style that aid rather than hinder proper flow in the line. It is best to use "long sweep" bends and "long turn" elbows. It is not necessary to use these fittings when changing from horizontal to vertical direction, but try to use the long sweep/turn fittings when there is enough room for them in the construction. Bends refer to cast iron drainage fittings, and elbows refer to threaded drainage (Durham) fittings.

CLEANOUTS

Because there is always the chance that a sewer line will become

Table 4-3. Horizontal Fixture Branches and Stacks.

BOCA TABLE P-601.2b*	
Diameter of Drain (inches)	Horizontal Branch Drain 1/4 in/ft. (dfu)
1 1/4	1
1 1/2	3
2	6
2 1/2	12
3##	32###
4	160

Includes horizontal branches of building drains.
No water closet shall discharge into a drain less than 3-inches.
Not over two water closets.
*Partial table as applies to dwelling units only.

Table 4-4. Approximate Discharge Rates
and Velocities in Sloping Drains Flowing Half Full.

Diameter of pipe inches	Discharge rate and velocity 1/4 inch/foot of slope	
	Discharge gpm	Velocity fps
1 1/4	2.41	1.26
1 1/2	3.91	1.42
2	8.42	1.72
2 1/2	15.3	1.99
3	24.8	2.25
4	53.4	2.73
*Partial table as applies to dwelling units only.		

clogged, it is necessary to install cleanouts (CO) at intervals in sewer and drainage lines. Cleanouts are required whenever there is a change in direction of the stack, or where the drain line under the floor changes direction.

A vertical stack must have its cleanout near the floor of a basement (6 inches above the finished floor). A cleanout for a line running underneath a concrete floor must be installed at least 2 inches above

Table 4-5. Size and Length of Vent Stacks and Stack Vents.

BOCA TABLE P-902.1a*						
Diameter of soil or waste stack (in.)	Total fixture units connected to stack (dfu)	Diameter of vent (in.) (Maximum developed length of vent in feet, given below)				
		1 1/2	1 1/2	2	2 1/2	3
1 1/4	2	30				
1 1/2	8	50	150			
1 1/2	10	30	100			
2	12	30	75	200		
2	20	26	50	150		
2 1/2	42		30	100	300	
3	10		42	150	360	1040
3	21		32	110	270	810
3	53		27	94	230	680
3	102		86	210	210	620
*Partial table as applies to dwelling units only.						

**Table 4-6. Minimum Diameters and Maximum Length of Individual
Branch, Circuit, and Loop Vents for Horizontal Soil and Waste Branches.**

BOCA TABLE P-902.1b*							
Diameter of horizontal branch (in.)	Slope or horizontal branch (in./ft.)	Diameter of vent (in.) (Maximum developed length of vent, in feet.)					
		1 1/4	1 1/2	2	2 1/2	3	4
1 1/4	1/4	NL#					
1 1/2	1/4	NL	NL				
2	1/4	290	NL	NL			
2 1/2	1/4	96	240	NL	NL		
3	1/4		97	420	NL	NL	
4	1/4			98	310	NL	NL
*Partial table as applies to dwelling units only. # NL means No Limit. Actual values in excess of 500 feet.							

BOCA Basic/National Plumbing Code/1984, Copyright 1983, Building Officials and Code Administrators, International, Inc. Published by arrangements with author. All rights reserved. (Used with permission).

the finished floor (this prevents the cleanout opening from being used as a floor drain). For the cleanouts, the vertical stack uses a tee; the underfloor line uses a wye plus a 1/8 bend and a short section of cast-iron drain line. The bell end is fitted with a threaded female adapter to accept a brass plug. When a cleanout is installed at a change of direction, only a wye is used. This occurs usually in a threaded, galvanized pipe drain line (Figs. 4-1 and 4-2).

Table 4-7. Size and Length of Sump Vents.

BOCA TABLE P-902.5*						
Discharge capacity of pump. (gpm)	Diameter of vent (in.) (Maximum developed length of vent, in feet)					
	1 1/4	1 1/2	2	2 1/2	3	4
10	NL#	NL	NL	NL	NL	NL
20	270	NL	NL	NL	NL	NL
40	72	160	NL	NL	NL	NL
60	31	75	270	NL	NL	NL
80	16	41	150	380	NL	NL
*Partial table as applies to dwelling units only.						
# NL means No Limit. Actual values greater than 500 feet.						

BOCA Basic/National Plumbing Code/1984, Copyright 1983, Building Officials and Code Administrators, International, Inc. Published by arrangements with author. All rights reserved. (Used with permission).

Table 4-8. Maximum Distance of Fixture Trap from Vent.

BOCA TABLE P-909.1			
Size of trap	Size of fixture drain	Fall per foot	Distance from trap
1 1/4"	1 1/4"	1/4"	3' 6"
1 1/4"	1 1/2"	1/4"	5'
1 1/2"	1 1/2"	1/4"	5'
1 1/2"	2"	1/4"	8'
2"	2"	1/4"	6'
3"	3"	1/4"	10'
4"	4"	1/4"	12'

Fig. 4-1. Drain cleanout. See also drain connections for sinks.

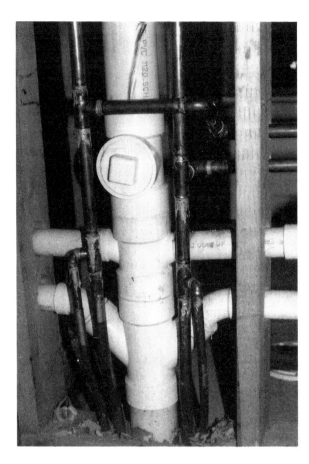

Fig. 4-2. Cleanout in riser. Note connections from sink traps.

The plugs, which are used to close these cleanout openings, are of brass with a raised square boss. A pipe wrench is used to break the plug loose. Many plumbers use grease instead of pipe joint compound for ease of removal. Four-inch plugs don't break loose easily. A cleanout is always provided where the main sewer line leaves the building: this allows direct access to the sewer line from the building to the street sewer. A horizontal line requires a cleanout at the far (high) end of the line. Cleanouts are required every 50 feet for 3-inch and smaller horizontal lines, and every 100 feet on 4-inch and larger horizontal lines. Where there is a plumbing fixture such as a sink or lavatory, the trap can be removed and the line cleaned out from there. This is especially useful at the end of a sewer line because it saves the installation of a cleanout.

VENT PIPING

For a drainage system to operate properly, it must be vented, or "ventilated." This means that air circulates in the vent lines and empty sections of the drainage and sewage systems. One thing this does is prevent any air pressure on the water in the traps of the fixtures. For this reason, every trap must have a vent. Another important function of the vent system is the removal of the so-called "sewer gas." This gas contains caustic chemicals, which—when combined with the moisture in the lines—form sulphuric acid, which is extremely corrosive to the metals in the system. Because of the "1/3 full" requirement, flow in the drainage and sewage pipes of air is in the opposite direction up these pipes and out the termination of the vent pipe to the atmosphere. Because drainage fittings are used in making up the vent lines, pitch (1/4 inch to the foot) is automatically provided for. No amount of pitch is required, but a certain amount should be provided.

Stack vents are extensions of the soil or waste stack above the highest horizontal drain connection (such as above all connections of a second floor bathroom) which continue up through the roof. Vent stacks provide air circulation in the drainage system and are run alongside or some distance away from the soil pipe stack, depending on whether there is room next to the soil pipe stack. The vent stack starts in the basement where it is tied in to the soil stack. In a dwelling, it continues vertically through the roof or, in some cases, may tie back into the soil stack.

The basement connection is made using a wye and a 1/8 bend or a 45-degree elbow. In a dwelling, this line usually is 2-inch galvanized pipe. Openings are left at locations adjacent to fixtures so that connection to the vent stack is easy.

An individual vent is to vent *one* plumbing fixture; this vent may connect back to a main vent or rise through the roof directly by itself. The maximum distance between a fixture trap and its vent is 30 inches for a 1 1/4 trap and 42 inches for a 1 1/2 trap. If an individual vent is to connect back into the vent stack, this connection (tee) should be at least 6 inches above the fixture overflow line, also called the *flood level rim*, which is the top rim of the fixture, above which water will overflow onto the floor. This prevents the vent from becoming a waste line for the fixture.

STACK TERMINALS

The termination of the stack is 1 foot above the roof. These terminals must not be closer than 10 feet from windows or doors, and must rise 7 feet above a flat roof which is used as something other than a roof, such as a sun deck. Commercially made roof vents are available for sealing the roof opening. Some for use in cold climates are larger than the pipe and are used to ventilate and warm the end of the stack above the roof proper. The hole cut in the roof is larger by 2 inches in diameter to allow attic heat to warm the stack to prevent frost buildup. Moist air from the vent system that freezes and accumulates can stop up this vent pipe.

WET VENT

When a portion of a vertical vent line also serves as a drain line, this dual section is known as a wet vent. When a kitchen sink connects to a vent, and a lavatory also connects to this same vent line but is lower than the connection from the sink, the section between these two connections is used as both a vent and drain line. At times this might cause a partial stoppage. One solution would be to enlarge the drain line if possible, and another choice is to vent each fixture separately and connect to the vent stack 6 inches above the flood level rim of the highest fixture. Many states permit these wet vents, and do not seem to have much trouble. Check with your local plumbing department to find out if wet vents are approved in your area.

Figures 4-3 and 4-4 show the plumbing layouts for one-and two-story homes, giving the sizes of the drain and vent lines. These layouts show all traps individually vented. This method will satisfy nearly all plumbing codes used in the United States. The lines will stay free of stoppages and the traps will keep their water seals because every trap has its own vent line, except floor drains which are not vented.

THE PLUMBING TRAP

All plumbing fixtures are required to have a trap. This is a fitting made in the shape that provides a water seal. Traps are **U** shaped or **P** shaped, providing a low place, or dip that holds water. When this trap is properly connected to a drain and vent line, it will prevent sewer gases from coming up in the sink, lavatory, or other fixture. It also allows rapid drainage of the fixture while preserving the water seal. Some installations having many fixtures with drain and vent connections might have more than one fixture on the same drain and vent line. For a trouble-free system, it is recommended that each trap have its own individual vent line.

The **P** trap is furnished in two styles: the common seal and the deep seal. This refers to the distance from the curved part (top dip) to the bottom of the pipe leaving the trap (crown weir). This distance in the common seal trap is 2 inches; in the deep seal it is 4 inches. Figure 4-5 shows the trap and its parts. The deep seal trap is used for abnormal conditions, such as extreme heat—which would evaporate the water seal—or where venting is not good. Most installations use the common seal.

All traps for a dwelling should be at least 1 1/2 inch, with the exception of lavatories, which can be 1 1/4 inch. Water closets have a built-in **S** trap. This is the only permitted use of the **S** trap. Bathtubs in older dwellings might have a drum trap. This drum trap is not recommended because of the chance of leakage of sewer gas into the bathroom. Do not use these traps. The running trap is in the form of a **U**. This is used on drain lines that are horizontal, such as the main sewer, and is placed near the exit of the sewer line from the dwelling.

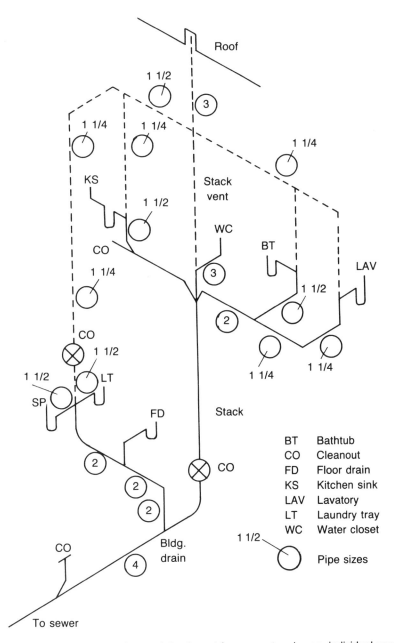

Fig. 4-3. Sanitary waste and vent piping layout for a one-story house, individual venting.

To ensure proper drainage and to eliminate siphoning away of the water seal, there is a maximum distance between the trap and its vent. For a 1 1/4 trap the distance is 2 feet, 6 inches; for the 1 1/2 trap the distance is 3 feet, 6 inches. A floor-type fixture such as a bathtub is vented by fitting a drainage tee in the horizontal line,

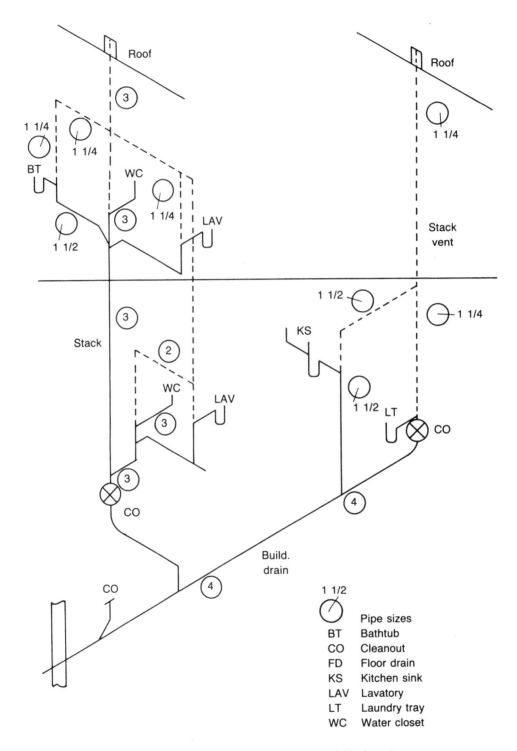

Fig. 4-4. Sanitary waste and vent piping layout for a two-story house, individual venting.

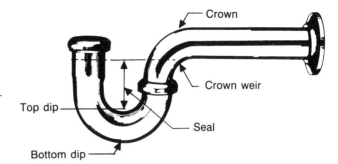

Fig. 4-5. Standard fixture trap with parts labeled.

then beyond that a 1/8 bend angles the line into the drain line. The side opening of the drainage tee points up, and the vent line then connects into the main vent riser (vertical line). This connection must be made at least 6 inches above the flood level rim of the fixture (Fig. 4-6).

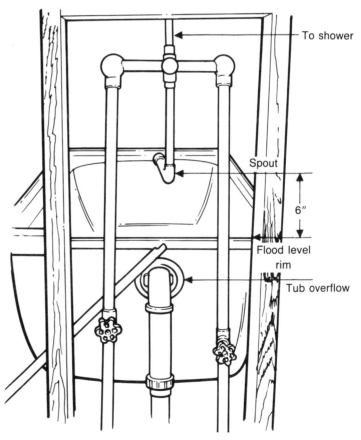

Fig. 4-6. Rough-in for tub and shower showing flood level rim.

When repairing older fixtures having traps that are obsolete or prohibited, use a modern approved type if at all possible. The height above the floor of the discharge of the trap (the horizontal part) shall not be higher than the connection of this line to the drain line. If the connection at the drain line is lower than the trap discharge, this arrangement becomes an **S** trap, which is prohibited. In this case, adding an extension to the tail piece (the part connected to the fixture) will make the trap lower and thus give the correct pitch of 1/4 inch to the foot.

Plastic drain lines, vent lines, and traps are now used. This material is satisfactory, but the codes of each municipality differ in some respects, and you must check with the plumbing inspection department to find out if plastic materials are approved.

SIZING WATER SUPPLY PIPING

Because the piping in a dwelling must be large enough to supply sufficient water at adequate pressure, pipe sizes need to be correctly determined. Sizing the piping in a one-family dwelling is routine. The number and size of the fixtures will be similar in all one-family dwellings. This book is not concerned with multiple dwelling buildings nor commercial installations.

A minimum size of 3/4-inch is required for the following installations:

● Water service from the water main in the street to the water meter.
● The first section of the inside piping beyond the meter (usually to the water heater or softener).
● To a sill cock (outside hose faucet).
● To the water heater.
● From the outlet of the water heater (the first section to the first branch line).

No concealed piping may be smaller than 1/2 inch. No more than three fixtures in the same bathroom may be supplied by 1/2-inch pipe (such as tub, lavatory, and water closet). The minimum branch pipe to a fixture must be 1/2 inch. Supply pipes to the individual fixture may be 3/8 inch or 1/4 inch, provided they are not concealed within the walls.

THE DANGERS OF CROSS-CONNECTIONS

There is a real and serious danger from cross-connections and backflow in a dwelling. Draining water lines creates a vacuum within them. This can suck dirty water, if, for example, a connected garden hose is left in a swimming pool. If the hose faucet has been left open while

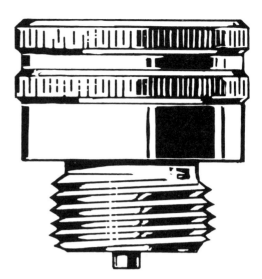

Fig. 4-7. Anti-siphon valve for outside sill cock.

filling the pool, and the water pipes have been drained, dirty pool water will be sucked into the clean water system. A hose connection vacuum breaker on the hose faucet will prevent this situation (Fig. 4-7).

The modern bathtub has no opening below the rim for a faucet assembly: the assembly is now installed 5 to 6 inches above the top of the tub rim. All modern fixtures provide for a minimum air gap of 1 inch. This is required by the Plumbing Code.

Dishwashers have an air gap fitting on the back rim of the kitchen sink that is chrome plated and matches the faucets. Where waste water flows directly into a drain line such as from a drinking fountain or air conditioner discharge, a special fitting is used to make the connection to the drain line. A special pear-shaped casting having slots all around with pipe threads on each end is installed in the drain line. This provides the required air gap in the drain line. Another air gap is a pipe nipple with one end cut at an angle and discharging over an open sink.

5

Materials
Used in Plumbing

The installation of plumbing fixtures and lines makes use of many and varied materials. Some of the most basic materials are pipe and fittings.

STEEL PIPE

Plumbing pipes are manufactured of many materials. Lead is still used for certain applications but is not found in dwellings built in the last 40 years. Most of these homes used galvanized steel (iron) pipe for the water lines, and the so-called "black iron" pipe for gas, steam, and hot water lines.

At this point, it should be explained that steel or iron pipe size is measured by the inside diameter (ID), not the outside diameter. This size designation is called the nominal size. The actual ID is never exactly this figure and is only approximate. As an example, 1/2-inch pipe has an ID of 0.622 inch and 3/4-inch pipe has an ID of 0.824. Much lumber is also designated by nominal sizes; measure a 2- x -4 stud and see.

All steel pipe 1/2-inch and larger is available in three wall thicknesses: standard, extra heavy, and double extra heavy. All these different wall thicknesses have the same OD for each size designation so that standard pipe dies can be used. Pipe fittings, elbows, tees, etc., come in sizes to match the pipe being used, both as to size and

Fig. 5-1. Representative group of malleable iron fittings. Courtesy Stockham Valves & Fittings.

finish—black or galvanized (Fig. 5-1).

Drainage fittings are specially made to allow the pipe to be screwed into the fitting and meet a shoulder. This is so that no ridge is left to collect debris. In addition, the threads of tees, elbows, wyes, etc., are at a slight angle to the face of the fitting, to give the pipe a pitch of 1/4 inch for each foot of the run of the pipe. This equals a 1-inch drop in 4 feet of pipe run. The pitch (slope) must not be any less or more than this 1/4 inch. Less will cause sluggish flow and more might suck the water out of sink traps because of the rapid movement of the waste water in the drain line.

COPPER TUBING

Copper tubing has supplanted steel pipe because of its ease of installation. The work is easier and faster; there is no threading of pipe and no heavy tools are used. Copper tubing is referred also by its nominal size, for example, 1/2 inch nominal. The ID of this size is 0.545 inch, closer to the 1/2-inch size than steel pipe. The inside surface of copper tubing is very smooth and a given size will carry more water than the same size steel pipe (Figs. 5-2 and 5-3).

There are three weights of copper tubing: K wall thickness—0.049; L wall thickness—0.042; M wall thickness—0.035. Type M is sometimes used for dwelling water lines when approved by Plumbing Code authority, otherwise type L must be used. Because all types have the same OD, the same fittings are used for each weight tubing. Plumbers designate copper tubing by its nominal size, i.e., 1/2 inch, 3/4 inch, etc. Pipe fitters, refrigeration and air conditioning mechanics,

Fig. 5-2. Wrot copper pressure fittings. Courtesy Mueller Brass Co.

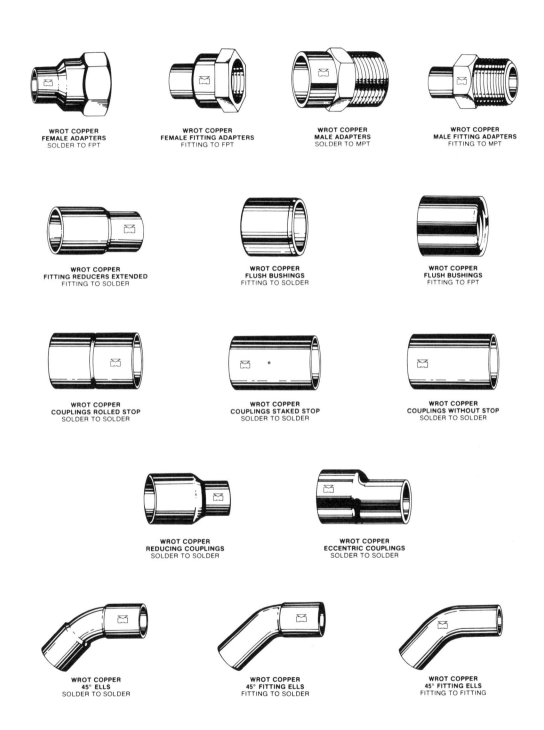

WROT COPPER
FEMALE ADAPTERS
SOLDER TO FPT

WROT COPPER
FEMALE FITTING ADAPTERS
FITTING TO FPT

WROT COPPER
MALE ADAPTERS
SOLDER TO MPT

WROT COPPER
MALE FITTING ADAPTERS
FITTING TO MPT

WROT COPPER
FITTING REDUCERS EXTENDED
FITTING TO SOLDER

WROT COPPER
FLUSH BUSHINGS
FITTING TO SOLDER

WROT COPPER
FLUSH BUSHINGS
FITTING TO FPT

WROT COPPER
COUPLINGS ROLLED STOP
SOLDER TO SOLDER

WROT COPPER
COUPLINGS STAKED STOP
SOLDER TO SOLDER

WROT COPPER
COUPLINGS WITHOUT STOP
SOLDER TO SOLDER

WROT COPPER
REDUCING COUPLINGS
SOLDER TO SOLDER

WROT COPPER
ECCENTRIC COUPLINGS
SOLDER TO SOLDER

WROT COPPER
45° ELLS
SOLDER TO SOLDER

WROT COPPER
45° FITTING ELLS
FITTING TO SOLDER

WROT COPPER
45° FITTING ELLS
FITTING TO FITTING

Fig. 5-3. Wrot copper pressure fittings. Courtesy Mueller Brass Co.

and other trades designate these same fittings and tubing by the actual OD of the tubing. The *inside* diameter of fittings fits the *outside* diameter of the tubing. There is an additional tubing designation used with type L called ACR (*Air Conditioning, Refrigeration*) tubing. These 20-foot lengths have sealed ends to keep out dirt and moisture, the enemies of a refrigeration system. The ACR tubing is type L cleaned and sealed.

Copper tubing is joined in three ways: soldering (sweating), using compression fittings, and using flare fittings. Most water lines in a dwelling — 1/2 inch and larger — are soldered, except where pipe unions are needed for disconnecting the tubing from a fixture. Water heaters and water meters will always use unions. Note that it is important to know that connections between copper tubing and iron or steel pipe *must* include a dielectric union or dielectric coupling (Fig. 5-4). Copper and iron, in touching each other in the presence of moisture, will start a chemical reaction at the point of contact, causing rusting or corrosion. A dielectric fitting will prevent this reaction.

The dielectric union has a rubber washer between the dissimilar metals, plus a fiber sleeve between the union collar and the brass half. The coupling has a plastic inside where the threads are. Both fittings thus effectively insulate/isolate the different metals from each other. Copper tubing is soldered using a propane torch available in hardware stores. On large installations, an acetylene torch is used. Its larger tank lasts longer and the cost is thus cheaper in the long run. Soldering techniques will be explained in Chapter 7. Copper tubing sizes in a dwelling will be 1/2- and 3/4-inch nominal, type L or M. The water main coming in to the house will be type K, soft, 1-inch nominal, up

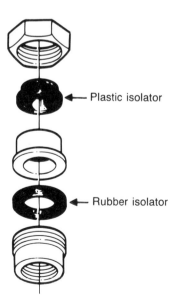

Plastic isolator

Rubber isolator

Fig. 5-4. Dielectric union used to separate dissimilar metals and eliminate corrosion at this joint.

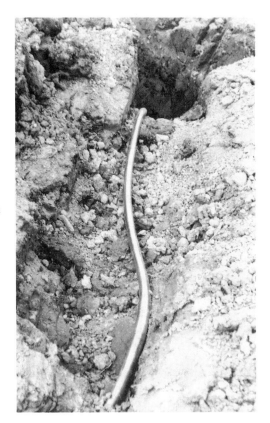

Fig. 5-5. Type K copper, soft, used as a water main to a building.

to the meter. The 3/4-inch nominal continues from there to feed the various fixtures (Figs. 5-5 and 5-6).

All fixtures, except the bathtub and water heater, are connected to the 1/2-inch branch lines using a shutoff valve (Fig. 5-7) and 3/8-inch OD riser tubes (Fig. 5-8)—chrome-plated soft copper tubing that is sold in assorted lengths. The shutoff valve is soldered to the end of the 1/2-inch branch line coming out of the wall. The leaving side of the valve is 3/8-inch compression (this is part of the valve). Compression fittings come in many styles—separate from valves—such as male pipe to compression, compression to compression, etc.

The valve connection will consist of a hex-shaped nut with flat top, a ferrule, and the mating end, which is part of the valve in this case. To assemble, slip the nut up on the tube, slip the ferrule up on the tube, and insert the tube end in the mating end on the valve body. Start the nut on the threads by hand, and turn it at least one full thread. These threads are very fine and are easily cross-threaded when started on the male threads, so always start by hand at least one full thread. Both parts must be perfectly aligned before starting the nut on the threads. These parts may be taken apart and reassembled many times, if done with care. Do not tighten excessively, or the ferrule will

Fig. 5-6. Type K copper, soft, stubbed up from concrete pour to supply fixtures in building.

Fig. 5-7. Stop valve, chrome, used to shut off water to faucet assemblies on lavatories and sinks. Courtesy Plumb Shop.

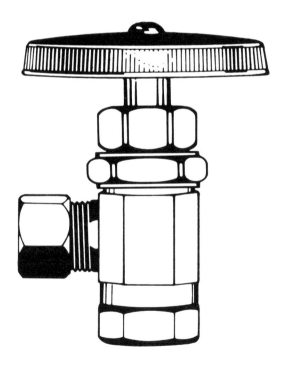

Fig. 5-8. Flexible chrome riser used from stop valve to the connections on sinks and lavatories.

be deformed and might leak when the nut is tightened a second time.

The third method of joining copper tubing is with flare fittings. These fittings are of cast brass having a pipe thread on one end, or flare threads on both ends. Usually the flare nut is sold separately, as opposed to compression fittings which are sold as an assembly, body, ferrule, and nut. Because there is no ferrule, the end of the tubing must be flared out to a 45-degree angle, or cone shaped. This matches the bevel on the end of the flare body, and the flare nut pulls the tubing flare surface down on this bevel to make an exceptionally tight joint. Flare fittings are of two grades: water fittings which are manufactured from brass bar stock on a lathe, and refrigeration fittings which are forged brass to withstand the much higher pressures used in this field.

PLASTIC PIPE

Plastic pipe has been on the market for many years, with improvements and new formulations continually being made to keep up with the latest needs of the industry. There are several types available, each having specific uses.

Polyethylene (PE). Polyethylene is black, flexible, and sold in coils. It can be used only outside for cold water.

Polyvinyl Chloride (PVC). Polyvinyl Chloride is rigid and suitable for cold water.

Chlorinated Polyvinyl Chloride (CPVC). CPVC pipe can be used up to 100 PSI and at 180 degrees F., thus it can be used for hot and cold water lines. CPVC requires that a primer (cleaner) be applied to the fitting and pipe end before the cement is applied.

Acrylonitrile-Butadiene-Styrene (ABS). ABS is black pipe, used in DWV (drain-waste-vent) systems.

Polyethylene (PE). Polyethylene is flexible thermoplastic (can be heated, bent and will hold the bend when cold). It comes in light tan or black. This type will also withstand 100 psi and 180 degrees F.

The advantages of plastic pipe are as follows; it is lightweight, easy to use, cheapest in cost, and has some insulating value. The few disadvantages are: not all types can be used with hot water because excessive heat will melt the pipe or make holes, causing a leak. Horizontal runs need closer spacing of hangers or pipe straps than galvanized pipe. Not all area jurisdictions allow plastic pipe, so check with your local plumbing inspection department (Figs. 5-9 and 5-10).

Common pipe sizes of plastic used in a dwelling are nominal sizes of 1/2, 3/4, and 1 inch. A smaller size of flexible PE (Polyethylene) having an OD of 3/8 inch is used to connect sinks, lavatories, and toilets to the stop valves underneath the fixture, and to the connections underneath the faucet.

Plastic pipe fittings are as numerous and varied as galvanized or copper fittings. And as with copper, there are adapters to convert from plastic to threaded pipe when needed. In fitting up plastic pipe, the length is assembled dry into the fitting and the assembly is lined up and set in place. When the assembly is as you want it, mark the fitting side and the piece of pipe inserted into it with a soft lead pencil. Make the two lines starting from the socket and extending over on the pipe as one continuous line. This is necessary because you must work quickly after applying the solvent to the parts. The marks allow you to line up the parts correctly (Fig. 5-11).

After dry assembly, dismantle the connection, and apply cement (solvent) to the outside of the pipe and the inside of the fitting (Fig. 5-12). Insert the pipe into the fitting socket, twist slightly in both directions to spread the cement evenly, quickly line up the pencil marks, and hold for 15 to 20 seconds. The parts must be held together because the pipe tends to push back out of the fitting. You are now at

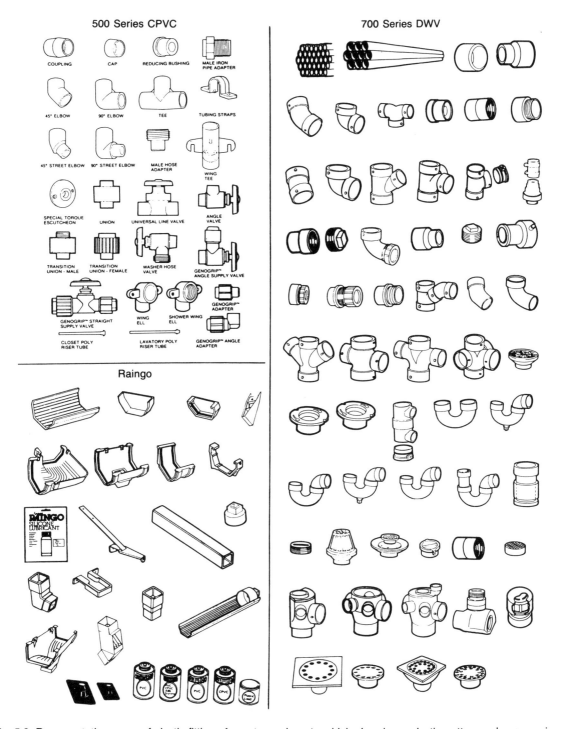

Fig. 5-9. Representative group of plastic fittings for water and waste which also shows plastic gutters and accessories, Raingo brand. Courtesy Genova.

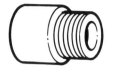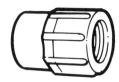

Fig. 5-10. Male and female adapter fittings for plastic to threaded pipe which are used for copper to plastic pipe.

the point of no return! The joint cannot be taken apart. The only recourse is to cut off the fitting, add a coupling, short piece of pipe, and a new fitting, and start again. Be sure to use the right primer and solvent (cement) for the type of plastic you are using, and make sure you have a good fit before applying the cement and making up the joint.

As stated before, plastic pipe must have hangers or other supports closer together than metal pipe has. Hangers should be spaced 32 inches apart. When plastic waste pipe carries hot water, as from a dishwasher, the pipe must be supported on continuous wood strips for its entire length. Pipe running vertically needs to be supported every 4 feet, using clamping hangers with arms extending out to rest

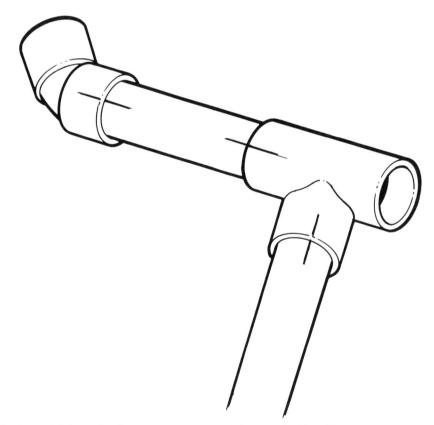

Fig. 5-11. Plastic pipe and fittings, showing pencil marks on both fitting and tubing. This makes it easier to align the fittings to face properly.

on a floor or other horizontal building member, or must be clamped to an upright member with a standard pipe clamp. Plastic pipe can be flared using a special plastic flaring tool and plastic tubing cutter. Plastic cutting wheels can be installed in a standard tubing cutter, in place of the original.

CAST-IRON SOIL PIPE

Cast-iron pipe has a very long life, and is impervious to most liquids. Many older dwellings have this pipe for the drainage and sewer systems. Most systems use the 4-inch size, and because this size will not fit within a 2-x-4 partition, a 2-x-6 wall must be built, where these pipes are to be run. Where allowed, copper or plastic DWV pipe is used, thus eliminating the extra-thick wall requirement.

Another advantage in using cast-iron soil pipe is that tree roots cannot penetrate the joints—as can happen with vitrified clay pipe—because they are sealed with oakum and molten lead. Cast-iron soil pipe is longer-lasting, and over the long run the total cost is less because of less maintenance.

Cast-iron soil pipe is furnished in two forms: the bell and spigot, and the no-hub. The bell-and-spigot style has a bell or hub on one end, and a spigot or plain end on the other. The plain end of one piece fits into the hub of another piece, and the oakum is tamped (caulked) in the annular space to within 1 inch of the top. Molten lead is then poured in to fill the remaining space, and caulked to form a water- and root-tight seal. Caulking irons are used for both the oakum and the lead by pounding on the caulking iron with a hammer.

Another sealing method uses a neoprene gasket inserted into the hub after being lubricated on both sides. The spigot of the next piece is forced in, using a special assembly tool that pulls the pipe sections together.

The no-hub type uses a neoprene sleeve into which the ends of both lengths are forced. A stainless steel band is then clamped around the sleeve and tightened using the screw clamps attached to the band. This band resembles the small hose clamps found in hardware and auto stores.

Connections using either type of neoprene gasket are somewhat flexible and must be supported on hangers set more closely together than necessary for lead caulked joints. Underground lines must also be supported carefully to avoid sags and reverse pitch. If not supported properly, the line might clog up and cause trouble.

VITRIFIED CLAY PIPE

In many older dwellings, clay sewer pipe was used outside the foundation and to the street sewer. A large problem with this pipe is that tree roots can penetrate the mortar in the joints and plug the line.

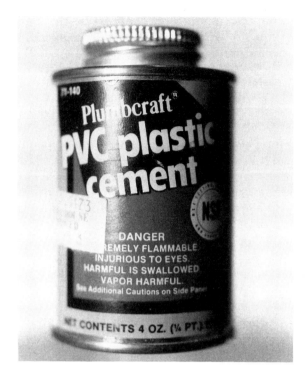

Fig. 5-12. PVC plastic cement. Note warning on can.

Clay sewer pipe is assembled in much the same way as cast iron pipe in that it uses oakum, but unlike cast-iron pipe, mortar rather than lead is used to fill the space between the bell and spigot. This mortar is then beveled to provide a smooth finish. Another method uses the oakum plus a commercial compound that is heated and poured into the annular space, but is not tamped in.

PIPE SUPPORTS

All pipe lines must be supported to prevent sags or possible breakage of fittings and pipes. Even underground lines must have adequate support. Buried drain lines must also be pitched downward in the direction of flow. If the line is bell and spigot, the bell (hub) must have soil dug out where the hub will rest so the straight section rests on tamped or undisturbed soil.

Above-ground piping has many of the same requirements. Correct pitch (usually 1/4 inch to the foot) must be maintained on drain and sewer lines. Because cast-iron pipe is very heavy, strong supports are needed, as are secure methods of attaching the hanger to the building structure.

Supports for lightweight pipe can be one- or two-hole pipe straps, ring hangers, and perforated strap. Use steel supports for iron or steel pipe and copper for copper tubing. Ring hangers can be hung from

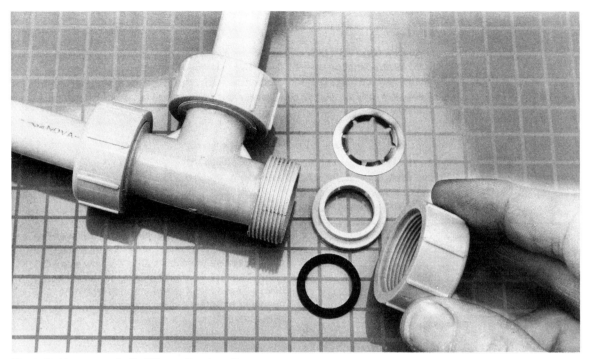

Fig. 5-13. Uncopper plastic fittings. Courtesy Genova.

the above strap or from a threaded rod attached to the building structure. Some ring hangers used with copper tubing are either copper plated or solid copper.

Clevis hangers are used for larger pipe sizes. They are in the form of an open **U** with a triangular top piece separate. A through bolt ties the pieces together, and a hole in the top of the triangular piece provides connection for a threaded rod for suspending the hanger from the building structure. In a residence, copper tubing is suspended from pipe hooks—heavy wire in a **V** shape with the top ends bent and pointed to be pounded into a floor joist.

Many times, because of the contact of the pipe with the joist, the noise of water flowing in the copper pipe is amplified. This can be quieted by moving the hook down a bit, putting a small piece of rubber between the hook and the pipe, and leaving space between the pipe and the bottom of the joist.

Another faulty installation that I found concerned a 2 1/8-inch copper air conditioning line held up by copper perforated strap. The pipe vibrated and was being worn through by the strap (the outline of the strap could be seen underneath the strap location). I cured this by also padding the pipe at the point of contact with the strap. As a rule, vibration will not cause this much damage, but it's best to use the rubber pad for both vibration and noise.

SPECIAL INTEREST PRODUCTS

Genova has recently come out with a new line of plastic valves and fittings. These are called Uncopper and will connect to CPVC, copper, polybutylene and galvanized pipe. They require no tools and are tightened by hand for a leakproof joint. Figure 5-13 shows an Uncopper tee partially disassembled to illustrate the adapters for the different kinds of pipe connections. The Appendix includes a complete listing of solvent weld pipe and fittings made by Genova.

The Plumb Shop Company has also developed a similar product, called the Poly-Lock System. These fittings connect plastic to copper and galvanized pipe. Some fittings do require a wrench on the metal nut of the fitting.

6

Tools

Some tools used in plumbing work are specialized; many others are standard tools that the homeowner might have on hand. Examples of the latter are small pipe wrenches, adjustable wrenches for nuts and faucet parts having flats—using an 8- or 10-inch size, and tubing cutters. The cold chisel, hammer, rule, and screwdriver are also common in almost every household.

Adjustable Wrench. Originally designed and manufactured by the Crescent Tool Company, this tool comes in 4-inch to 15-inch sizes. The wrench is set over the nut or hex faucet part and adjusted snugly over the flats. Pressure is exerted on the handle, on the side opposite the movable jaw. This prevents the jaw from breaking. For a non-slip hold, use a box wrench.

Allen Wrench. This is a piece of hexagon steel bar bent into an **L** shape with one short leg and one long leg. The various sizes range from those so small the hexagon shape cannot be seen to those with the distance across the flats of 1 inch or more (Fig. 6-1).

An infinite variety of screws, valve seats, and bolts use hexagon-shaped sockets that will accept these wrenches. Almost nothing else will loosen headless Allen socket screws that are set flush with the surface of material.

Sets of Allen wrenches come in all forms. Some are made like a pocketknife, with three or more wrenches on each end of the holder. Bolts on each end of the holder go through ring ends on each wrench.

Fig. 6-1. Straight hex wrench. Courtesy Ridge Tool Co.

Hex jaw design gives multi-sided, secure grip on all hex and square
nuts, unions, valve packing nuts, and even flathead gas cocks. Jaws
are smooth for plated nuts, fit in tight places.

This allows each wrench to swing out like a pocketknife blade. Other
types have one end extra-long; some have screwdriver handles. Another screwdriver type has a ball-hex end and may be used at a slight
angle.

Basin Wrench. To reach the connections on a sink or lavatory faucet underneath, this wrench is very handy. The shaft has a toothed
hook end that can be reversed to loosen or tighten the connections
on the faucet base. A sliding handle allows its use in confined spaces.

Bolt Die. This die will cut threads on a rod of the correct diameter
for the specific die you are using. The rod is clamped in a vise and
the die, in a holder. The die is pushed flat against the end of the rod,
and the die pushed and turned to get it started on the rod. Cutting
oil should be used to help chamfer the end of the rod to start the die
easily. If chips build up, the rotation is reversed half a turn before going forward again.

Bolt Tap. The tap is used to cut threads in a drilled hole in metal.
The tap is operated similar to the die. Be careful; the tap is slender
and very brittle. Do not force the tap. Each size tap requires a specified drill bit to drill the correct size hole. There are printed charts that
give the correct drill bit for each size tap. Too small a hole will break
the tap and too large a hole will give a sloppy fit. Example: A 1/4-20
tap requires a No. 7 drill. The designation "1/4-20" means the bolt
is manufactured from 1/4-inch rod and there are 20 threads to the
inch. Drill bits are manufactured in inches and fractions of an inch,
in a number series, and in a letter series. Drill bits are now manufactured in metric sizes also.

Box Wrench. This wrench is in the form of a ring with the inner
circle having 12 sides. This is to fit on a six-sided bolt or nut to allow
working in close places. Six-sided wrenches are made, but are not com-
monly used—they do not round off the corners of the hex as easily.
Some wrenches have a box end and an open end and are called, for
instance, a "9/16 inch box/open" wrench with both ends the same
size. Other wrenches are box both ends or open both ends. In these
cases, each end of the wrench is a different size, such as 1/2 inch
by 9/16 inch. You would ask for a "half-nine box wrench."

Closet Auger. This special auger, similar to a sewer auger or snake,
consists of a brass tube curved at one end. A snake with a corkscrew
end runs through the tube and the top end has a crank on it. The snake
part is pulled out of the top and only the screw end sticks out. When
inserted into the toilet trap, the handle is cranked and pushed down

at the same time to feed the screw end through the trap and hopefully snag the obstruction.

Cold Chisel. This tool is made from hexagon or square steel rod and has a chisel-shaped end for chipping steel or masonry. *Caution:* Always wear goggles when using this tool.

File. A file is used to dress metal, or to file coarse wood or plastic. Always use a file handle because the pointed tang can cause a bad injury if it accidentally digs into your palm or wrist.

Flaring Tool. Certain copper tubing fittings, called flare fittings, need a tool to form a flared end on the copper tubing used with these fittings (Fig. 6-2). The tool consists of a flare block having two hinged halves, which, when closed, form a series of holes of varying sizes to accommodate a range of tubing diameters. After a flare nut is put on a length of tubing, the tubing is clamped in the block by a swing bolt and wingnut at the open end. The tubing holes are countersunk on the flare block, and a flare yoke is hooked onto the block. A cone-shaped mandrel on a threaded stem is screwed down to meet the end of the tubing and form it to match the angle of the mandrel and countersink. This forms a perfect flared tubing end. Be sure to put the flare nut on the tubing before making the flared end, or you will have to start over.

Hacksaw. This is a common household workshop tool that comes in varying qualities. Buy a medium or better grade. Blades have various numbers of teeth per inch, such as 14, 18, 24, and 32. Thin-walled tubing needs the 32-teeth-per-inch blade; a coarse tooth blade would catch on the thin wall.

Machinist's Vise. Most home workshop will have a small vise. Some of these vises have pipe jaws of a sort, but are not too good for gripping pipe well enough to hold it while cutting threads with a thread cutter (Figs. 6-3 and 6-4). Standard pipe vises and threading dies can be rented from most rental shops.

Pipe Cutter. This tool is the larger version of the tubing cutter. A moveable jaw on a screw thread stem with a **T** handle has a steel cutting wheel that cuts through the pipe. The solid part of the tool

Fig. 6-2. Flaring tool for soft copper tubing. Courtesy Ridge Tool Co.

One Integral Unit . . . Parts can't get lost

Mfrs. Code No. 785461

These advanced-design RIDGID Flaring Tools give smooth, uniform flares . . . faster, too . . . with minimum effort, even on large sizes. Large, comfort-grip feed screw handle turns easily. Hardened steel flaring cone, eccentrically mounted in precision bearings, produces rolling action for even metal flow . . . gives uniform flare walls without galling. Flare can then be ironed by continued cone action. Heat treated flaring bars are precision-ground. Tubing hole sizes are clearly marked. Rugged yokes slide to desired size. Yoke clamp screw fits into centering hole . . . locks bars, yoke and tubing into alignment. Stop pins keep yoke on flaring bars at all times.

Mfrs. Code No. 785461

Handy for threading 3 common sizes of pipe or conduit. Compact threaders, with steel dies that reverse for close-to-wall threads.

| 36515 | 30-A | 3/8"-1/2"-3/4" | 8 1/4 | |
| 36540 | 31-A | 1/2"-3/4"-1" | 10 | |

Fig. 6-3. Three-way pipe threader which carries three sizes of pipe dies. Courtesy Ridge Tool Co.

00-R, 111-R & 12-R Exposed Ratchet

Unusually handy, efficient drop-head dies. Head locks in or releases by pull of ratchet knob. Separate sets of alloy steel chaser dies, quickly removed or reversed for close-to-wall threads. Unless otherwise specified NPT dies are furnished. NPSM straight dies are available.

Fig. 6-4. Drop head ratchet threader which has a pumping action and is more convenient. Courtesy Ridge Tool Co.

Gives fast, clean pipe cutting by hand or power. Extra long shank protects adjustment threads. Extra large handle for quick, easy adjustment. Balanced frame of special malleable iron. Equipped with tough blade cutter wheel. Can convert to 3-wheel cutter by replacing rollers with cutter wheels.

Fig. 6-5. Heavy-duty pipe cutter. Courtesy Ridge Tool Co.

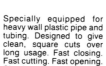

Specially equipped for heavy wall plastic pipe and tubing. Designed to give clean, square cuts over long usage. Fast closing. Fast cutting. Fast opening. Simply push handle in to snug up cutter wheel to pipe. When cut is completed, just press release nut and cutter wheel slides smoothly away from pipe. No. 134-P cuts through 7/16" wall thickness. Nos 131-P and 132-P also cut thin wall PVC and flexible plastic with No. E-1740 special wheel.

Fig. 6-6. Plastic tubing and pipe cutter. Courtesy Ridge Tool Co.

Nine models for cutting 4" through 12" pipe in tight quarters where minimal cutter rotation is necessary.

Mfrs. Code No. 785461

The RIDGID Hinged Pipe Cutters are designed for rapid cutting through cast iron and steel pipe. Each model features rugged cast iron frame, long feed handle for better leverage, pipe guides for square cuts, closed frame design with easy operating latch for quick and positive engagement on pipe, four cutter wheels and a pipe handle for applications requiring extra leverage. Additional cutter wheels for cutting cast iron, standard steel pipe and heavy-wall steel pipe are available separately. Four cutter wheels and extra pipe handle packed with each cutter.

Fig. 6-7. Large hinged pipe cutter. Courtesy Ridge Tool Co.

has rollers that back up the cutting wheel. The tool is set over the pipe and tightened with the cutter set on the mark made on the pipe. The cutter is rotated around the pipe as the **T** handle is tightened, thus cutting through the pipe. Do not tighten much as you make each rotation (Figs. 6-5, 6-6, and 6-7).

Pipe Dies. Pipe dies, similar to bolt dies, come in nominal sizes, 1/8-inch to 4-inch. These dies can be rented, as can a motorized pipe machine. There are many styles of die stocks (the die holder and handles); some are part of the pipe machine. Other die stocks have two handles and are started on the pipe end by pushing and turning far enough for the dies to start cutting—then turning is enough to make the dies advance on their own.

Another style is the ratchet with one handle. To start this die, the heel of the left hand is pressed on the head of the stock and the ratchet handle is operated to start the die. The handle is then "pumped" up and down to continue the cutting. Almost always the cutting is stopped when the outside edge of the die is flush with the end of the pipe for all styles of die stocks. There is a knob that can be lifted and turned to reverse the action of the ratchet handle, and the stock can be removed from the pipe by turning it counterclockwise.

Pipe Reamer. The reamer has a cone-shaped cutting end that is inserted into the pipe end (Fig. 6-8). This has either straight or spiral grooves with sharp edges to ream the ridge that is left after cutting the pipe with a cutter. The reamer is also mounted on a ratchet handle similar to that used on the pipe dies. The reamer end is pushed with the heel of the left hand during reaming. Ream just to remove the ridge, no more.

Pipe Wrench. Most people are familiar with the pipe wrench (Figs. 6-9 through 6-11). Sizes range from 6 inches to 4 feet in length. The moveable jaw can tilt a little, which allows it to catch and grip the pipe between both jaws. At this point the more pressure put on the handle, the more tightly the wrench grips the pipe. As this digs into the pipe it leaves marks, so do not use on chrome pipe. Strap wrenches using a leather strap can be used for polished or plated fittings and pipe.

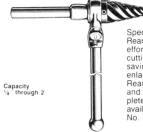

Fig. 6-8. Spiral ratchet pipe reamer. Courtesy Ridge Tool Co.

Capacity
⅛ through 2

Special spiral design of 2-S Reamer cuts into metal with least effort — fast, clean cuts, long cutting life. Makes easy, time-saving work of reaming pipe or enlarging conduit box outlets. Reams sheet metal — smooth and easy without chatter. Complete with handle. Reamer unit available alone for use in RIDGID No. 00-R ratchet handle.

The original heavy-duty pipe wrench, known for its serviceability. Replaceable jaws are made of hardened alloy steel. Full floating hook jaw gives instant grip and release. Handy pipe scale and large easy-to-spin adjusting nut allow fast, one-hand setting to pipe size. Comfort grip, malleable iron I-beam handle.

Fig. 6-9. Heavy-duty pipe wrench. Courtesy Ridge Tool Co.

Fig. 6-10. End pipe wrench. Courtesy Ridge Tool Co.

Mfrs. Code No. 785461

Designed with an offset jaw and longer handle swing to ease work in tight places, these wrenches offer the quality features of famous RIDGID Straight Pipe Wrenches: replaceable jaws, full floating hook jaw, easy-spin adjusting nut, pipe scale and malleable iron I-beam handle.

Mfrs. Code No. 785461

Aluminum handles make these heavy-duty wrenches almost 40% lighter than similar wrenches with malleable iron handles. Parts are identical to those of RIDGID Straight Pipe Wrenches. Ideal for over head work.

Fig. 6-11. Aluminum pipe wrench, straight. Courtesy Ridge Tool Co.

Fig. 6-12. Bench yoke vise. Courtesy Ridge Tool Co.

Unusually handy and efficient. Convenient pipe rest and bender. Red yoke base of strong special malleable iron. Highest quality alloy steel jaws. Capacities, 1/8 through 6 inches.

Pipe Tap. This tap is similar to, but not interchangeable with, bolt taps. All pipe threads are tapered, which allows them to be "made up" tightly to prevent leaks at the joints. While all taps are subject to breakage, pipe taps are larger diameter (the 1/8-inch nominal size pipe tap is actually 3/8-inch diameter) and are quite strong. It still pays to be careful when using them.

Pipe Vise. Unlike the machinist's vise, the pipe vise can only be used on round materials. Most pipe vises have three legs that fold for carrying; some have a shelf underneath the vise to hold tools. The vise can be the yoke style, hinged on one side with a hook on the other side to catch on the base when the vise is closed. Another style is the chain vise. This has a base with teeth in a **V** shape and a chain to wrap around the pipe and hook into a slot. Each chain link has a boss on each side. These catch in the slot in the base. A hinged lever underneath the base is turned to pull the fixed end of the chain down to hold the pipe tightly (Figs. 6-12 through 6-14).

Plunger. This is a rubber cone-shaped cup on a handle, used to

Fig. 6-13. Bench chain vise. Courtesy Ridge Tool Co.

Mfrs. Code
No. 785461

Chain tightens by handy top crank handle that's anchored to base. Jaws of tool steel hardened for long wear. Handy pipe rest and bender. Capacity ⅛" thru 8".

A portable work bench with integral steel tray and legs that fold for easy carrying. Tray makes it extra rigid when set up. Large vise base overhangs front legs so threader handles swing clear — lots of room for dope pot, oil can, slots for hanging tools; pipe rest, three pipe benders, ceiling brace screw for extra rigidity. Efficient yoke vise, alloy steel jaws, hardened for firm grip and long wear.

Mfrs. Code
No. 785461

Fig. 6-14. Tristand yoke vise. Courtesy Ridge Tool Co.

force obstructions out of and on through a drain or toilet. A style made especially for toilets has an extension of rubber as part of the plunger cup, to better seat in the toilet bowl. This style cannot be used over a flat drain as in a sink, but the sink style will work in a toilet.

Propane Torch. The propane torch is available in all home centers and hardware stores. It is used for, among other things around the house, soldering copper tubing. Always use caution when working with an open flame. *Always* recheck after you have finished to see that nothing is still smoldering.

Seat Refacing Tool. When faucet seats become worn, the refacing tool may be used. It is only recommended for refacing seats that are not removable—for example, if they are part of the faucet body. Usually the refacing tool will radically change the shape of the seat it is refacing and the new washer will not seat properly to shut off the water. There is no alternative when the seat is not removable, except refacing or buying a new faucet. Be sure the new faucet does have a replaceable seat.

Seat Wrench. This **L** shaped wrench is used to remove faucet seats. Most seats have square holes to accept this wrench. If you have a hexagon hole in the seat, you can use an Allen wrench. When installing a new seat, put a little pipe joint compound on the threads for easy removal the next time.

Socket Wrench. A special socket wrench is needed to remove the bonnet from a tub faucet assembly. Sometimes a standard deep socket can be used. If so, you will need to turn it with a pipe wrench, because the standard socket handle will not fit.

Spud Wrench. This is a short cast wrench having wide jaws. It is used for working on sink traps to loosen the slip nuts.

Strap Wrench. Mentioned previously, this wrench is used to work on polished and plated fittings (Fig. 6-15). It is similar to a chain wrench, except that it has a leather or woven strap.

Mfrs. Code No. 785461

For use on polished pipe and tubing — protects nickel and chrome finish. Strong I-beam handle and solid head, all one piece. Handy hang-up hole. Easy to attach and use. Straps are easily replaced . . . easy to use.

Fig. 6-15. Strap wrench prevents marring on chrome. Courtesy Ridge Tool Co.

Mfrs. Code No. 785461

Grooved Rollers for Close Flare Cut-Offs

Fig. 6-16. Tubing cutter used for copper tubing. Courtesy Ridge Tool Co.

Enclosed feed protects against clogging and jamming. Only 5″ long, open or closed, this cutter features a spare cutter wheel in handle and fold-in reamer. Frame is lightweight, high-strength aluminum alloy. Cuts copper, brass, aluminum tubing and thin-wall conduit. Also available with HD wheel for SS and steel tubing. Rollers smooth tubing ready for soldering.

These 8 benders for free-form bending of soft copper and aluminum tube meet all government specifications. Spring wire is proportioned to tube size to allow shorter radius bends on small tube.

Fig. 6-17. Spring tubing bender which slips on tubing to bend without kinking. Courtesy Ridge Tool Co.

Mfrs. Code No. 785461

6 sizes for Soft or Hard Copper, Brass, Aluminum, Steel and Stainless Steel Tube

Fig. 6-18. Lever-type tubing bender which bends 1/4-inch copper tubing. Courtesy Ridge Tool Co.

These lever-type benders are versatile, accurate and easy-to-use. Correctly measured, bends will be accurate to blueprint dimensions within $\pm 1/32$″. Scale on link eliminates extra measuring, assures fast tube positioning for accurate finished dimensions. Forming head shows angle of bend in $22\frac{1}{2}°$ increments from 0° to 180°. "Gain Marks" on handle give accurate tube measurement before cutting . . . no wasted material. Handles are still wide apart when making 180° bend.

Tubing Cutter. This cutter is used to make a straight cut on copper or brass thin-wall tubing, rather than heavy brass pipe (Fig. 6-16). Most can cut up through 1-inch nominal tubing. There are also small tubing cutters, for working in confined spaces.

Tubing Bender, Spring. This is a coiled spring with a flared end (Fig. 6-17). The spring is slid over the tubing, then carefully bent. Each tubing cutters that will cut tubing through 5/8-inch OD for working in confined spaces.

Tubing Bender Lever. This style bender has a half-circle head with a groove corresponding with the size of the tubing being bent. One style has a follower shoe with a matching groove and a second handle. The tubing is inserted under the shoe and in the groove in the head, and the handles are brought together to guide the tubing around the groove in the head to make the bend. Another style has two han-

96

dles, one that operates a hook over the groove. As the handles are squeezed the hook holds the tubing in the groove, then the tubing itself is pulled around the groove in the head, or the bender is pulled around and the tubing held stationary.

All three styles of benders only bend one size of tubing each. A few benders have two sizes of grooves for two sizes of tubing, but these are awkward to use and usually cost more. Professional plumbers and pipe fitters use larger benders of the first lever style to bend rigid (hard) tubing, thus eliminating many fittings and soldered joints.

7

Working With
Pipe and Fittings

When repairs are made and the plumbing system is extended, nearly every situation will require working with pipe and fittings. Many older homes have threaded, galvanized pipe for the plumbing lines, and threaded black iron pipe for gas and heating lines, plus the necessary fittings.

GALVANIZED IRON AND BLACK IRON THREADED PIPE

Threaded iron pipe was used extensively for many years and requires some skill; detailed drawings and explicit text will help you repair and install this type of pipe. Threaded pipe requires a vise, pipe wrenches, a pipe cutter, dies, and a reamer. Some vises are on a tripod while others clamp onto a post or column in the basement. (Refer to Chapter 6 for the different types of vises available.) All pipe tools can be rented at local rental shops. You will need all five items to make your work easier. Sawing steel pipe with a hacksaw and removing the burrs is the hard way to go, especially if you have many threads to make. The pipe cutter makes a square cut and the reamer is fast and accurate.

Because iron pipe has no "give," measurements must be accurate. Each pipe size has its own distance the pipe enters the fitting. For example, 1/2-inch pipe enters a fitting approximately 1/2 inch. Also the distance from the face of an el (elbow) to the center of the other open-

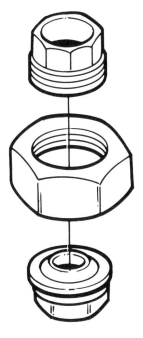

Fig. 7-1. Parts of an iron pipe union.

ing is 1.12 inches, usually taken as 1 inch. These measurements are used to measure for a length of pipe in order to make an offset in a line to go around an obstruction. As an example, the offset is 32 1/2 inches, center to center (C-C). If the pipe enters each elbow 1/2 inch, this is 32 1/2 inches less 1/2 inch twice, or 31 1/2 inches. This is the length of pipe you would need.

If both els are in place (this is not likely, as will be explained later) a measurement can be taken "face to face" (F-F), which in the example above will be 30 1/2 inches. Add the "make-up" of 1/2 inch for each end, which will again give 31 1/2 inches for the length of pipe needed. Referring back to the two els already in place and the line continuing in both directions, it will be impossible to install a pipe between two threaded fittings. In this case you will have to get two shorter pieces of pipe and a pipe union to make up the correct length.

A pipe union consists of three parts. There are two end pieces with female threads—one piece has male threads on its large end, the other piece has a large end with no threads. To hold the two pieces together is a center ring or collar. The collar is slipped on the pipe section, and this section is screwed into the elbow. The union piece having no threads is screwed on the end of the pipe. Then the other short pipe is screwed into the other el and the other union half is screwed on. The union ends are brought together and the union collar is tightened to complete the assembly. Two wrenches are needed to tighten the collar, one to hold the union half that the collar is screwed onto and one to tighten the collar (Fig. 7-1).

Unions are used in many situations where a pipe section cannot be turned, as when a water heater is connected to the gas and water lines. A union can be used when a pipe section has rusted through or has frozen and burst. Cut the piece out with a hacksaw and replace it with two pieces of pipe and a union. The union can be placed near one end of the space and a 3- or 4-inch nipple used to connect the union to the el, then only one piece of pipe has to be threaded for the connection to the other el.

There are many styles of pipe dies. A common style is the three-way threader. The most popular size for the homeowner is the 1/2-, 3/4-, and 1-inch. This head has these three dies mounted in one casting at 120 degrees to each other. Opposite each die is a guide hole to line the die correctly with the pipe. The head is put on the pipe with the alignment hole first and the die is shoved up to contact the end of the pipe. This alignment hole will accept the pipe snugly if the correct die is selected.

Be sure to ream the pipe before starting to thread it. If there are burrs on the outside of the pipe, file them off before starting to thread. The die will start easily when any outside burrs have been removed. Grasp the two handles and press the die against the pipe end as you turn clockwise. Cutting oil, which can be found in hardware stores, is needed to help cut perfect threads. In an emergency any oil may be used, even cooking lard; hand threading is slow and the dies will not overheat.

Continue turning the threader until the pipe is flush with the surface of the dies. Threading one thread past the dies will not hurt, but is not necessary. Too long a thread will hit bottom in the fitting, won't "make up" tightly, and will leak. Too short a thread might not start in the fitting. In this case, return the pipe to the vise and cut the proper length of thread.

After threading, unscrew the die counterclockwise from the pipe. Wipe the new threads with a rag to remove any chips and cutting oil. Pipe threads are different than bolt threads. Pipe threads have a slight taper that allows joints to be made up liquid- and gas-tight.

Another type of die, the drop head ratchet threader, has a handle that will accept various dies such as 1/2-, 3/4-, and 1-inch sizes. These die sets can be ordered with any size die from 1/8-inch to 1 1/2-inch. Each handle takes a different range of die sizes. The handle incorporates a ratchet mechanism so that when operated the one handle need only be pushed down in a pumping motion. This might be somewhat easier than the three-way threader, and can be used in confined quarters on pipe already in place in a building. The handle can be reversed to unscrew the die from the pipe by lifting a spring-loaded pin, turning it a half turn, and releasing it.

Figure 7-2 illustrates the method of cutting a pipe to length using a pipe cutter (a large version of a tubing cutter). A pipe cutter is used to cut pipe by hand or in a pipe machine. The pipe cutter is placed on the mark on the pipe and the cutting wheel is tightened against the pipe. Make two turns around the pipe to form a groove. (Make sure the cutter wheel makes a complete groove, and does not "form a thread.") If the wheel tracks correctly, tighten the cutter handle a quarter to a half turn and go around twice again. Turn the handle just enough to provide drag and go around, tightening as you go until the pipe has been cut off. If you are cutting just a small amount from the pipe end, be sure that you do not hit your arm or hand on this stub as you rotate the handle because it could easily gash you. When cutting off a long length, hold the piece so that it does not fall on your foot or against your leg. Safety is an important consideration at the workplace or in your home. Do not hurry or you could make a mistake or hurt yourself. In either case you will lose the time you thought you would save.

The next step is to ream the inside of the pipe using the reamer. A round file will work, but a pipe reamer will do the job better and more quickly. Figure 7-3 illustrates a ratchet-type reamer, used with a pumping action. Ream just enough to remove any burrs. When threading, start the die head on the end of the pipe. Push and turn the die head to get the dies started biting in to the pipe. About two turns should be enough. Figures 7-4 and 7-5 illustrate this method. Use plenty of cutting oil. Continue threading until the dies are flush

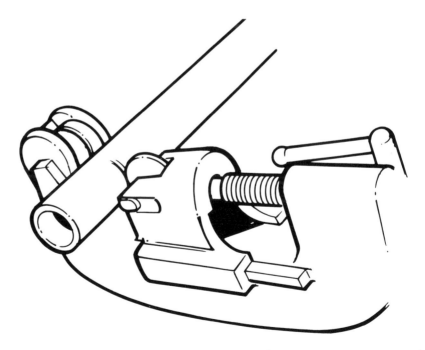

Fig. 7-2. Pipe cutter starting to cut off an iron pipe section.

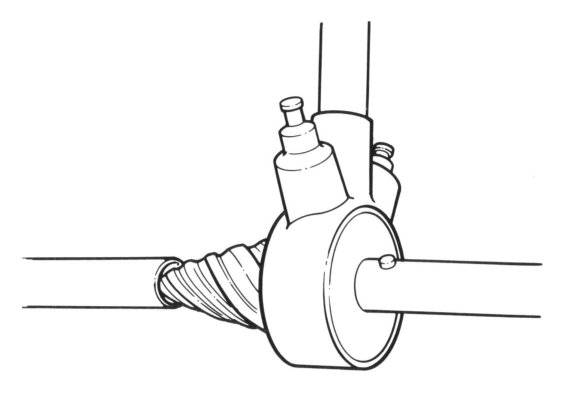

Fig. 7-3. A spiral reamer removing burrs from the cut pipe.

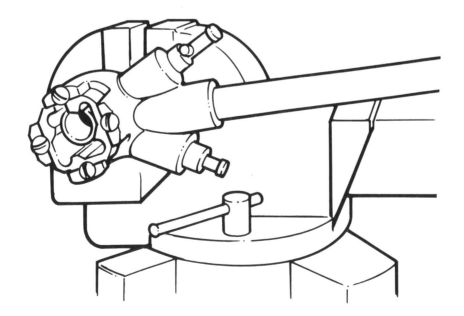

Fig. 7-4. Threading dies started on the end of the pipe.

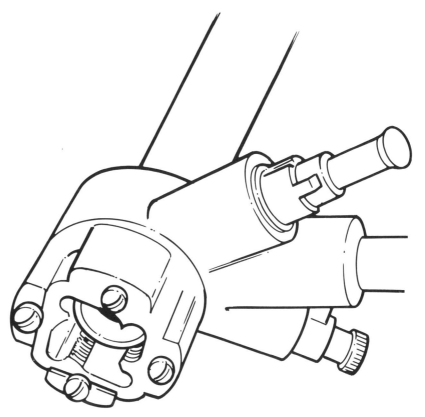

Fig. 7-5. Close-up of threading die on end of pipe. Threading continues until pipe end is flush with die face.

with the end of the pipe. Dies in good condition will make a thread properly when stopping the threading at this point.

Making up the pipe assembly is accomplished by using two wrenches. For 3/4- and 1-inch pipe use the medium size, usually 12- and 14-inch pipe wrenches. These two wrenches will handle almost all pipe work up through 1-inch pipe. Large pipe, 2-inch and larger, will be found on bathtub drain lines (galvanized) and boiler heating lines (black iron). For these lines you will need two 18-inch wrenches and possibly a 2-foot (sometimes called 24-inch) wrench. Do not use too large a wrench on small pipe or you might deform the pipe and cause a leak. You might need a larger wrench to disconnect rusted joints. In this case it is alright to use the larger wrench.

Note: Sometimes frozen (tight) threaded joints can be loosened by heating just the fitting. This will expand the fitting from the pipe end and release its hold on the pipe. Be extremely careful when heating the pipe with a torch. Protect any flammable materials with sheet metal and continue to check for at least a half hour after you have extinguished the torch. Charred wood can burst into flame after you have left the area. Be sure to check!

You can work on pipe without using a pipe vise if you work on the floor. Sections of pipe with fittings on them can be taken apart by putting a pipe wrench on the pipe near the fitting, with the fitting to your right. The open side of the wrench jaws must face *up* (hold the wrench and place the pipe into the open jaws). Adjust the wrench to hold the pipe and turn the pipe slightly as you tighten the wrench jaws. There will be some looseness in the jaws—this is normal. When the pipe starts to turn, the jaws will grip tightly. Put the other wrench on the fitting you want to remove; face the open side of the jaws down this time. Press down on the wrench on the fitting; the other wrench is backed up by the floor, and will either lie flat or can be raised. Figures 7-6 and 7-7 show the position of the wrenches. I like to use the larger wrench on the fitting for more leverage.

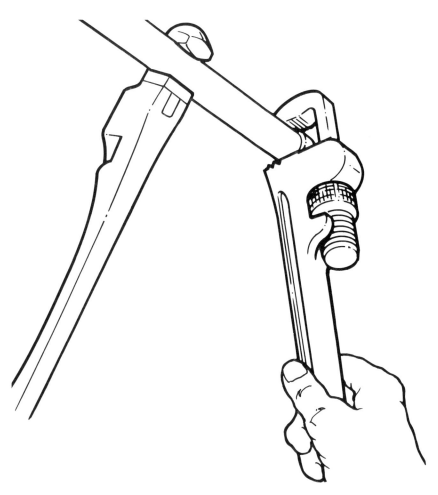

Fig. 7-6. Two pipe wrenches being used to remove a coupling from 3/4-inch galvanized pipe. The left-hand wrench is on the ground and acts as a vise in this case.

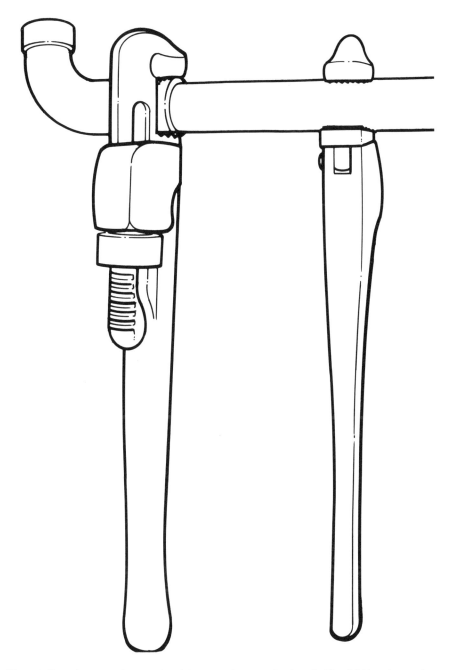

Fig. 7-7. Two pipe wrenches used to tighten an el onto a pipe length. The right-hand wrench, on the ground, acts as a vise also.

When raising the wrench on the floor up on its handle end, put your left foot on the handle to prevent slipping. You'll need a little practice, but once you get the hang of it you will have no problem.

Making up a fitting is just the opposite because the fitting is on the *left* end of the pipe and the floor wrench is to your *right*. This is a little awkward for a right-handed person, but plumbers and other mechanics learn to be ambidextrous. When an assembly of threaded fittings must be assembled, each piece must be tightened separately before tightening the next joint to assure that each joint is assembled tightly enough.

There are many formulations of pipe joint compounds on the market. Some are lead-based and some use other ingredients. One of the best products is Teflon joint tape. This is a very slippery substance (also used in cooking utensils), that is wrapped around the male pipe threads of the pipe. The pipe is then screwed into a fitting, valve, or other female connection.

Because the Teflon tape is very slippery and has no adhesive, the starting end must be held against the threads, while the rest of the tape is wound tightly around the threads. Press the end of the tape down into the threads to secure it. Make two turns around to provide two layers on the threads. The 1/8-, 1/4-, and 3/8-inch pipes need only one thickness of tape. Take care that the first joint is made up tightly, or it will turn when the second joint is made up. Back up (hold back) the first joint with a wrench when tightening the second joint. To Teflon's advantage, it is very clean to use and works extremely well when used carefully.

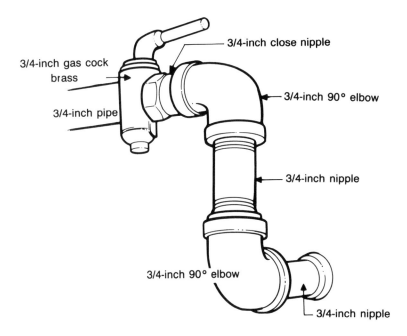

3/4-inch close nipple

3/4-inch gas cock brass

3/4-inch 90° elbow

3/4-inch pipe

3/4-inch nipple

3/4-inch 90° elbow

3/4-inch nipple

Fig. 7-8. Assortment of black iron pipe fittings, including a gas stop cock (valve).

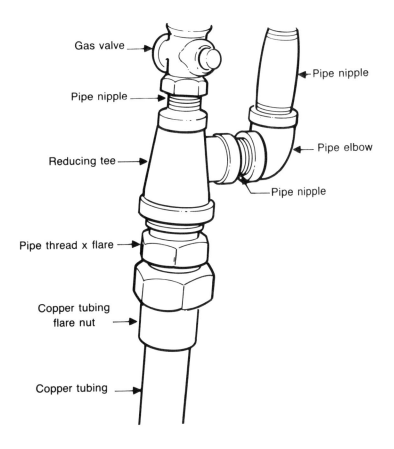

Gas valve

Pipe nipple

Pipe nipple

Reducing tee

Pipe elbow

Pipe nipple

Pipe thread x flare

Copper tubing
flare nut

Copper tubing

Fig. 7-9. A copper gas line coming into a house and adapted to black iron pipe. This connection has no dielectric fitting because moisture is not present.

Other types of joint compound are a bit easier to use than Teflon, but are also messier. These are painted on the male threads using a small brush. As mentioned before, *do not* connect two different metals together because corrosion will occur. Metal to plastic, however, is the exception and will not cause corrosion. It will be useful to refer to Chapter 6 as you read this chapter.

Figures 7-8 and 7-9 illustrate typical pipe connections using black iron pipe to connect lines for a gas furnace and a gas fired clothes dryer. Figure 7-10 illustrates the tightening of a black iron pipe union on a gas line to a furnace. The left wrench is tightening the union ring, while the right wrench is holding back on the union half having male threads on the larger end. The ring has a flange that goes over the left union half (not shown), and pulls it into contact with and snug against the right union half. If the right-hand wrench is not used, the whole union might turn, which would cause a leak.

Figure 7-11 illustrates a saddle tee that may be used instead of cutting into a copper line and soldering in a sweat tee. With this fit-

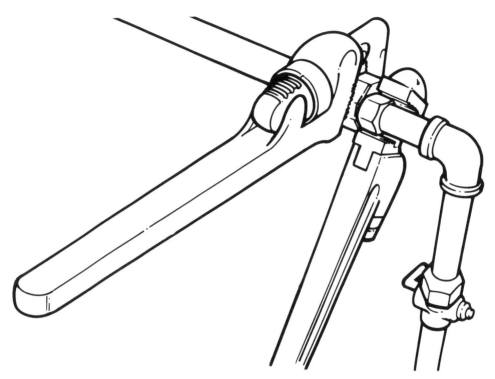

Fig. 7-10. Tightening a black iron union on a gas line.

Fig. 7-11. Saddle tee, used to tap into a copper or iron water line. Used for connecting automatic washer hoses.

ting, a hole is drilled in the tubing and the saddle clamp and rubber gasket are set in place. The back-up plate is then attached and tightened using the four bolts. These saddle tees are also made for iron pipe. Both types come in many sizes.

COPPER TUBING AND FITTINGS

Working with copper tubing and fittings is much easier than working with threaded pipe. To work with copper tubing, you will need a tubing cutter, a reamer (part of the cutter), sand cloth, solder, flux, and a propane torch and tank. A vise may be handy but is not necessary.

Copper tubing comes in three wall thicknesses: type K is the heaviest at .065 inches, L is .045 inches, and M is .038 inches. All dimensions refer to the 3/4-inch size tubing. Type K—the soft temper type—is used for the water supply line from the city mains to the dwelling. The soft type K is supplied in 60-foot rolls, which are usually long enough to reach from the main to the dwelling. Type L is used in a dwelling in the hard temper for hot and cold water lines. These lines are usually 1/2-inch and 3/4-inch sizes. The soft 3/8-inch OD size is used to pipe gas barbecues, gas dryers, and in the chrome finish as risers to sinks, lavatories, and toilets.

Note: Copper tubing as used in plumbing is designated by the nominal size, such as 1/2-inch and 3/4-inch. Smaller sizes are called by their outside diameters (OD), such as 1/4-inch and 3/8-inch. The refrigeration and air conditioning trades refer to copper tubing and fittings by the actual OD, such as 5/8-inch instead of 1/2-inch, and 7/8-inch instead of 3/4-inch—in other words, the nominal designation plus 1/8 inch. Refer to Chapter 5.

Fittings used with copper tubing are also copper (wrought copper), with a few exceptions that are cast in brass or bronze. There are many configurations of fittings to choose from for nearly every situation. Common styles are: 90 and 45-degree els, tees with all openings the same size or reducing tees, and adapters that adapt from copper to threaded pipe. Soldered connections are explained here; other connection methods will be discussed later in this chapter. Fittings for soldering are designated either as "sweat" or "solder." The plumber will call for a "1/2-inch sweat, by 1/2-inch MIP 90-degree el." This is a 90-degree elbow. One end has 1/2-inch male (outside) threads to screw into a coupling, elbow or other female (inside) threads. The other end of the elbow (sweat) is formed to accept the end of a length of 1/2-inch copper tubing. A straight fitting with these same ends could be used to extend a length of galvanized iron pipe.

Caution: Because iron and copper are dissimilar metals, they will react with each other in the presence of moisture (water) and cause corrosion. This type of joint will start to leak within six months. As mentioned previously, special dielectric unions and couplings must be used where dissimilar metals need to be joined.

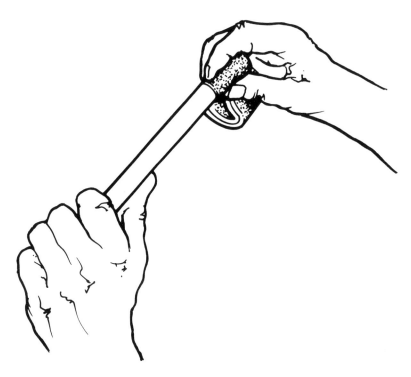

Fig. 7-12. Sanding copper tubing held in the hand, using sandcloth, a cloth-backed sanding material.

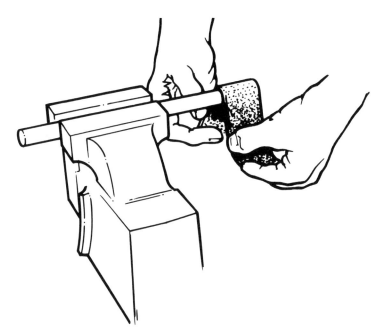

Fig. 7-13. Sanding copper tubing clamped in a vise using sandcloth.

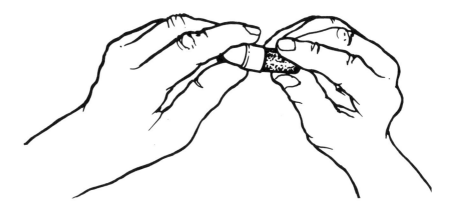

Fig. 7-14. Rolled-up sandcloth used to clean the inside of a fitting.

When soldering copper tubing to copper fittings, it is important to have everything very clean. This is accomplished by shining the end of the tubing and the inside of the fitting with sandpaper or better yet, sandcloth (cloth-backed). Sandcloth is more flexible and can be rolled into a small roll to sand the inside of fittings (Figs. 7-12 through 7-14). Wire brushes are available for use on the inside of fittings and the outside of tubing. Each brush fits only one size, so more than one set might be needed. Sandcloth fits all sizes. After the copper has been shined, do not touch these surfaces because dirt and oil on your hands will prevent the solder from adhering.

Spread soldering flux (a paste) on these cleaned surfaces using an "acid brush," a small brush with bristles 3/8-inch wide and a metal handle (Figs. 7-15 and 7-16). Buy two or three; they are cheap and convenient. A common brand of flux is No-Korode, which lives up to its name. Another type is called Laco Self Cleaning Flux. This flux is corrosive, but the claim of the manufacturer is that the tubing and fittings do not need to be sanded. I have used both brands, and would recommend the No Korode. A small can cost about 50¢. The flux and solder are available in all hardware stores.

For use with tubing and fittings, buy either 50-50 or 95-5 wire solder, 1/8-inch diameter, solid. Do not buy acid-core or rosin-core. Some wire solder comes in the 1/16-diameter size. This is too small for plumbing work—you are constantly needing to unwind more length because it is smaller and goes faster.

Measure the tubing and cut it to length; clean the tubing end and the inside of the fitting with sandcloth. Apply flux to both parts and assemble. If a tee is being installed, it is recommended that all connections be soldered at the same time. If you solder just one joint and then later do the others, you might melt the solder out of the first joint. Any previous joint should be wrapped with a wet rag to keep it cool and prevent leaks while doing the other joints of the same fitting.

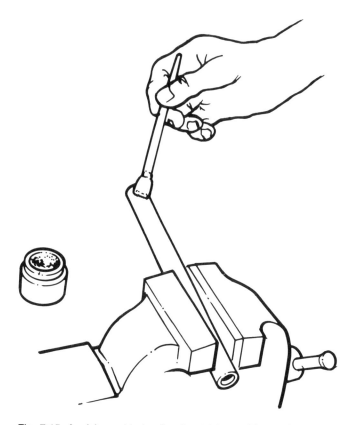

Fig. 7-15. Applying soldering flux (paste) to a tubing end.

Fig. 7-16. Applying soldering flux to the inside of a fitting.

Unwind about 4 inches of solder so that you can hold the roll; light the torch with the lighter and adjust the flame to the point where it is not noisy. Apply the flame to the base of the fitting so that the inner blue tip just touches the copper of the fitting. Play the flame all around the circumference of the fitting while touching the end of the solder to the end of the fitting—keeping it hot but not overheated. Overheating the fitting or jarring the joint will cause a leak.

Soon the solder will start to melt and you can feed it into the annular space between the fitting and the tube (Fig. 7-17). When the temperature is right the solder flows easily into the annular space. The amount of 1/8-inch solder needed is about equal to the fitting size: for example, a 1/2-inch fitting will need about 1/2 inch of solder. When you see the silver ring completely around the tubing, the joint is finished. All joints can be soldered in any position, even when the fitting is looking down, because capillary action causes the solder to be pulled into the annular space. Refer to Chapter 10.

Caution: A joint cannot be soldered (as in repairs) when either water or air under pressure is in the tubing. Sometimes white bread can be stuffed into a tube to stop a water trickle while you solder the joint. I have not tried this, but once I had to plug a line to solder on a gate valve. I used a "Fuller ball" (part of an old-style faucet) obtained from a hardware store. This ball has a hole through the center and I put a long, thin bolt through the ball, added a washer and nut, and tightened the assembly. This expanded the ball inside the tube, which stopped the water flow. By removing the top of the gate valve I was

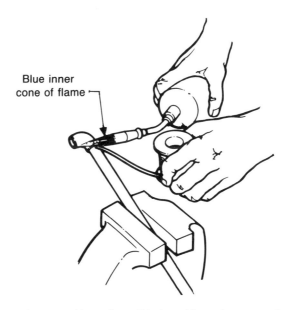

Blue inner
cone of flame

Fig. 7-17. Soldering fitting to tubing using solid wire solder and a propane torch. Note blue inner cone of flame that touches the fitting.

able to remove the stem and gate, leaving room to remove my water plug after the soldering was finished.

There are two other types of connection methods used for copper tubing: compression and flare. Because compression fittings do not need special tools to assemble; they are easily used in any situation. Sizes up to 1/2-inch nominal are sold in hardware stores. The compression fittings are more expensive than sweat fittings, but only require a tubing cutter and two wrenches to install.

The proper way to assemble a compression fitting onto copper tubing is as follows: cut the tubing to length, remove the nut and compression ring (ferrule) and slide, first the nut (open end facing the end of the tubing), then the ferrule after the nut. Push the end of the tubing into the socket of the fitting body. While holding the tubing in place, push the nut and ferrule down and start the nut on the body by turning it clockwise. Because compression threads are very fine, it is necessary to turn the nut *two turns by hand* onto the fitting body. If the tubing is aimed straight into the body the two turns will be easy. If the nut will not start or turns hard, the tubing is not aligned. Usually the nut can be turned up snug. If you use a wrench, it is very easy to cross thread the nut on the fitting body and ruin both parts, so be sure to turn the nut the full two turns by hand. Use two wrenches of a size comparable to the torque needed to make the connection leakproof. For the 1/4-inch and 3/8-inch nuts use a 6-inch wrench. Refer to Figs. 7-18 through 7-21.

Fig. 7-18. Compression fitting. This fitting is sold complete, including body, ferrule, and compression nut.

Fig. 7-19. Compression nut, then ferrule, have been slid onto tubing, ready to complete the connection.

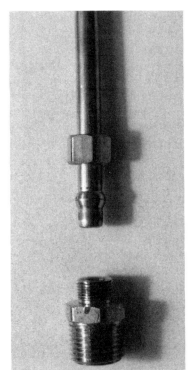

Fig. 7-20. The connection has been made and taken apart to show the proper deformation of the ferrule for a tight joint.

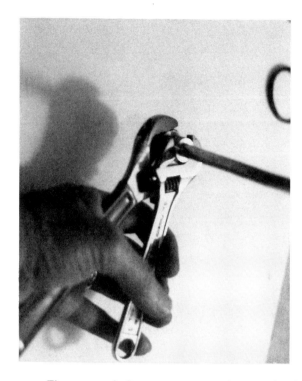

Fig. 7-21. A handy method of tightening a flare or compression joint using two wrenches. The two wrench handles are squeezed to give a tightening action. This is easy to use in a tight place.

The second alternate connection method is the flare type. To use this method you will need a flaring tool, which consists of a flare block and mandrel. This tool can be rented or purchased for about $15. Flare fittings are the most expensive of the copper connection types. The flare nut is sold separately from the body; compression fittings come with the nut and ferrule attached to the fitting body. Follow Figs. 7-22 through 7-29.

To use flare fittings, cut the tubing to length, slip a flare nut on the tubing with the open end facing the tubing end. Open the flare block by loosening the thumbscrews on each end and insert the tubing end. Adjust the tubing end to extend 1/16 inch above the block face (the side having the 45-degree bevel at the hole face) and tighten the thumbscrews to clamp the tubing in place. Slide the mandrel over the block until the flare cone is centered over the tubing end. Spin the cone down until it touches the tubing end; slowly continue forcing the cone into the tubing end until you feel resistance. Do not force the cone further.

Back off the mandrel and open the flare block; you now should have a perfect flare. As with any new procedure, it does take some practice. A flare nut and a 6-inch length of tubing will let you make many practice flares. The flare must be of a size that will enter the flare nut easily, not too large nor too small.

The final adjustment of the flare will be made when the flare nut is screwed onto the flare fitting body. Torque needed is slightly more

116

Fig. 7-22. Flare block and anvil. This special type needs no screw clamps. Tapered sides on block and anvil clamp the tubing tightly as the anvil forces the flare shape on the tubing end.

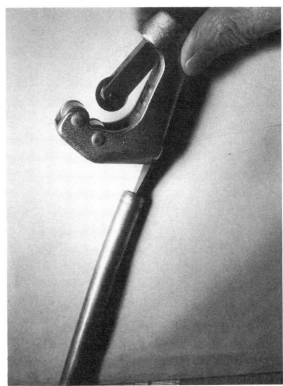

Fig. 7-23. Tubing has been cut off and is being reamed to remove burrs.

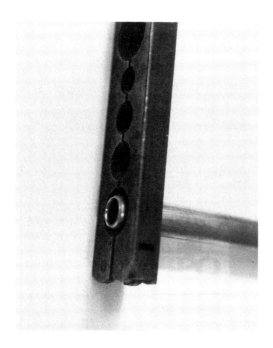

Fig. 7-24. Tubing is clamped in flare block ready to be flared. Note that tubing projects above block 1/16 inch.

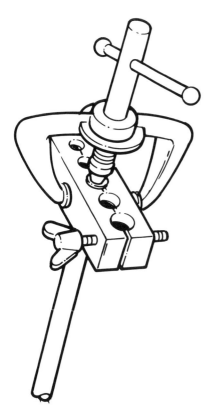

Fig. 7-25. Flare block with screw clamps and anvil ready to flare the tubing clamped in place.

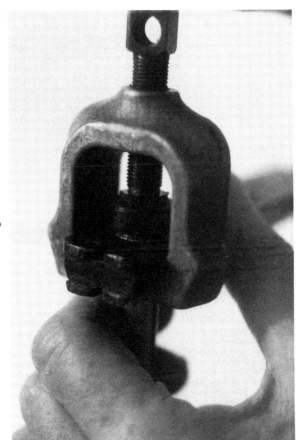

Fig. 7-26. Flare has been formed. Tubing can now be removed.

Fig. 7-27. Shows tubing in flare block with perfect flare.

Fig. 7-28. Tubing removed from flare block to show the shape of the flare.

than that used for compression fittings. Many tubing cutters now have a groove in the rollers that will allow a damaged flare to be cut off the tubing with little waste.

Flare fittings come in two grades: "water fittings" and special "refrigeration grade." Water fittings, both the flare nut and flare body

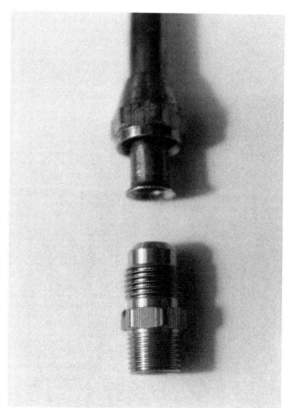

Fig. 7-29. Flare nut on tubing ready to be connected to flare fitting body. These are "water fittings."

are machined from brass bar stock. Refrigeration grade fittings are *forged* brass and will withstand pressures up to 600 psi. There are advantages in using flare fittings. For example, a ferrule is not needed—when a ferrule has been damaged or leaks for some other reason, a new ferrule must be used and possibly the end of the tubing must be cut off also. If none is available, it means a trip to a hardware store to get another one because, even though ferrules are cheap, the joint cannot be repaired without one. The flare made from the tubing itself is always available unless the tubing is so short that a flare cannot be made.

Because a flare cannot be made on hard tubing, the tubing end must be annealed by heating it to a dull red and allowing it to cool in the air. Anneal at least an inch for this purpose. Flare connections are known to form a stronger, more leakproof joint.

Caution: Always ream the tubing end before starting to form a flare. Form the habit of sliding the flare nut on the tubing even though the other end is not attached. If you do this each time, you will not have to cut the new flare off to slip the nut on the tubing. Even the "pro" can forget sometimes.

Both hard and soft tubing can be bent using tubing benders— one style for hard, and another for soft tubing. Soft tubing can be bent

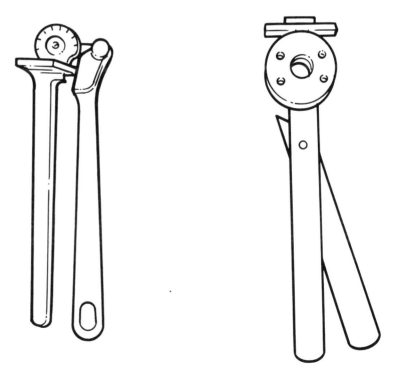

Fig. 7-30. Tubing benders for 1/4-inch copper tubing. The left bender is for *soft* tubing, the right for *hard* tubing.

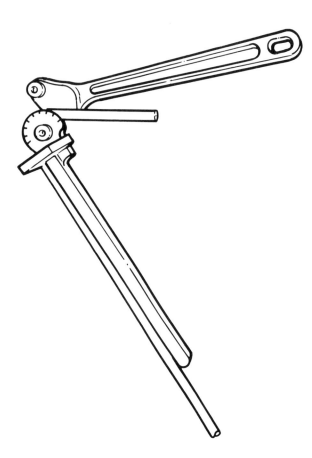

Fig. 7-31. Soft tubing bender showing tubing being bent.

in a shorter radius than can hard tubing. These benders are shown in Figs. 7-30 through 7-32. Soft tubing can also be bent using a spiral spring that slides over the tubing to keep it from being flattened at the bend.

PLASTIC PIPE AND FITTINGS

In the last decade plastic pipe and fittings have won approval by more municipalities and plumbing inspection departments, and have been incorporated into their building codes. Plastic pipe and fittings are the easiest and cheapest method of installing plumbing system. If you plan to use *any* plastic plumbing materials be sure to ask at your plumbing inspection department if these materials are approved.

Different types of plastic require different solvents and cleaners, so make sure to buy the proper materials for this. Solvent, as the name implies, actually dissolves the mating surfaces, so when the surfaces are joined they become one integral piece. This takes place in a matter of seconds, so you must work quickly and accurately.

Measuring, cutting, and assembling plastic pipe is much like working with copper or iron pipe. Only the material and assembly is differ-

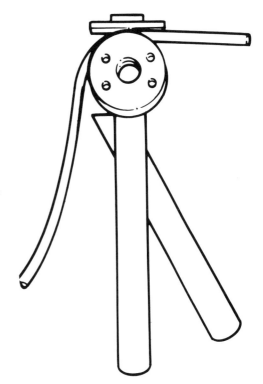

Fig. 7-32. Hard tubing bender clamping tubing while left hand pulls tubing around in the bender groove for the amount of bend needed.

ent. One disadvantage is that once the fitting and pipe are joined together, they cannot be taken apart. The fitting will have to be sawed off the pipe, thus losing the length that was inserted into the fitting *and* the fitting. If this happens, cut off enough pipe to allow a coupling and a short nipple to restore the original length. (Refer to Figs. 5-7 through 5-9).

When joining pipe to fittings, measure carefully, allowing the extra length for insertion into the fitting at both ends. Insertion depth is measured with a rule, since the depth varies with the fitting size. Usually depth corresponds with the size of the fitting, a 1/2-inch fitting has insertion depth of 1/2 inch.

Make up the assembly *dry* for the arrangement you need. Some fittings might not allow complete insertion until cement has been applied to both parts and has softened both surfaces, so make allowances for this condition when assembling. When you have completed the assembly, make a pencil mark on each fitting and pipe connection, starting on the fitting and continuing in a straight line onto the pipe. This will allow the proper alignment needed for the fitting to face the right direction. After you apply the solvent to the mating surfaces you have only 15 to 20 seconds to assemble and align the two parts.

PRECAUTIONS AGAINST FREEZING OF PIPES

In all areas except tropical and sub-tropical, such as the southern states and Hawaii, it is imperative that water pipes and drainage pipes be protected against freezing. The insulation of pipes will not prevent freezing, it will only delay this action.

In recent years sections of the country have experienced extremely cold winters and previously unheard-of freezing temperatures. Many houses had been built with the water lines passing through unheated attics. As the outside temperatures dropped below freezing the pipes burst and caused extensive damage to the rooms below. It is necessary to route all water pipes through heated areas to prevent damage. Both copper and plastic pipes will expand slightly when frozen and might only bulge, but take no chances and keep the pipes warm at all times.

The insulation of hot water pipes will save you money by reducing heat loss. You can also add a water heater blanket, which gives additional insulation and will pay for itself in a year or two. The insulation of cold water pipes will also eliminate the dripping of condensation on basement floors. The best insulation is the foam preformed type. Made for all pipe sizes, it is slit on the side and can be cemented closed after it has been installed. Elbows and tees are covered by cutting the insulation on a 45-degree angle and cementing the two pieces together at the fitting. For iron pipe fittings, cut away some of the

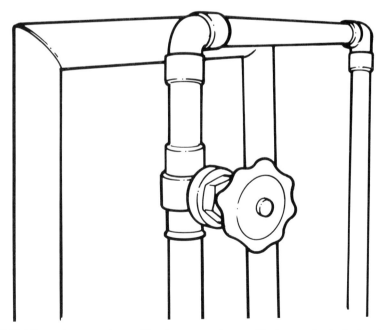

Fig. 7-33. Water pipes entering and leaving a water heater. The larger pipe is the insulated hot water line. Note the shutoff valve in the cold water line.

inside of the foam to accommodate the larger size of the fitting. Copper and plastic fittings are covered without allowances for the fitting thickness because the fittings are thin and no cutting is needed. Figure 7-33 shows insulation installed on a water heater and the hot water pipe leaving the heater.

INSTALLING FLUE PIPE FOR GAS WATER HEATER

Water heater flue pipes are either 3-inch or 4-inch, and the length is usually 30 inches. The pipe should slope upward to the connection to the chimney. To extend the life of the heater, buy the best quality available. Each section fits inside the next one. Be sure to use three short sheet metal screws at each joint, No. 8 or 10 × 1/2 inch long.

In almost all installations the water heater flue pipe enters the chimney *above* the furnace flue pipe. This is usually required by inspection department rules, and must be followed. If you are removing an old heater that used other fuel, you might have to make a hole in the chimney. If so, use a carbide drill bit to remove the brickwork. Be careful when you drill into the flue lining. Drill a series of 1/8-inch holes in the liner and chip out the opening, using furnace cement to seal.

8

Common Plumbing Problems and Repairs

Problems with water and sewer systems are varied, but the two major problems are leaks and clogged drain lines. Leaks can cause extensive damage to buildings and furnishings. Sometimes a quick-fix is needed immediately, but usually a valve can be closed to stop the flow. Clogged lines are not as potentially damaging as leaks are, but need to be taken care of promptly.

FINDING AND REPAIRING LEAKS IN PLUMBING LINES

Leaks in plumbing lines are sometimes as hard to find as leaks in roofs, if the lines are concealed within the walls. In both cases, the water will travel some distance before it is noticed. In houses with basements, pipes rise up into the hollow partitions and thus may pinpoint the location of the leak. In a bathroom, the leak often originates from a shutoff cock (valve) under the toilet tank. This water can travel to the wall behind the fixture and to the inside of the wall and down to the basement. Concealed pipes might require much detective work in tracking down the leak.

Temporary repair devices are available in hardware and home repair stores. The best device consists of two pieces of curved steel, 4 to 6 inches long, plus a rubber strip covering the pipe split or hole. The metal pieces hook together on the back side and are clamped tightly around the leaking pipe. The front side has flanges with holes

Fig. 8-1. Pipe repair clamp. Leak is covered by rubber pad.

to accept two or more clamping bolts, to tightly compress the rubber pad. This is the best type of temporary repair device, and can be classed as semi-permanent (Fig. 8-1).

Note: Any repair that does not replace the defective pipe or fittings is only temporary and cannot be forgotten, but must eventually be replaced by new pipe, fittings, or valves.

Other temporary repairs:

● A piece of rubber sheet 1/8 to 1/4 inch thick and of a size to cover the damaged section, and one or more screw-type stainless steel hose clamps. If the pipe is split, use a longer piece of rubber and more clamps.

● For a pinhole, use electrician's plastic tape. Wrap the tape at least 6 inches on both sides of the hole. This is only temporary, and the water pressure will force its way through the tape layers.

● A fitting leaking where the threads of the pipe enter can be quick-fixed using epoxy putty applied at the threaded part of the pipe and up onto the fitting. Keep the water off if possible. It is best to apply two layers.

THAWING FROZEN PIPES

The best and safest method of thawing frozen pipes is to direct an electric heater or a heat lamp toward the frozen pipe. Be sure to open a valve or faucet so that the steam can escape.

Caution: Thawing a pipe with an open flame is very risky. If you use this method, be extremely careful to avoid igniting wood in the area. Use a heat shield behind the line you are heating. The shield can be of metal or other non-flammable material. In addition, do not leave the area without making very sure that there are no glowing embers that might re-ignite after you have left. Keep checking back occasionally for at least a half hour. If possible, soak the wood with water.

REPAIRING LEAKING FAUCETS

Faucets come in many styles and two types. The first type has two handles, one for hot water and one for cold water. This is probably the most common type in use today. Repair parts are available everywhere, from a faucet washer to the packing, **O** ring, seat, and including the washer—all for about $1.60. The faucet stem might cost up to $2.50, but this item is needed only once during the life of the faucet—if at all. Open the faucet halfway; if the stem can be wiggled from side to side, the threads on the stem or the faucet body are worn. In this case, it is worth a try to buy a new stem and try it in the body. If the new stem fits very loosely, the body threads are worn and the complete faucet should be replaced.

Many cheap faucets do not have removable seats. In this case only, you might have to resort to using a seat dresser. The seat dresser is used to "renew" the seat surface. Most of the dressers on the market radically change the shape of the seat from its original shape. The cross section of the normal seat is half-round, like the top edge of a drinking glass. Most seat dressers form a slanting surface, which is not satisfactory because the faucet washer cannot conform to this surface.

All removable seats can be replaced, and this is the only permanent repair. Most hardwares have replacement seats in stock. Take the old seat with you, and match the size as well as the thread size. The store will have a metal plate having many tapped (threaded) holes so you can get an exact match. The thread match is important because the new seat must fit exactly in the faucet body.

Figure 8-2 illustrates all the parts in their relative positions, including the removable seat. Figures 8-3 through 8-5 show the faucet being taken apart, and the use of a seat removal tool is shown in Fig. 8-6.

Another single faucet uses a diaphragm instead of a washer. A stop ring is also used around the diaphragm instead of a washer. This faucet works the same way as the washer type. If you have a problem finding the diaphragm in the hardware or home improvement store, try a plumbing supply company.

A third single faucet has a stem cartridge similar to the single-handle faucet cartridge, but for only one water supply—hot or cold.

128

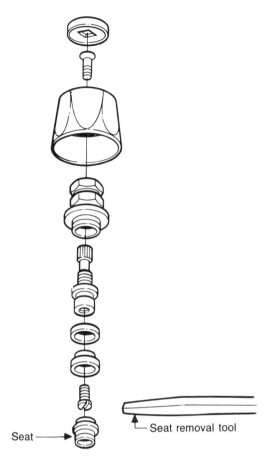

Fig. 8-2. Exploded view of lavatory faucet assembly. Note the seat and seat removal tool.

Seat ⟶

Seat removal tool

The **O** rings and the seat and spring can be replaced easily. Repairing tub/shower two-handle faucets (Fig. 8-7) is similar to repairing other two-handle faucets. The main difference is that the stem of each faucet is longer because it has to extend from behind the tile or other wall finish of the tub area (Fig. 8-8).

Clay tile around the elongated faucet stem might interfere with removing these parts because the packing nut is larger and is inside the wall finish, and the finish might be tight around the nut. In this case, it will be necessary to *carefully* chip the clay tile area interfering with the removal of the stem. To do this, use a screwdriver with a 1/8-inch-wide blade and gently chip away very small pieces of the tile about 1/8 inch square. For work like this, I use electrician's pliers to tap on the screwdriver handle. Using the pliers eliminates blows that are too strong and that might break the tile further than you want. Clay tile is very fragile, which is why very small pieces rather than

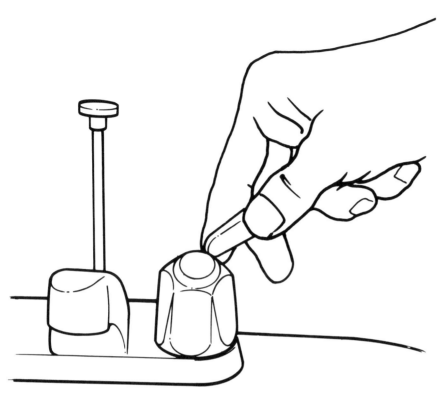

Fig. 8-3. Removing the plastic cover from faucet handle. This has the designation "C" (cold) on it.

larger pieces must be chipped away. Remove only enough to use a deep socket wrench or adjustable wrench on the hex part to loosen it (Fig. 8-9). The white plastic sleeve is threaded into the stem cavity. The exposed end of the sleeve accepts the escutcheon plate that covers the opening in the wall.

Note: Certain faucet assemblies on lavatories, sinks, tubs, and laundry trays (tubs) are supplied with lever handles instead of symmetrical or round handles. In the case of lever handles, either lever is pulled forward toward the front of the fixture to open the faucet — whether hot or cold. This indicates that there are different threads on each faucet stem: the hot faucet has right hand threads, while the cold faucet has left hand threads. Therefore, when replacing stems the correct "hand" (either left or right) must be specified. Most new two-faucet assemblies will have the same threads on both faucet stems. Recently, expensive brass and gold-plated faucet assemblies have been made available. These have the lever handles as described and will have the different "hand" stems.

Many faucet assemblies are now made almost entirely of plastic with a chrome finish. As shown in Fig. 8-10, the internal plastic parts,

Fig. 8-4. Removing the handle screw, Phillips-head type.

Fig. 8-5. Removing the faucet stem, which includes stem, washer, and jamb nut.

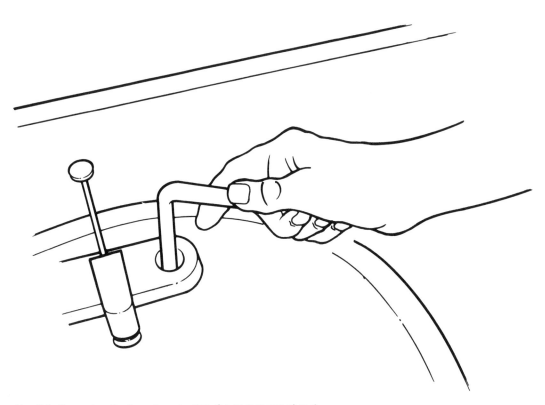

Fig. 8-6. Removing the faucet seat using the seat removal tool.

the packing gland and cartridge, are not separable. In the assembly shown, the handles require only a quarter turn from full closed to full open because of the arrangement of the internal ports in the cartridge. Illustrated in Fig. 8-11 are the chrome-plated body (plastic), the faucet body, and the seat below the threads.

Single-lever faucets consist of a replaceable cartridge that comes as a kit for that specific make and model faucet. After turning off both the hot and cold stop valves under the fixture, replacement is easy. Directions are always given.

After you remove the lever handle by loosening the Allen setscrew, lifting the handle off lets you unscrew the bonnet. The control assembly can now be lifted out, whether it be a ball, disc, or cartridge. Beneath the control assembly you will find two rubber seals mounted on springs, located in recesses in the bottom of the faucet body. All new parts furnished with the repair kit should now be installed in the reverse order that you removed the old parts. If there are **O** rings of large diameter included in the repair kit, they may be intended for the swing spout. This spout can be removed by lifting and turning. Carefully pry out the old **O** rings without damaging the metal grooves, and put on the new **O** rings. Then assemble the swing spout and other parts and check for leaks, after turning on the hot and cold stop valves.

132

Fig. 8-7. Exploded view of tub faucet assembly.

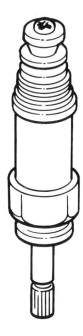

Fig. 8-8. Jamb nut and stem assembly removed from faucet.

Fig. 8-9. Chipping ceramic tile edges away so that jamb nut and stem may be removed.

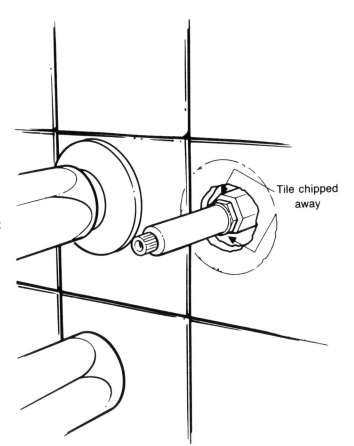

Tile chipped away

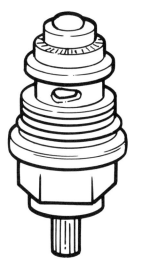

Fig. 8-10. Quick-acting laundry tray faucet—a one-piece part.

Your single-handle faucet will now be like new. Figures 8-12 through 8-15 show, step-by-step, how to replace the cartridge assembly.

There are many brands of single-handle faucets for kitchen sink, bathroom lavatory, and tub. All operate on the same principle, the lever handle moves the control plate for water temperature and flow desired. The brands with the lever action operate better than those that require that the knob be pulled up to turn the water on.

Replacing A Lavatory Faucet

This procedure is one of the easiest of all repair jobs. It is as simple as: disconnect and remove, install and reconnect. Most replacement projects involve removing an old two-handle faucet and installing a

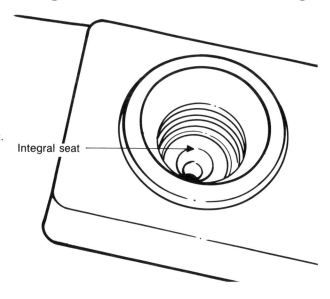

Fig. 8-11. Seat and faucet body of laundry tray faucet. The seat is integral with the body (not removable).

Integral seat

Fig. 8-12. Removing the cap of a single-lever kitchen faucet. A special wrench is supplied with the replacement kit.

single-lever faucet. Doing this replacement on a lavatory is easier than on a kitchen sink because there is no garbage disposal to interfere.

The first step is to turn off the supply faucets under the lavatory. If there are none, close the main valve controlling the water entering the house. Because the work will take some time, turn off your gas water heater (turn the valve on the heater to "Pilot"). If the heater

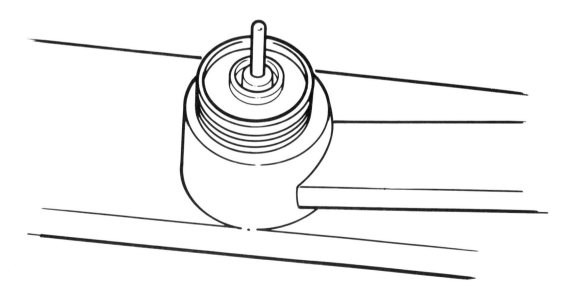

Fig. 8-13. The cap removed.

136

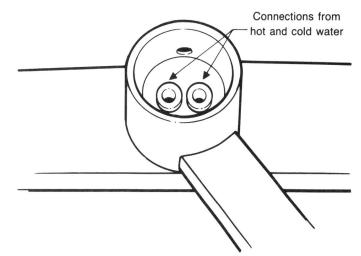

Fig. 8-14. Internal parts are removed to show the connections from the water supply lines.

is electric, turn off the power to the heater. With the water off, disconnect the hot and cold risers going to the underside of the old faucet base. A small amount of water will drain out of the risers. Opening the faucets above will help to drain the lines.

Use a basin wrench to loosen the nuts under the lavatory ledge that hold the faucet assembly to the ledge. Lie on your back under the lavatory (use a pillow to pad the hard edge of the cabinet floor). The basin wrench head flips over for turning the nuts in either direction, and grips much as a pipe wrench does. These large nuts and washers usually slip down over the tubing connections. The faucet assembly is now free. At times the plumber's putty may hold the faucet. A putty knife worked around the edge can help loosen the base. Work carefully so as not to chip the porcelain. Carefully clean the surface, since a hard plastic gasket will be installed under the new faucet base.

The supply risers of the new faucet will come through the center opening of the lavatory and the hold-down studs through the two end holes. Large washers are used on these 1/4-20 studs to cover and span the large holes. The washers may either be slotted to be slid over the studs with the nuts already on, or only have a 1/4-inch hole in the center. Figure 8-16 shows the stud beside the tubing (this is the old faucet, a single lever, but with the tubes extending through the outer holes).

Many single-lever faucets come with short (10- to 12-inch) copper lines. Extension lengths can be soldered on, or compression couplings can be used. If you will solder extensions on, couplings are available at refrigeration wholesalers. (Refer to Chapter 7 for soldering methods.) The compression couplings are easier because no sol-

Fig. 8-15. Faucet internal parts, an exploded view.

Fig. 8-16. Stud, part of the old faucet hold-down method.

dering is required. The shutoff valves have compression fittings on their outlets.

With the faucet tightened down firmly, measure the copper tubing length. Remember that the tubing enters the fitting recess about 1/8 inch. After cutting, slip the nut on the tubing, then the ferrule. Insert the tubing end in the fitting recess and start the nut. Be sure the nut is started straight because the fine threads make it easy to "cross-thread" and damage both pieces. If you can tighten the nut two full turns, the parts are not cross-threaded. Also follow this "trick of the trade" when starting the nuts on the compression couplings and on any other threaded items. In this manner, you will be less likely to damage any threads.

Some faucet assemblies will have 1/2-inch male pipe threads on the copper ends. You can use riser tubes that connect to these ends. Hardware stores stock this style, or you can cut these ends off and solder or use compression couplings. It is possible to connect almost any piping material or fitting to any other with the adapters now available. Genova makes Uncopper fittings that will connect copper, iron pipe, and plastic in any combination to suit your needs. Many hardwares and home centers stock this Uncopper line of fittings for the do-it-yourselfer. Figures 8-17 through 8-20 show some of the procedures for this replacement operation. Genova offers booklets describing methods of using their products.

POP-UP DRAINS

A great improvement over the rubber drain plug and chain is the "pop-

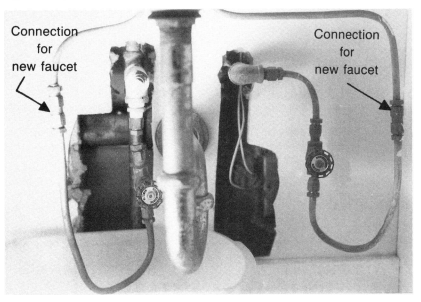

Fig. 8-17. Connections under a lavatory. A new faucet is to be installed to replace a defective single-lever type. Note the new faucet connection points.

Fig. 8-18. New faucet ready for installation. Notice the studs that hold down the new faucet on each side of the copper water lines. The lines had to be extended as shown, by soldering on extra tubing.

up" drain assembly. This consists of a rod having a flat or round head for grasping, located behind the spout on a lavatory assembly. Pulling up on this rod moves a lever arrangement extending horizontally into the drain pipe, just below the lavatory bowl. In a seesaw motion, this rod raises or lowers a stopper to open or close the lavatory drain.

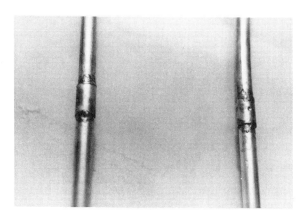

Fig. 8-19. Close-up of soldered connections to extend the lines.

Fig. 8-20. The new faucet has been installed and tested for leaks.

Figure 8-21 shows the linkage arrangement. The stopper itself is about 3 inches long. Originally the stopper in Fig. 8-22 had a hole in the lower end for the control rod to engage, but due to the need to remove and clean it without disassembling the linkage, the bottom side of the stopper hole has been cut away. This allows the stopper to be removed for cleaning. A thin rubber gasket under the stopper edge forms a seal with the drain opening. Other stoppers are made of brass or die-cast metal, and their weight allows them to seal without a gasket.

The opening in the drain line (it resembles a tee) is sealed by a packing gland where the horizontal control rod enters the drain line. The seesaw action is made possible by a ball of plastic or metal on the rod where it enters the drain line. The packing gland nut and packing seal and hold this ball in a recess. Tightening the gland nut snugs the ball in place and provides resistance to hold the lever assembly in any position.

REPAIRING OR REPLACING THE TUB DRAIN

The tub drain assembly is a simple mechanism, but it must be adjusted correctly. The linkage has to be the specified length, otherwise the tub either will not drain or will not hold water. As with all mechanical devices in the home, the installation and servicing instructions should be retained, just in case adjustments to a piece of equipment are needed.

Tub drain assemblies take two forms:

● The stopper is within the drain pipe from the tub and is directly below the end of the overflow pipe where it meets the horizontal pipe from the tub drain connection. This mechanism is all behind the tub itself. The drain opening in the tub is covered by a strainer.

● The stopper is visible in the tub drain and pops up and down, similar to a lavatory pop-up. This pop-up part can be easily removed and replaced for cleaning. The other part is removed by detaching the lever assembly from the tub and lifting it out. The lever assembly of

141

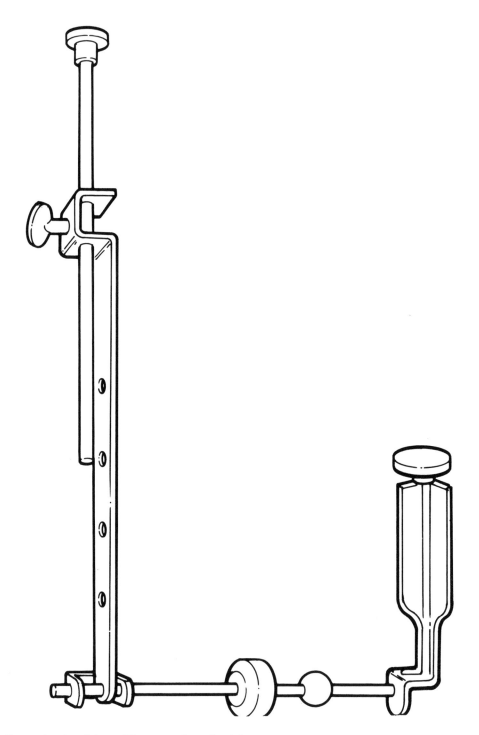

Fig. 8-21. Pop-up lavatory linkage. The pop-up is at the right.

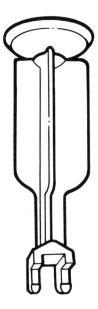

Fig. 8-22. Lavatory pop-up plug. It is all plastic except for the chrome top that shows here.

the first type is removed the same way (Fig. 8-23).

With both types, adjustment is accomplished by lengthening or shortening the lift linkage. There is a **U** shaped yoke and a 1/4-inch threaded rod that goes through the bottom of the yoke. On each side of the yoke on the rod are nuts. These nuts can be loosened to permit the necessary adjustment to be made. If you have no illustrated instructions, this adjustment can be made through trial and error. Make only small adjustments each time. Notice the rubber gasket behind the tub at the faceplate.

The faceplate through which the control handle extends can become worn on the concealed side. On each side of the control lever on the concealed side of the face plate are two humps cast in place. A washer, spring, another washer, and a cotter pin put pressure on the washer, which rides on the humps. This holds the control handle in the up or down position, whichever is desired (Fig. 8-24).

UNPLUGGING BATHROOM DRAINS

Figures 8-25 through 8-29 illustrate the operation of unplugging a bathroom lavatory with either a plunger or, with the trap removed, a snake. When unplugging a lavatory, try the plunger first, snake second, and chemicals last. This sequence is important because if you try chemicals first and they are not successful, you will be working with dangerous and caustic materials. *Caution:* Wear rubber gloves and goggles if working with dangerous chemicals.

The trap illustrated is plastic and the nuts can usually be tightened by hand. It is better, however, to use Channellock pliers for a tighter fit. The **P** trap attached to the lavatory (Fig. 8-25) is removed

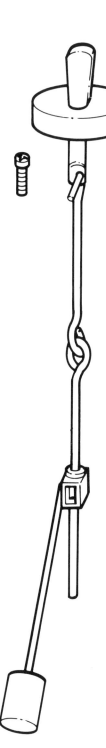

Fig. 8-23. Tub drain plug and overflow plate. Drain plug is concealed behind the tub wall at base near the drain.

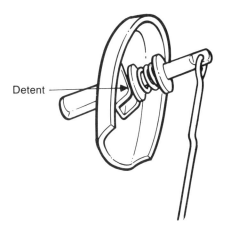

Fig. 8-24. ''Detent hump'' that holds the drain plug in either the open or closed position.

so the drain line can be unplugged or just cleaned. The trap can be loosened (Fig. 8-26), and the horizontal section removed so the trap can be "rodded" properly (Fig. 8-27). The snake is inserted and worked down through the drain more easily if the tail piece is not removed

Fig. 8-25. An all-plastic trap. The tail piece attached to the lavatory is metal.

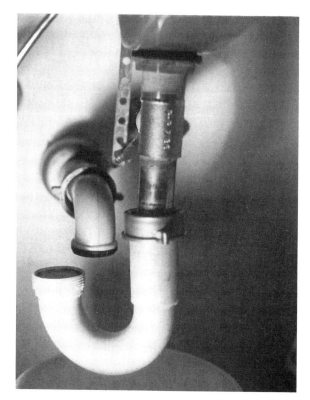

Fig. 8-26. Removal of the trap has been started, prior to using a sewer snake to unplug the line in the wall.

Fig. 8-27. The complete trap has been removed so that the snake can be used easily.

146

Fig. 8-28. The snake has been inserted into the plugged drain line. Notice the crank handle with the set screw which allows the snake to rotate so as to hook the clog.

(Fig. 8-28). Any elbows that can be removed make using the snake easier and more efficient.

SEWER CLEANING

Cleaning sewers (rodding) is a necessary operation at times, particularly if materials and chemicals are put down the house sewer lines. Remember that some items advertised as disposable are *not* disposable! This includes baby diapers, sanitary napkins, and facial tissues. It also includes hair and cooking grease. Hair is a problem mainly in the lavatory, shower, and bathtub, while cooking grease usually clogs kitchen sinks. Gather any hair left in the lavatory before the water is let out of the bowl, and gather the hair before draining the tub. In the kitchen, it is good practice to collect meat drippings in a jar or can, then dispose of it in the garbage.

The small but necessary tasks just mentioned will save you time and trouble. Plumbing problems often arise at the most inopportune times. If you cannot clear a clogged toilet yourself, you will need a plumber, at considerable cost (even in daylight hours). Problems are

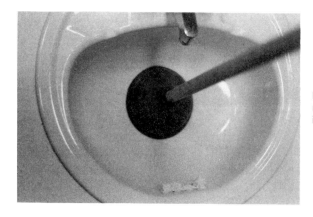

Fig. 8-29. Using a plunger. This tool should be used before removing the trap; it might unclog the stoppage without having to remove the trap.

avoidable if proper and regular maintenance is given to all of your mechanical equipment.

All sewer drainage lines are required to have clean-out openings (cleanouts) at regular intervals to allow for rodding out the line. These openings have a 3-inch pipe plug with a square boss you can use a wrench on to loosen the plug. Plugs at floor level (a violation of the Plumbing Code) might have a square recess. Wrenches are made to fit this recess, and you might be able to rent one. The Plumbing Code requires the cleanout, if in the basement floor, to be 1 inch above the finished floor. This prevents the cleanout from being used as a floor drain.

Main sewer lines under the basement floor or in a crawl space will require a long sewer snake or a motorized snake. This motorized snake requires some skill and experience to use; you might require a plumber. Plumbers who specialize in drain cleaning will sometimes go up on the roof and rod the vent risers from there. This way a better, more thorough job can be done. It also eliminates the necessity of bringing the rather bulky rodding equipment into the house, down to the basement, and through finished recreation rooms.

SUMP PUMPS

The sump pump (Fig. 8-30) is a real necessity for many homes. Some houses have basements below the level of storm sewers, other houses need to remove the water that collects at the weeping tile (4-inch perforated drain pipe laid around the perimeter of the house outside the basement wall footings). This last condition is common where the surrounding soil is mostly clay because clay soil does not absorb water readily.

Sump pumps generally come in three models: pedestal, submersible, and sumpless. The pedestal and submersible models, of necessity, must be set in a sump. Sumps are usually 24 inches deep and 18 inches in diameter. Larger commercial models will have larger

Fig. 8-30. This view shows the motor and manual switch for testing the operation of the sump pump. Warning and nameplate labels are shown here.

sumps to accommodate them. Domestic submersible models are rated at 2270 gallons per hour (gph) at a 10-foot head for the 1/3-hp motor. For the 1/2-hp motor and a 10-foot head, the capacity is 3240 gph. The pedestal model is the same for the 1/3-hp motor. The 1/2-hp motor is rated at 3600 gph at the 10-foot head.

The submersible models are completely in the sump, only the discharge pipe and the electric cord extend above the floor level. Be sure that the electric circuit feeding the pump is protected by a ''slow blow'' fuse; this type fuse will hold when the high current inrush occurs as the motor starts. In one case a family left on vacation and decided to have two sump pumps. They made the mistake of connecting both pumps to the same circuit. The first pump failed and blew the fuse, which prevented the second pump from operating. The basement then flooded 2 feet deep and damage was extensive.

There is now on the market a battery-operated sump pump that is ideal if the power goes out frequently. This system costs about three times the price of a standard pump, but it could save you a great deal in the long run.

Another style, "the sumpless sump pump," sits in a vertical 6-inch tile that is connected to the weeping tile that circles the house foundation beside the footings. There is no open sump. These pumps are very reliable—some have been operating for over 20 years with no problems.

Getting rid of the water discharged from the sump pump is sometimes a problem. I had this situation in my new house. The pump discharge line extended about 8 inches through the wall to the outside. The pump would discharge water on the ground just outside the foundation, and this water would sink into the ground and find its way down to the weeping tile. The pump would restart and pump more water out to repeat the cycle again.

My final solution was to get permission from the city to tap into the storm sewer manhole in front of my house. I then changed the direction of the pump discharge line to the opposite side of the basement, through the basement wall, down in the ground, and from that point to the manhole. In cooperation with my neighbor, we trenched out to the manhole, tunneled under the sidewalk, and drilled a series of holes in a 4-inch circle through the side of the manhole. We then broke out this 4-inch circle. In return for my neighbor's help, we also connected his pump discharge into the same 4-inch plastic line going to the manhole. The pipe connection to the manhole was cemented to seal the joint watertight. I also installed a boiler drain cock (faucet) in my own basement at the end of the iron discharge line, near the ceiling of the basement. Here I connected a garden hose as a relief connection in case the line coming out of the side of the wall froze. The hose could be directed outside or into a floor drain; one drain *was* connected to the sanitary sewer.

9

The Domestic
Water Heater

Water heaters come in many styles and sizes, and use various types of fuels. Because of the small price differential, it might be wise to consider buying a 40-gallon size as a replacement for a 30-gallon heater. Families grow and appliances such as dishwashers or automatic clothes washers are added—increasing hot water needs.

For normal household uses, the water temperature should be a maximum of 130 degrees F. and a minimum of 120 degrees F. The only appliance that would need higher temperatures is the automatic dishwasher. Many brands of dishwashers, however, have an auxiliary electric heater and have no need for high temperature water from the main heater.

A gas-fired heater has a faster recovery (ability to heat another tank of cold water) and you might be able to get by with a setting of 120 degrees F. Both heaters have adjustable thermostats. The gas model has a knob mounted on the front of the thermostat cover with marks such as "hotter" or "cooler." The knob can be turned toward either mark to make the adjustment. Turn the knob only a small distance and try this setting for two or three days before changing it again.

Most modern heaters have what is called an "energy cut-off," which shuts the heater off. Because even this device can fail, the temperature and pressure (T & P) relief valve is always mandatory to protect against water heater explosions. Many manufacturers require that

Fig. 9-1. Temperature and pressure (T & P) relief valve. Courtesy Watts Regulator Co.

a T & P relief valve (Fig. 9-1) be installed to validate the warranty. Some areas require a check valve in the water supply line to the heater, to prevent damage to the water meter.

An approved water pressure reducing valve (Fig. 9-2) is needed if the water pressure exceeds 80 psi. High water pressure will damage appliances and waste the potable water. Water conservation is a national concern. Thirty percent less water flows at 50 pounds than at 100 pounds.

Before buying a new water heater, decide what type of fuel is available. Gas is cheaper, and recovery of the heater will be faster. If gas is not available, stay with electricity. If you are only replacing a defective heater and will use the same fuel, there is no need to con-

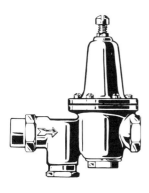

Fig. 9-2. Pressure reducing valve to reduce high water pressure in a house. Courtesy Watts Regulator Co.

tact the utility. If you are changing to another fuel, contact the utility before buying the heater. Electric water heaters are usually on a timer, controlled by radio signals from the utility. Many times the heater is on a separate meter at a lower rate. The gas utility usually has no restrictions, but contact them to be sure.

Chapter 7 explains how to disconnect and reconnect the piping to the heater correctly, and how to install the flue pipe from the gas water heater to the chimney.

GENERAL INSTRUCTIONS

Hot water heaters (Figs. 9-3 and 9-4) do develop leaks and generally need replacement rather than repair. Heater tank leaks occur on the outside of the tank, underneath the insulation and the metal cover. These leaks *can* be repaired using a repair plug, but one leak is the beginning of more. You will save trouble and expense by replacing the heater with a new one.

When buying a new heater, be sure the one you choose will fit in the same space as the old heater. Another point to consider is that the hot and cold connections may be reversed on the top of the new heater. You can turn the heater slightly so that the two lines can cross each other, but do not turn the heater so far as to put the access panel against the wall. As when doing anything permanent, think out each step beforehand.

A normal installation will have unions in both water lines as well as the gas line. If not, you will have to cut the pipes with a hacksaw. Do the disconnecting *after* all the water has been drained. *Caution:* The old heater will weigh as much as one third more than a new one due to scale and sediment. Also, once you disconnect the water lines, the heater might fall over since the lines have been keeping it upright.

Copper water lines are easy to work with and fittings are available for any type of connection. For galvanized pipe, a special tank union is available; one end has a male pipe thread, and the union section has female threads to accept the pipe. At this time, consider adding a valve in the cold water supply to the heater for servicing, if there was none in the old installation.

Remove the flue pipe and the draft diverter (a hood-shaped sheet metal section set directly on top of the heater). These parts should be replaced, although most heaters will come with the diverter furnished. Buy heavy-gauge flue pipe; it will last longer. It is best to get help in removing the heater, especially from a basement.

After the area has been cleared, set the new heater in place. If the hot and cold connections match up with the pipe arrangement, you are in luck. It might turn out that the pipes match for hot and cold but are spaced differently. If so, then go to the hardware store and purchase flexible lines with connection fittings on each end. These come in different lengths and will be ideal for crossed connections.

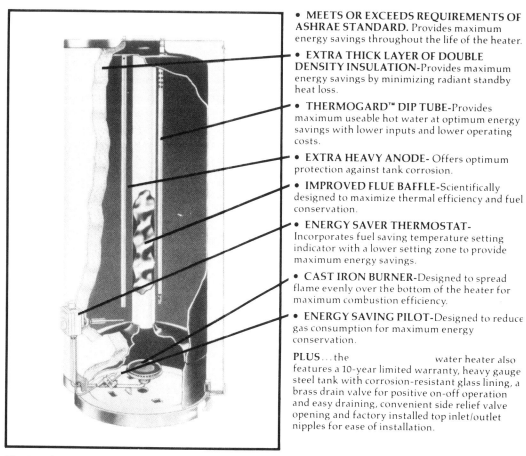

• **MEETS OR EXCEEDS REQUIREMENTS OF ASHRAE STANDARD.** Provides maximum energy savings throughout the life of the heater.

• **EXTRA THICK LAYER OF DOUBLE DENSITY INSULATION-**Provides maximum energy savings by minimizing radiant standby heat loss.

• **THERMOGARD™ DIP TUBE-**Provides maximum useable hot water at optimum energy savings with lower inputs and lower operating costs.

• **EXTRA HEAVY ANODE-** Offers optimum protection against tank corrosion.

• **IMPROVED FLUE BAFFLE-**Scientifically designed to maximize thermal efficiency and fuel conservation.

• **ENERGY SAVER THERMOSTAT-** Incorporates fuel saving temperature setting indicator with a lower setting zone to provide maximum energy savings.

• **CAST IRON BURNER-**Designed to spread flame evenly over the bottom of the heater for maximum combustion efficiency.

• **ENERGY SAVING PILOT-**Designed to reduce gas consumption for maximum energy conservation.

PLUS...the   water heater also features a 10-year limited warranty, heavy gauge steel tank with corrosion-resistant glass lining, a brass drain valve for positive on-off operation and easy draining, convenient side relief valve opening and factory installed top inlet/outlet nipples for ease of installation.

Fig. 9-3. Cutaway of a gas water heater.

If you have copper plumbing, you might want to make the connections by using copper fittings and soldering all connections. Remember that the flexible lines come complete with union-type ends and do not need much work to make the connections, though they might be more expensive. These flexible lines are also available for galvanized lines.

Replacing a water heater is not difficult. First turn off the water supply to the heater. Near the top of the heater will be a shutoff valve. Close this valve, then open the drain valve at the bottom of the heater. Also open a hot water faucet to allow the water to drain easily from the heater. Attach a hose to the drain valve if you need to lead the water away from the area.

When the heater has completely drained, you can disconnect the hot and cold water lines. These lines should have pipe unions to allow easy disconnection. If not, you will have to saw both pipes. If the pipes are copper, you can use a tubing cutter. You will need a cutter for reassembling the lines anyway, so buy or rent one. Good tubing cutters cost about $10 to $15. If you buy, buy a good one.

If the heater is electric, make sure the power is off at the electrical panel. Remove the fuses or trip off the circuit breaker, then disconnect the wires at the junction box on the side or top of the heater. After removing the connections, pull the cable or conduit free of the heater. Tape the bare wire ends in case someone turns the power back on.

If the heater is gas, you must shut off the gas to the heater. Many heaters have a manual gas cock (valve) ahead of the control on the heater. The valve will have a pipe union between it and the control box. Turn the valve to the off position and disconnect the union.

Caution: As with any work of this nature, keep your mind on the work at hand. Do not let your mind wander or you could forget a vital step in the procedure and have an accident. If there is no shutoff valve, you might have to shut the gas off at the meter. Be aware that all gas

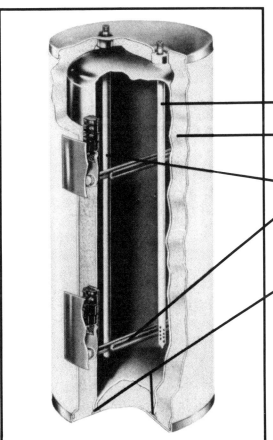

- **MEETS OR EXCEEDS REQUIREMENTS OF ASHRAE STANDARD-**Provides maximum energy savings throughout the life of the heater.
- **DIFFUSER DIP TUBE-**Delivers better draw for more useable hot water.
- **EXTRA THICK LAYER OF DOUBLE DENSITY INSULATION-**Provides energy savings by minimizing radiant heat loss.
- **EXTRA HEAVY ANODE-**Protects against tank corrosion.
- **PHOENIX™ LOW-WATT DENSITY DIRECT IMMERSION ELEMENT-** Eliminates burn-out due to overheating from lime build-up. Ceramic terminal block won't melt.
- **INSULATOR PADS-**Protect tank from radiant heat loss.

PLUS...the   water heater also features a 10-year limited warranty, fingertip temperature control with overheat protection, and heavy gauge steel tank with corrosion-resistant glass lining. Complete unit is U.L. listed.

Fig. 9-4. Cutaway of an electric water heater.

pilots in the building must be shut off *before* you shut off the main valve at the meter. When you are done, the main valve is opened first and then each pilot is *individually* turned on and relighted. This is very important.

Either type of heater will have connections on the top marked "hot" and "cold," but there is a chance that those on the new heater will be reversed. Do not turn the heater around to install it unless the front of the heater is fully accessible for servicing and lighting. There are flexible lines 12 to 18 inches long available, and you can cross these to fit the reversed connections with no problem. This is much easier than repiping in either copper or galvanized pipe.

In most water heaters there is a copper or plastic "dip tube" inserted into the cold supply opening of the heater. If you wish, this tube can be moved to the hot supply pipe of the heater and the cold water supply connected to this pipe. I do not like to do this unless there is no other way to make the connections, because the labels of the openings are then wrong. The purpose of the dip tube is to lead the incoming cold water supply directly to the lower part of the heater tank, forcing the hot water to the top.

Certain water heaters incorporate a magnesium anode. This anode gives up its magnesium metal to prevent the tank from giving up its metal. This sacrificial action extends the life of the heater tank and prolongs the useful life of the heater.

With electric water heaters, you must be more cautious. You *must* first turn off the electric power to the heater, then carefully remove the two small panels from the front of the heater. These are held on by sheet metal screws. Most heaters have two thermostats, one for each heating element. Yours might have only one thermostat. The thermostat will have a central shaft with a screwdriver slot and a pointer. The dial has degrees marked on it, so turning the shaft adjusts the pointer to a different setting in degrees. Be careful not to touch any exposed wires or wire terminals when adjusting the thermostat, even though you have turned the power off. Also be careful not to let the cover touch any exposed wires when you remove or replace the cover. Adjust the thermostat slightly and try it for a few days before readjusting it.

Electric heaters have easily replaceable heating elements, sold in many hardware stores. It is necessary to buy a replacement where the mounting method (flange or screw-in) fits exactly, so the fit will be leak-proof. Also, element wattage rating must be the same as the old element. After installation, check for leaks before reconnecting the wiring.

Both the gas and electric heaters have a drain valve near the bottom of the heater. The valve should be opened periodically to drain the sediment and rust from the heater, which will help prolong the life of the heater. And again, the T & P (temperature and pressure) relief value is vitally important for safety reasons. As with any mechanical device, failure is always a possibility. If the heating device, whether a gas burner or electric element, does not shut off when the water reaches the 140-degree range and continues to increase the temperature of the water to the boiling point and higher, the heater "runs wild," and will cause excessive pressure and temperature.

THE GAS-FIRED WATER HEATER

In many areas, the most common and cheapest fuel is natural gas. The gas-fired heater is supplied in 30- and 40-gallon sizes. Heaters have warranties of up to 7 1/2 years, but, depending on water conditions, do not last out the warranty period. Hard water is considered less corrosive than soft water (and more healthful for drinking). It also scales everything, including water heaters and tea kettles. When a gas water heater, new or old, is started up after being filled with *cold* water, there will appear to be a water leak because water will drip from the flue pipe, which goes up through the center of the heater. This is only condensation of the water formed when natural gas is burned, it is not a leak.

Standard black iron pipe should be used to pipe the gas line. Because the gas line is on the side of the heater near the floor, solid pipe is better than a flexible line. Damage to the flex line is possible, therefore it should not be used. After completing the gas connection, turn on the gas but do not turn on either the pilot or the main valve. Check for leaks using thick soap suds or a child's bubble solution. Brush this solution on all joints and watch for bubbles. Be sure to look very closely; a gas leak is extremely dangerous. *Caution:* Never under *any* circumstance use a match or other open flame!

In gas heaters usually the only thing that would require attention—other than a leak in the heater tank—is the thermocouple. The main gas valve might fail, but very rarely. Thermocouples are stocked by most home centers and hardware stores. Take the old one with you for matching. A universal style is available. Match the tubing length; somewhat longer tube can be used, but it cannot be shorter. The thermocouple is mounted alongside the pilot burner by bolts or a threaded bushing. The other end is attached to the main gas valve. This is an electrical connection, so do not tighten excessively.

Turn the main gas valve on the pipe ahead of the valve on the heater to OFF (handle of valve will be crosswise of the pipe). Turn the heater gas valve to OFF. Open the access door and remove the thermocouple. You might have to take off the pilot (possibly the main burner also) to remove the thermocouple. All these parts are usually rusty; use care and they will come loose. There is no danger if the gas is shut off in two places.

When you are ready to relight the heater, turn the main gas valve to OPEN; turn the heater valve from OFF to PILOT. If you removed the pilot burner, the short pilot tubing will be full of air and you will use two or more matches before the gas will ignite. The pilot orifice through which the gas flows is very small and might take 30 seconds to fill with gas. Hold the button on the valve down for the 30 seconds then try the match. When the pilot flame has been established, slowly release the button. If the pilot stays lighted, turn the heater valve from PILOT to ON. The main gas flame will light if the thermostat is calling for heat.

THE ELECTRIC WATER HEATER

In areas where natural gas or liquified petroleum gas (LPG) are not available, the electric water heater is the only type to use. All tables of cost comparison show that electric water heating is the most expensive form of energy. Removal and replacement procedures are the same as described before. It is necessary to disconnect the wiring from the heater connections.

Before touching any of the wiring, be sure the fuses have been removed or the circuit breakers have been tripped off. If the replacement heater is electric, the problem is simple. The electric cable connects to a junction box, usually on top or near the top of the heater casing on the side. Remove the cover from the junction box. Again check that the wires are not live. You should have a pocket voltage tester with which to test the wires in the box.

In some heaters, the wires are attached to bolts and held tight by a washer and nut, in others, the wires are under terminal screws. In either case, disconnect the wires. There will be three wires: one black, one red, and one bare (the bare wire is attached to the metal casing of the heater and not to a terminal). At times, but not correctly, the wires might be: one black, one white, and one bare. Consider the white wire to be red.

The cable is held to the box by a clamp extending inside the box. A locknut is screwed on the clamp to hold it in the box. There are notches in the locknut edge; use a screwdriver to tap the locknut loose. Tap with a pair of pliers on the screwdriver handle. If you can't reach the locknut easily, loosen it by turning the body of the clamp on the outside of the box. Loosen the clamp from the cable before trying to turn the clamp. Use water pump pliers (Channellock brand is best) to turn the clamp. This will allow you to remove the old heater and set the new one in place. It might be necessary to put a thin block under one leg of the heater for leveling, if the floor is uneven.

Many years ago, electric water heaters were controlled by a time clock owned by the utility. In these cases, it was necessary to set the two thermostats quite high to have enough hot water to carry over when the power was shut off. There was a switch that could be turned on in case more hot water was needed, but this power was metered at the regular rate. The power that was not metered was supplied at a fixed monthly cost. Some systems might still be connected this way, but now most heaters are on a separate meter and have a special relay. This method only shuts off the power during peak loads on the utility system by using radio signals.

Many heaters come with a high setting even now. To prevent being scalded, set the thermostats lower. To do this, turn off the power to the heater circuit and remove the access plates from the side of the heater—one near the top and one lower down. You will see the end of the element and close by a small scale with a central screw and a small pointer. Move the pointer toward "colder" one or two divisions on both thermostats. Because this is trial and error, use the heater for a while on this setting before lowering the settings any more. Be sure to replace the covers before turning the power back on, because there are exposed live terminals carrying 240 volts.

If you eventually have gas brought into the dwelling, you might want to install a gas-fired heater to replace the old electric heater. Be aware that the electric water heater might have been installed at a distance from the chimney *and* the gas supply. In this case, the heater location should be within 6 to 8 feet from the chimney and the gas line. There is no problem in extending the water lines. The access door must face out so the pilot can be lighted and the main flame observed. Chapter 7 gives additional instructions.

If you are using galvanized pipe for the water lines, you will need an assortment of pipe nipples in various lengths and 3/4-inch nominal size; add two 3/4-inch galvanized tank unions if none were used originally. You will need a roll of Teflon tape to use on the pipe threads.

Note: If you are using this tape with copper adapter fittings (thread on one end and a solder end on the other) on the heater top, you must solder a 6- to 8-inch piece of copper tubing in the adapter and then apply the Teflon tape to the fitting threads and screw the fitting into the heater. If you screw the fitting into the heater and then solder copper tubing into the fitting, you will destroy the Teflon tape. There are no cautions when using the tape with galvanized pipe threads. Because Teflon tape has no adhesive, it should be stretched tightly as you wrap it around the threads; this will help it to stay on the threads. Use two turns on pipe 1/2 inch or larger.

After you have made the connections to the water lines, turn on the water and test for leaks. Open a hot water faucet so that air can escape while the tank is filling. Make absolutely sure that the tank is full before lighting the gas flame or turning on the electricity or the oil burner, depending on the fuel used. Set the thermostat(s) to deliver 130-degree water to all faucets and other connections. This will usually be high enough for everything except the dishwasher, which might have its own auxiliary heater.

THE OIL-FIRED WATER HEATER

Heaters using fuel oil are practically obsolete. A power burner such as on an oil-fired furnace will have such a low firing rate that operation is unsatisfactory. Those having what is known as "pot type" burner are equally unsatisfactory because they tend to soot up badly and give off an oily odor. If at all possible, try to install an electric water heater, or better yet, a gas heater.

REGULAR MAINTENANCE

Hot water heaters only require minimal maintenance. Drain the heater tank regularly to remove the sediment that accumulates over time. Do this once a month to start, then if the water comes clear, try every other month. This will depend on the type of water supplied to the heater. You might have to attach a hose if a drain is not close by, or if the heater is in the first floor utility room. In case the valve leaks and cannot be made to stop, buy a "hose end cap" from the hardware store. These are made for use when a series of sprinklers are connected by short lengths of hose to water a large area. The last sprinkler needs this end cap. Screw this cap on the heater drain valve outlet. It will stop the leak. It will pay you to buy an insulating blanket to wrap around the outside of the heater casing.

Note: Do not cover the top of the gas-fired type. The electric heater might have its top covered because there is no flue pipe to ignite the cover of the insulating blanket.

SOLAR WATER HEATERS

The use of solar energy for heating domestic hot water is practical for all areas except the states in the northern tier. Solar panels can be used to supplant the domestic water heater where there is enough sunshine to warrant the cost of installation. In the areas where freezing conditions are encountered, the *indirect* system must be used.

The indirect system is more expensive because it must have a heat exchanger as part of the system. The device separates the water in the solar panel, which has antifreeze and water to prevent freezing of the water in the panel and its connecting piping.

Solar panels in warm climates do not need to have this indirect system, but instead can use the water from the panel directly. Most solar water systems need either gas or electric heater/storage systems to provide backup when conditions are not right for solar heating of the water (no sun, extremely cold weather, or heavy usage of hot water). These are special storage units having a heating element or gas burner and large storage tank (Fig. 9-5).

Solar Energy Installations

Panels, pumps, check valves, storage/heater tanks, and related

THE DOMESTIC WATER SOFTENER

Where the water supply is hard to very hard, water softeners are necessary. In hard water, laundry does not come clean because detergents do not make suds, and therefore leave a soap curd on fabrics. Washing, bathing, and shampooing in hard water will leave a film and solid particles on the skin. Dishes and flatware are left water spotted and might even be etched in severe cases. Water heaters, boilers, and tea kettles become caked with calcium and magnesium deposits.

The water softener will solve this problem using a chemical reaction known as "ion exchange." This removes the calcium and magnesium from the water, replacing them with sodium. The material used for this process is called zeolite, a resin in the form of small beads. In action the zeolite, precharged with sodium ions (chemically charged particles), attracts calcium and magnesium ions from the hard water and replaces them with sodium ions.

The softener must be "recharged" at intervals, depending on the hardness of the water, the type of equipment, and use by the occupants. Ordinary table salt (sodium chloride) in solution is run through the zeolite bed (backwashed) to recharge it. Many water softeners are automatic, and will perform the recharging and return the system to normal with no attention, except to replace the salt when needed. This operation is set to be done late at night, when water is not needed.

Another type of water softener is provided by a water softener service company on a replacement basis. "The Culligan Man" is an example. Self-contained tanks are provided by the servicing company and are exchanged at regular intervals by a service person. This might be more expensive, but will save the investment and maintenance costs of owning a softener.

Note: The recharging of a water softener will damage the septic tank, field, and soil in the area, so the discharge from the backwashing of the softener should not be allowed to flow into the septic system. Persons who, for medical reasons, must reduce their sodium intake are advised to *not* drink softened water because the sodium content is very high. Softened water is not usually supplied to the kitchen cold water faucet that supplies water for cooking and drinking.

Both types of water softeners, the permanent and the rental unit, need to have a bypass valve between the supply and outlet lines, plus a valve in each of these lines between the bypass valve and the softener. This is to allow water use while the unit is being serviced. A new water softener will have complete installation and operating instructions packed with it.

Special filters are available to remove iron, odors, and other undesirable substances in the water supply. They are usually installed under the kitchen sink or in the basement. Replacement cartridges are available where the filters are sold. One shutoff valve is needed ahead of the filter to allow the cartridge to be changed.

LIGHTWEIGHT COLLECTORS. YOU
DON'T NEED A CRANE.

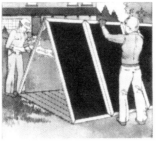
YOU CAN EVEN PUT COLLECTORS
IN THE BACK YARD.

The concept of solar water heating is a practical solution for conserving energy with resultant energy cost savings for more than 70% of the United States. In fact, the solar belt stretches from Florida in the South to as far as Montana in the North.

The savings will vary depending on the amount of sun available, the number of solar panels used in the installation, the amount of hot water used per day and local utility rates. Savings of 50% to 80% are not uncommon.

**solar water heaters...
an idea whose time
has come.**

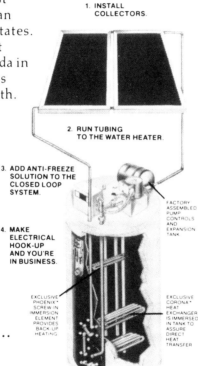

1. INSTALL COLLECTORS.

2. RUN TUBING TO THE WATER HEATER.

3. ADD ANTI-FREEZE SOLUTION TO THE CLOSED LOOP SYSTEM.

4. MAKE ELECTRICAL HOOK-UP AND YOU'RE IN BUSINESS.

FACTORY ASSEMBLED PUMP CONTROLS AND EXPANSION TANK

EXCLUSIVE PHOENIX* SCREW IN IMMERSION ELEMENT PROVIDES BACK UP HEATING

EXCLUSIVE CORONA* HEAT EXCHANGER IS IMMERSED IN TANK TO ASSURE DIRECT HEAT TRANSFER

Fig. 9-5. A solar water heating system using an electric water heater storage tank, pump, solar panels, and one electric element in the tank. A special heat exchanger is immersed in the tank also, which circulates hot liquid.

materials are available for installing a solar energy system. Many companies provide complete installation kits for the do-it-yourselfer.

The indirect system consists of a closed circuit that includes the solar collector, piping, and heat exchanger. A circulating pump circulates the water through these. The liquid in this system is a mixture of water and antifreeze as in an automobile radiator.

A booster heater is almost always required in cold areas to provide hot water during long periods of cloudy and cold weather and long nights. Sometimes the heat exchanger consists of 1/2-inch soft copper tubing, wrapped around the outside of the tank, soldered to the tank, and connected to the solar connector and pump. A commercial heat exchanger inserted *inside* the tank—much the same as in an electric water heater—is more efficient. The heat exchanger serves the purpose of transferring heat from the water/antifreeze solution to the clean domestic water in the tank. The storage tank will need to be 80- to 120-gallon capacity.

The tank has four openings, two for the clean water and two for the antifreeze solution. The antifreeze connections lead to a coil inside the tank, through which this solution circulates to heat the clean water, so the two water systems are kept separate.

The direct system is somewhat more efficient as the domestic (clean) water circulates through the collector and is heated directly by the sun. *Note:* This direct system can be used *only* where freezing weather does not occur. A frozen collector could be expensive to repair, or replace.

The solar collector panel is generally installed on the roof, although ground level is satisfactory. Disadvantages of ground level installations are that the collectors are susceptible to vandalism and the possibility that a building might be constructed in such a position as to shade the collector from the sun.

The collector must be securely mounted on the roof. Reliable collector manufacturers are able to furnish mounting hardware for use on any type of roof construction. The collector must be mounted on the south side of a pitched roof. The angle above the horizontal that the collector face must be set at is the local latitude plus 10 degrees. As an example, Chicago at 42-degree latitude plus 10 degrees equals 52 degrees from horizontal. This is the setting for the collector frame.

Solar collector panels are readily available from suppliers. The standard sizes are from 3 × 6 feet to 4 × 12 feet. The frame is about 6 inches deep, usually of aluminum. The plate and tubing, which are bonded together, are painted flat black for maximum heat absorption. The covering is preferably glass, but may be plastic. If glass is used, it should have a low iron content so it is more transparent. Glass admits solar radiation, but is opaque to long-wave radiation. This radiation (energy) is trapped inside the collector box and heats the water or water/antifreeze mixture. Plastic does not trap the long-wave energy, as does glass, and it deteriorates rapidly. In cold climates, two layers of glass are recommended.

Another system has a piping arrangement that allows the storage tank to be mounted on the roof or in the attic. Because the tank is at the high point of the system, a circulating pump is not needed because the liquid circulates by gravity. This system is known as a "Thermosyphon" solar water heating system. The disadvantages of this system is the great weight of the tank and its contents (750 to 1200 pounds). It requires very sturdy supports to spread its weight over a larger area than the storage tank covers, which is about 10 to 12 square feet. This gives a possible weight per square foot of 100 pounds on the roof area. It is better to install the storage tank in the utility room or basement and circulate the liquid using a pump.

Piping materials used for the system can be copper or brass pipe and galvanized threaded iron pipe. Plastic pipe is prohibited. It is better to purchase a heat exchanger, rather than soldering copper tubing to the outside of the storage tank. High water pressure from the supply must be *reduced,* using a water pressure regulator. As in a standard water heater, the T & P relief valve is required. Automatic air relief vents must be installed at all high points in the system and drain cocks installed at all low points. All equipment must be accessible for service or replacement. The storage tank must be labeled with the maximum test and operating pressures. This label will also give the manufacturer's name, address, and any other information required—such as capacity and year of manufacture.

Mounting the equipment to the roof requires care to prevent leaks from developing in the roof, which could cause damage to the building interior. The supports must be arranged so lag bolts can be screwed through the support brackets and directly into the rafters. Enough lag bolts should be used to insure that the equipment will not break loose during high winds, snow load, or other acts of nature. In the Midwest, with the collector panel set at 52 degrees from the horizontal, the collector will not lie close to a pitched roof nor a flat roof, so high winds could sweep against the back of the collector and tear it loose from its support brackets.

Figure 9-6 shows a commercial building that is heated and cooled by a solar energy system. This complete surface is the solar panel array. Figure 9-7 is a closer view of the panel array, and Fig. 9-8 is a

Fig. 9-6. A view of a very large solar panel array on a public building. This system provides heat in winter and cooling in summer.

Fig. 9-7. A closer view of the solar array. Because the heat produced is not hot enough to operate the cooling system, the system was made oversize to offset its reduced capacity.

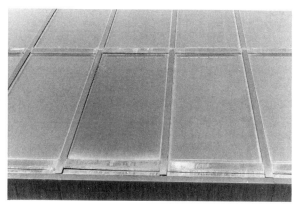

Fig. 9-8. A close-up of two of the panels. These are 3 by 6 feet in area.

close-up of the panels. The cooling equipment can operate at only 50 percent of its rated capacity because of the lower temperature water supplied to it. This is an absorption refrigeration system that normally operates using steam at about 230 degrees F, hence its reduced capacity. The complete system is designed oversize to compensate for the reduced capacity of the mechanical equipment.

10

Repairing
and Replacing
Bathroom Fixtures

Some repairs to bathroom fixtures were covered previously. This chapter will cover repairs and replacement of all fixtures. Keep in mind that very old fixtures do not conform to the present plumbing codes.

THE BATHTUB

Many older tubs have the faucet assembly below the rim of the tub, and the faucet can be submerged in dirty water if the tub is full to overflowing. New tubs do not have a faucet hole in the tub; the faucet assembly is above the tub 4 to 6 inches.

If you are replacing the older type tub, you will need to make a piping assembly to mount behind the finished wall at the drain end of the tub. Decide if you want the shower or only the tub faucet. You might want to make provision for adding a shower head later and plug that opening for now (Refer to Fig. 4-6).

In the older tub, the water lines will usually come up from the basement directly to the faucet connections. These lines will have to be disconnected in the basement and extended to come up inside the partition wall at the end of the tub recess. When you do this work, install shutoff valves in both hot and cold lines for ease of servicing. It might also be necessary to move the old tub drain connection to line up with the new tub drain location.

Unless the old tub is pressed steel, the best way to remove it is to break it up into small, easily handled pieces. *Caution:* Be sure to wear safety goggles because small pieces of metal can fly into your eyes. Take no chances; if you get something in your eye, go and have it removed as soon as possible. Iron is especially dangerous.

Use a 3-pound sledge to crack the tub. Pressed steel tubs cannot be broken, but they are lightweight and can be carried by two men. You might find that the new tub is longer or shorter than the old one. Either cut away under the point where the tub end fits or add a flat surface to match the wall finish. Make these adjustments at the end opposite the drain. The tub might also be wider or narrower from front to back. If so, the floor might need to be patched or cut away. To eliminate some of these problems, look for various brands that will fit the space better. Take the dimensions of the space with you for comparison with available sizes. Footed tubs were shorter, so you might have trouble finding one to fit.

Before setting the new tub, nail a piece of 2 × 4 along the back wall of the space, 3 1/2 inches above the floor, to support the back edge of the tub. To avoid cutting and patching the wall where the faucet and shower head will be, consider a fiberglass bath-shower module. This is the tub and surround (the walls of the tub area up to about 6 feet) in one piece. Some come in two pieces, the tub and the surround. These assemblies are completely satisfactory.

You can now break into the wall to install the faucet and shower head assembly. For both the faucet and the shower pipe, you will need to install a 1- x -8 backer board of the length to span two studs. When you mount the board, the faucet height is 4 inches above the tub rim and the shower head will be 6 feet above the floor. Use a drop ell (a 90-degree elbow having ears with holes to screw to the backer board) for the shower and faucet for support.

You will have to caulk all around the tub edges where it contacts the wall, and the joint where the tub base contacts the floor. You will need to buy floor tile to match the present tile if the new tub is narrower and leaves a space there. Depending on the wall finish, you might need to paint drywall or replace a number of wall tile as well. Take samples of both floor and wall tiles to a store that sells clay tile. You might be able to get a very close match.

If the walls surrounding the tub are in bad condition, you should consider either a whole new tub and surround or a new surround (plastic) and a new pressed steel tub. Talk with a salesperson at the plumbing supply or hardware store.

For a modern-style tub there will be only the tub removal and replacement; the plumbing will be in place. You might need to make some adjustment to connect the tub drain to the old drain line below. The faucet assembly can be changed to the single-lever style, but the wall will have to be opened up and patched to do this. If clay tile was used, the present holes for the hot and cold faucets must be

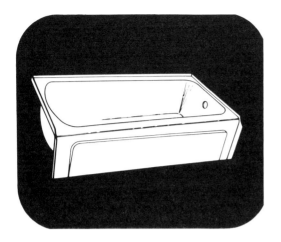

Fig. 10-1. PVC bathtub. These are very hard to distinguish from a steel tub. Courtesy U. S. Brass Co.

Fig. 10-2. Premium wall surround. Used for replacement or for new work using a steel or plastic tub. Courtesy U. S. Brass Co.

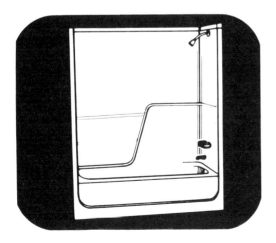

Fig. 10-3. One-piece fiberglass tub/shower. This lightweight unit can be used for old or new construction. Courtesy U. S. Brass Co.

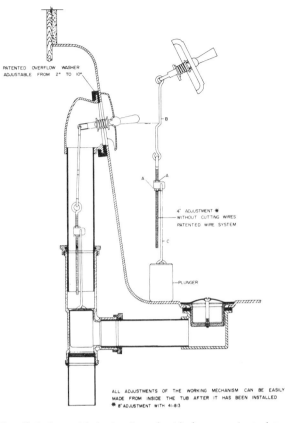

PATENTED OVERFLOW WASHER
ADJUSTABLE FROM 2" TO 10"

B

A   A

4" ADJUSTMENT ✱
WITHOUT CUTTING WIRES
PATENTED WIRE SYSTEM

C

PLUNGER

ALL ADJUSTMENTS OF THE WORKING MECHANISM CAN BE EASILY
MADE FROM INSIDE THE TUB AFTER IT HAS BEEN INSTALLED
✱ 8" ADJUSTMENT WITH 41-813

1. Assemble shoe, tee, head, shoe plug and tubes to the bathtub in the regular manner and attach strainer to shoe.

2. Preset plunger/wire assembly to the approximate required length by following these steps:

   A. Loosen locknuts "A".
   B. Hold plunger/wire assembly with the offset in wire "B" in line with centerline of tub overflow and adjust wire "C" until plunger rests on bottom of bathtub as illustrated.
   C. Tighten locknuts "A" against reinforced Celcon adaptor. In most instances, no further adjustment is necessary.

3. The plunger/wire assembly can now be installed through the head. Align the holes in the faceplate with those of the head and insert screws. Tighten screws with moderate force, the patented head gasket is made of the finest grade soft rubber and will seal easily.

4. Check operation of plunger by raising and lowering the handle. Readjust if necessary.

Fig. 10-4. Assembly instructions for trip lever waste and overflow. Courtesy Gerber Plumbing Fixtures Corp.

patched. Do the rough-in for the single faucet and then repair the wall.

Figure 10-1 illustrates a PVC bathtub. This tub is lightweight and easy to install. In Fig. 10-2 is a premium wall surround. This can be used as a replacement for damaged walls in the tub alcove or used with a new tub. For a remodeling job or as a replacement, Fig. 10-3 shows a one-piece fiberglass tub/shower assembly. This also can be used as a replacement for an old unit, or for a complete bathroom in new construction.

Assembly instructions for a Trip Lever Waste and Overflow manufactured by Gerber Plumbing Fixtures Corp. are given in Figs. 10-4 and 10-5.

FIXTURE CLEARANCES

Clearances of bathroom fixtures from adjoining walls or other adjacent fixtures are given and required by the National Plumbing Code. Clearances for single homes are given in Figs. 10-6 and 10-7.

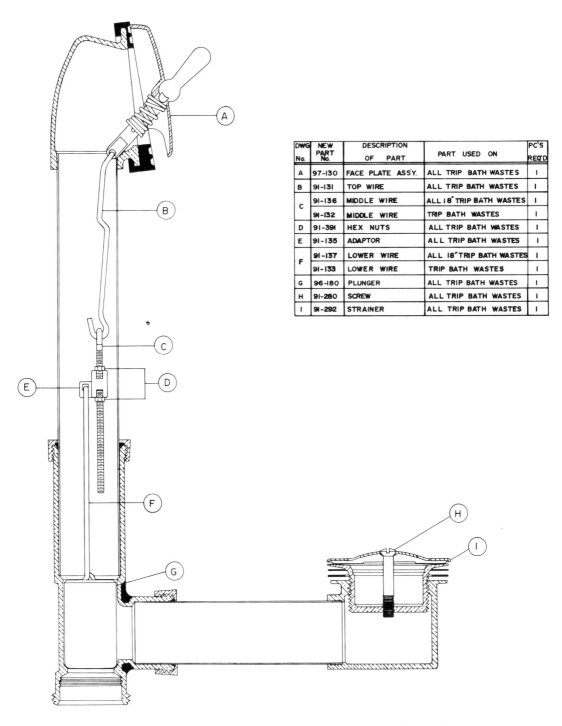

DWG No.	NEW PART No.	DESCRIPTION OF PART	PART USED ON	PC'S REQ'D
A	97-130	FACE PLATE ASS'Y.	ALL TRIP BATH WASTES	I
B	91-131	TOP WIRE	ALL TRIP BATH WASTES	I
C	91-136	MIDDLE WIRE	ALL 18" TRIP BATH WASTES	I
	91-132	MIDDLE WIRE	TRIP BATH WASTES	I
D	91-391	HEX NUTS	ALL TRIP BATH WASTES	I
E	91-135	ADAPTOR	ALL TRIP BATH WASTES	I
F	91-137	LOWER WIRE	ALL 18" TRIP BATH WASTES	I
	91-133	LOWER WIRE	TRIP BATH WASTES	I
G	96-180	PLUNGER	ALL TRIP BATH WASTES	I
H	91-280	SCREW	ALL TRIP BATH WASTES	I
I	91-292	STRAINER	ALL TRIP BATH WASTES	I

Fig. 10-5. Parts list for trip lever, waste and overflow. Courtesy Gerber Plumbing Fixtures Corp.

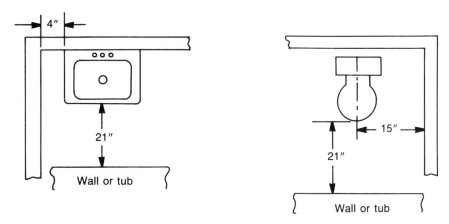

Fig. 10-6. Fixture clearances, bathroom.

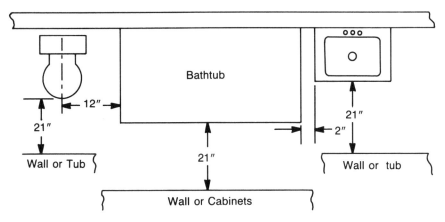

Fig. 10-7. Fixture clearances, bathroom.

PLUMBING FIXTURE CLEARANCES

Water Closet. Clearance must be set a minimum of 15 inches from the center of the bowl to any wall or partition, and 12 inches from the center of the bowl to the outside edge of a tub apron. There must also be a minimum clearance of 21 inches from the front of the bowl to any finished wall, door, or other plumbing fixture.

Lavatory. Clearance must be a minimum of 4 inches from its edge to a wall and a minimum of 2 inches from its edge to the edge of a tub. There must also be a clearance of 21 inches from the front of the lavatory to any finished wall, door, or other plumbing fixture.

Shower Compartment. Clearance must be a minimum of 24 inches for easy entry and exit from any finished wall, door or other plumbing fixture.

When installing new (or old) plumbing fixtures, it is important to "rough in" the pipes to the fixture location exactly. If this is not done, difficult changes might have to be made, such as cutting into the wall to change the location of water line stub-outs. The worst alteration is to have to change the location of the closet bend to move a water closet over just a few inches because of the tub, shower stall, or lavatory.

Water closet rough-in from the center line of the outlet to the wall is normally 12 inches. Ten- and 14-inch rough-ins *are* available. The width of the toilet tank is very important to know, because there might be interference with a lavatory, tub, or wall. All fixture manufacturers furnish rough-in sheets for their products.

SHOWER BATHS

This type of bath is currently the most favored. The shower takes less water than a tub, unless it is allowed to run for a long time. It is faster and more convenient than a tub bath, and many people enjoy feeling the force of the water.

The shower can be a separate stall or can be incorporated with the tub by means of a diverter valve in the faucet assembly. The separate shower stall saves space in the bathroom, and is often installed in a private bathroom serving one or perhaps two bedrooms. The main bathroom will have a complete tub shower, lavatory, toilet, and vanity counter top and drawers.

Water controls for the shower are made in three different styles:

● The standard two-handle valve combination
● The single-handle control (all the control is from the one knob—hot, cold, volume, and off)
● Temperature is thermostatically controlled after the desired temperature is set, plus on and off.

Showers in hotels, motels, and other public facilities usually use the thermostatic control style to prevent scalding from very hot water. This very hot water could be caused by a malfunction of some remote device in the system, or by a great demand for cold water that would leave only hot water at the shower head. Even though hot water in the home is provided at about 140 degrees F., it is wise to install the thermostatic style valve for safety, especially if children use the shower by themselves.

Hand-held and solid mounted shower heads are popular. These heads can be made to pulsate, give a sharp needle spray, and various other types of spray patterns. The hand-held type is convenient for all-over use. When finished, it is hung from a bracket at the shower mount. Installation is easy. The old shower head is removed and the new head installed, or the end of the hose is installed on the 1/2-inch male end of the shower pipe.

Certain shower heads are part of the shower pipe. The connection is a ball and socket design, the ball is on the end of the shower pipe and the socket is part of the shower head. In this case, the existing shower pipe will have to be replaced. This part, a bent chrome-plated 1/2-inch pipe is threaded on both ends. Unscrew the old pipe: put thread compound or Teflon tape on one end of the new pipe and screw it into the fitting that is hidden inside the wall. Use the hole in the wall to guide you. Prepare the other end with tape or compound, screw the head or hose end on, and check for leaks. Make sure that the bracket that will hold the hose-type head is in correct position to accept the head easily.

THE BIDET

The bidet, a low-set bowl resembling a toilet, is equipped with hot and cold faucets, and is used for personal hygiene after using the toilet. This fixture has been in use in Europe for many years and has found favor in the United States in recent years. It is about as large as a toilet, but does not have a tank. It has a spray that cleanses the body while the person sits astride and faces the faucets. The drain line only needs to be 2 inches.

THE TOILET

Because the toilet (water closet) is essential to a dwelling, it has to be maintained and repaired occasionally. Many older dwellings have only one bathroom, therefore the toilet must be in operating condition at all times. Most problems are minor—for example, water runs all the time or parts of the flushing mechanism or the ball cock stick and do not operate properly.

A major problem is a plugged-up toilet. This requires a plumber's rubber plunger (Fig. 10-8). A special type made just for toilets has a round, cone-shaped center that creates a better seal in a toilet but will not work in a lavatory, tub, or sink. A standard plunger will work well for minor stoppage.

A better tool to use for major stoppages will be the closet auger (Fig. 10-9). This consists of a J shaped tube that contains a flexible sewer snake with a a crank on the handle end and a corkscrew shape on the bottom end. When purchased, this bottom corkscrew end is pulled all the way out of the J shaped end and hooked into a ring near the top of the tube.

To use the auger, unhook the corkscrew end and pull out on the crank handle to draw the snake up out of the top of the tube, leaving only the corkscrew end exposed (Fig. 10-10). In this position, insert the corkscrew end into the toilet trap (this can be seen in the front or rear of the toilet bowl). Start cranking on the handle clockwise as you force the snake down farther into the closet bend under the floor. This bend is the elbow leading away from the toilet. If you feel resistance you have hit a stoppage. Try to snag the stoppage with the cork-

Fig. 10-8. Using a rubber plunger (plumber's helper) on a water closet bowl. Do this before using a snake.

screw end. If you snag something, pull up on the crank handle at the same time turning it clockwise. It is best to pull the corkscrew end up to the J bend of the auger, then withdraw the auger to see if you have snagged anything.

If you have not snagged anything, insert as before, still cranking

Mfrs. Code No. 785461

**Simplest way
to clear closets
and urinals.**

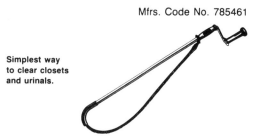

Fig. 10-9. Closet auger.

The No. K-4 Closet Auger for closets and urinals is precision-built to give years of reliable service. Designed to save time, assure profitable results, it is sturdy, light weight and easy to use. Plastic bowl protector. Corrosion-resistant brass tube. Comfort-grip plastic handles. Replaceable 3′ bulb auger cable.

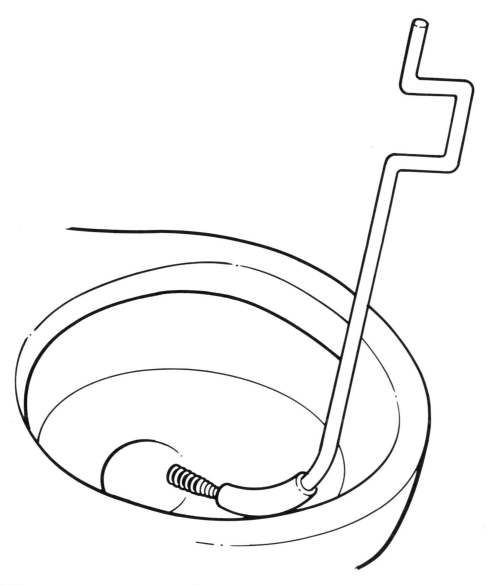

Fig. 10-10. Closet auger in use in a water closet (toilet).

clockwise. If you get the handle in as far as it will go, it will help to pull the handle only all the way out, then force it back without cranking. This might force the stoppage on through to the sewer, thus clearing the line. With the toilet tank lid off, flush the toilet, but be ready to push down on the tank ball to stop the flush (the bowl could overflow if the stoppage has not be cleared completely). If the flush ends with a "gulp" the stoppage has been cleared. Flush the toilet a few more times to be sure everything has been cleared. If not, repeat the rodding with the auger and rubber plunger.

Some toilets are prone to stoppages because some passage inside the toilet trap has a point of porcelain sticking out into the passageway that can snag toilet paper. If the problem occurs frequently, you should remove the toilet bowl from the floor and inspect for a point in the passageway of the toilet bowl casting.

A general rule is that a tennis ball should be able to be passed through the trap and not get stuck. Some toilets have a 1 3/4-inch passageway and might not accept a tennis ball. Other brands have a 2 5/8-inch passageway and will accept a tennis ball. The *only* item other than human waste that should be put down a toilet is toilet paper. Toilet paper is made so that it will disintegrate upon contact with water. Note that most toilet papers are now made especially for use with septic systems.

Because the toilet is constantly used, the operating mechanism

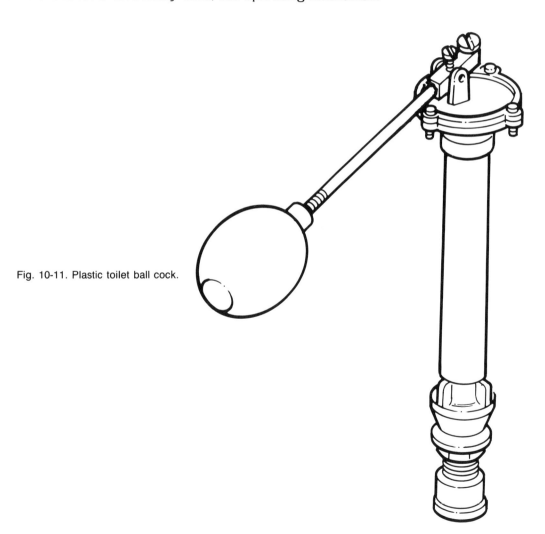

Fig. 10-11. Plastic toilet ball cock.

MANSFIELD 08 ANTI-SIPHON BALLCOCK

INSTALLATION INSTRUCTIONS

1. Shut off the water supply. (There is a shut-off valve between where the supply pipe leaves the floor or wall, and where it enters tank.) Turn valve handle clockwise.

2. Flush toilet and continue to depress flush lever to drain toilet tank. Use a sponge or cloth to remove any remaining water from tank.

3. Unscrew the water supply line coupling nut from ballcock shank (extending from bottom of tank). A small amount of water may flow from coupling at this time. Normally, the supply line coupling nut will slide back onto supply line to be reused. If replacement is necessary, a new coupling nut is provided.

4. The ballcock is secured to the bottom of the toilet tank with a locknut. Unscrew and remove. Reach inside toilet tank and pull ballcock up to remove.

5. Take new Mansfield ballcock out of package. Unscrew coupling nut and locknut from shank, leaving the black rubber gasket in place. A float rod is provided in the package. Screw it into lever on top of ballcock. (Some tanks may require a longer threaded float rod which can be obtained the same place this ballcock was purchased.)

6. Insert new ballcock — placing shank through hole in bottom of tank. Steady ballcock with one hand while threading new locknut onto shank. Turn ballcock so that float rod and float will not interfere with flush valve in middle of tank. Use a wrench to tighten locknut. DO NOT OVERTIGHTEN.

7. Dispose of the old coupling nut washer (which may be stuck to the end of supply line). Install new coupling nut washer provided and connect coupling nut to threaded shank of ballcock. Use a wrench to tighten coupling nut. DO NOT OVERTIGHTEN.

8. Locate refill tube connector at top of ballcock. The plastic refill tube should be pushed onto this connector. The opposite end of refill tube should then be clipped into overflow tube of flush valve.

9. Your new Mansfield ballcock is ready to use. Turn on water by slowly turning supply line valve handle counter-clockwise. Watch for a few minutes and examine for leaks. With no leaks apparent, flush toilet and check its operation.

Sometimes slight adjustments have to be made to allow more water in tank. This can be done by bending float rod in an upwards direction.

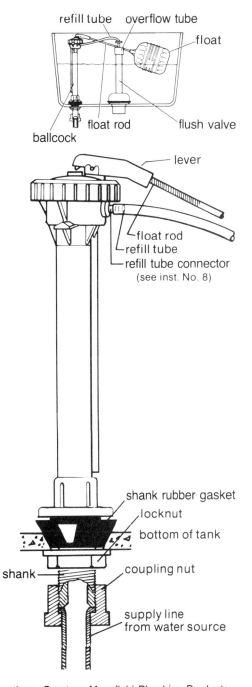

Fig. 10-12. Mansfield No. 08 Anti-Siphon Ballcock installation instructions. Courtesy Mansfield Plumbing Products.

in the tank will wear and leak or refuse to work at all. The ball cock (the valve that allows the tank to fill and shuts off when the tank is full) has parts that can be replaced easily. The older ball cock has parts that look complicated, but are just an arrangement of seesaw levers to raise or lower a washer onto a seat to turn on or off the flow of water. This valve is controlled by the float ball, made of either copper or plastic (metal balls tend to spring a leak and thus take on water and will not float) that rises or falls as it controls the water level (Fig. 10-11).

Figures 10-12 through 10-14 illustrate a Mansfield 08 Anti-Siphon

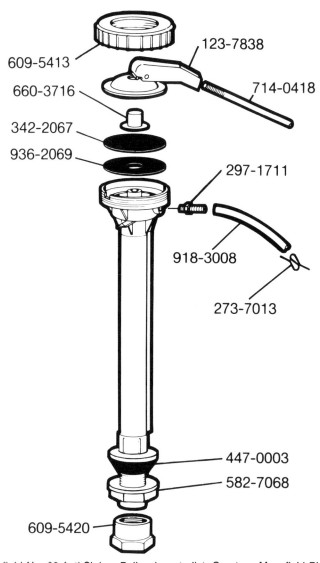

Fig. 10-13. Mansfield No. 08 Anti-Siphon Ballcock parts list. Courtesy Mansfield Plumbing Products.

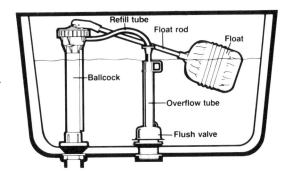

Fig. 10-14. Cutaway of toilet tank showing component parts. Courtesy Mansfield Plumbing Products.

Ballcock. Included are detailed instructions for installation.

The ball cock can be taken apart easily. On some models the screws have flat ends that allow you to turn them with your fingers. Turn off the water supply at the stop valve before starting work. When taken apart, the valve plunger will have a split leather washer around its center (this serves the same purpose as an **O** ring in a faucet). At the bottom of the plunger is the bottom washer and screw, also similar to that in a faucet. All these parts are available in kit form.

A newer ball cock model is the diaphragm type. This has fewer moving parts because there is only the diaphragm and a plug with a washer to press against the water inlet. Three or four screws hold the top plate on. Some styles have a screw collar that takes the place of the screws and ears where the screws go. This collar screws onto threads on the top of the ball cock body to hold the assembly together.

Both these styles have a float ball with its float rod. The float ball actuates the ball cock in response to the water level. To adjust the water level, the float rod is bent. For a lower water level, bend the rod down, for a higher level, bend it up. Use two hands, one near the ball cock and the other near the float ball. The rod is slender, so it is easy to bend. Bend only a small amount at a time and try before bending again. Many toilet tanks have the correct level marked on the inside rear tank wall. A one-piece tank/bowl toilet is shown in Fig. 10-15.

A third style is the float cup. As with all ball cocks, there are different heights for use in different depth tanks. Too high a model will not fit, and one too short will be under water and will not be approved. The float cup style has a cup-shaped container that floats on the water and takes the place of the float ball and float rod. There is an adjustment clip by which the float cup is raised or lowered to adjust the water level. Four types of toilet flushing action are shown in Fig. 10-16.

To remove any type of ball cock, turn off the water stop valve, flush the toilet, and sponge out the rest of the water. Unscrew the slipnut from the inlet pipe and let it slide down the tube. Grip the bottom of the ball cock shaft with locking grip pliers—with the handles up against the inside wall of the tank. Use an adjustable wrench to

179

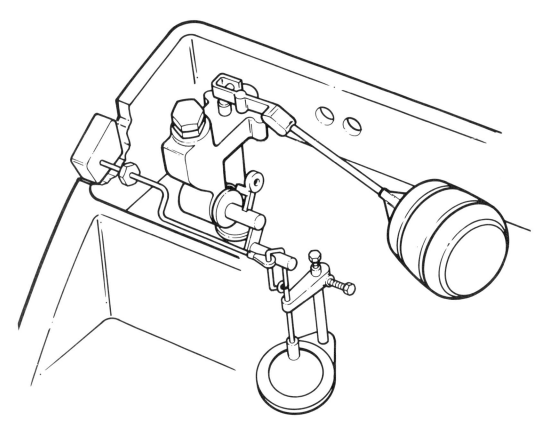

Fig. 10-15. Ball cock and flush ball mechanism in a one-piece toilet (i.e., toilet bowl and tank are one piece).

loosen and remove the retaining nut on the underside of the tank. You can now lift out the ball cock without having to bend the 3/8-inch water tube from the stop valve to the tank. If you are lucky, the original slipnut will have the same threads that will let you use it on the new ball cock. Be aware that you can use the toilet even though there is no water in the tank. Half a pail or more of water from another source will flush any toilet. Pour water into the toilet bowl rapidly to simulate flushing.

The tank ball or flapper ball holds the water in the tank and releases the water when the flush handle is pushed down. The original of this mechanism is the tank ball. The ball is hollow rubber, the bottom half being a half-round ball with a 1-inch hole in its bottom. The upper half is a cone shape with the small end at the top. A 1/8-inch brass rod is screwed into a brass insert molded into this top. This rod, which is about 4 inches long, has a tight loop formed at its top. Another 1/8-inch brass rod is hooked into the flush lever. The bottom end has a larger loop formed flatwise and is around the rod screwed into the tank ball. When the flush handle is pressed, this rod lifts the tank ball from its seat.

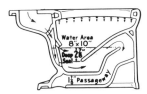

WASHDOWN action closets are noisy. The washdown bowl is no longer acceptable in many municipal codes and Kohler has ceased production of washdown closets.

QUIET

REVERSE TRAP closets are quieter than the washdown models. Their outward appearance and flushing action are similar to better siphon jet action closets; but they have a smaller water area, passageway and water seal.

QUIETER

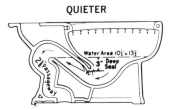

SIPHON JET action closets are the next in quietness. Their advanced styling ensures a generous supply of water from the rim for a thorough flush, while providing a flushing action that is quieter than washdown and reverse trap closet actions. Kohler closets including the Wellworth, the wall-hung Cayuga, Bolton Aqua-Vent and the Welland, Kingston and Corwyn have siphon jet flushing action.

QUIETEST

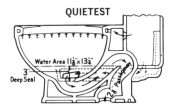

SIPHON ACTION closets are the quietest toilets Kohler makes. Top quality and advanced engineering combine quietness with the thorough cleaning of siphon action in such one-piece Kohler closets as the Rochelle, Champlain and Pompton.

Fig. 10-16. Types of flushing actions in current water closet bowls. Courtesy Kohler Co.

When the flush handle is released, the brass rod fastened to the flush lever slides down the rod from the tank ball. The ball floats due to its hollow shape. Because of the arrangement, the tank ball can float and allow the tank to empty to complete the flush.

This sliding rod arrangement is fine as long as all the parts are lined up properly. If not, the ball will not seat tightly, which causes the "noisy toilet" problem. For this reason the flapper ball was developed. A clamp with two ears is fastened around the overflow tube base. The flapper ball has two legs with holes in the ends, which hook over the ears of the clamp. The action of the flapper ball is the same as the tank ball, but the flapper is raised by a chain instead of rods. Correct seating is accomplished by adjusting the clamp and the side-to-side movement of the flapper ball as it drops into place.

At times the seat below the ball might have lime, scale, or other roughness. Clean the seat with steel wool or a scouring pad. For either type of ball, if the ball feels mushy, replace it.

Toilets are available that have a flush mechanism that can be used as a water saving device. This device has a connection to the tank ball from the flush handle arm, which allows you to pull up on the flush handle and reseat the tank ball in mid-flush to stop more water from leaving the tank. This control use is optional because the toilet will flush normally with no further action once the flush handle is pushed. The short flush should only be used when there is no solid waste to dispose of. Figure 10-17 illustrates the Deluxe Water-Saver Toilet, designed to use less water for each flush.

Removal and replacement of the toilet seat sometimes is a problem because of the difficulty of removing the nuts from the hinge bolts. Metal bolts are the worst because they corrode badly. You might have to saw these bolts off to remove them. You can try penetrating oil or Liquid Wrench; be sure to let the bolts and nuts stand overnight to allow the solutions to do their work. If the nuts are recessed, you will need to use a socket wrench. If the bolt also turns, hold the bolt head with locking grip pliers.

To saw through the bolts, try to remove the seat and cover by removing the screws in the hinges. Put tape on the bowl edge where you will be sawing to prevent saw marks. Use a coarse saw blade in your hacksaw. It might be easier to remove the blade, wrap one end with tape for a handle, and saw with the blade alone. Do not force anything because you might crack the bowl itself. Bowls cost at least $50. Most seat bolts are now made of plastic. These can still be covered with corrosion but will not give as much trouble as the metal bolts. Some bolts have slotted heads that are reached from the top side and covered by a snap cover for appearance purposes. In all cases do not force anything.

Replacement of an old or broken toilet is quite simple. First, buy a new toilet and a new wax ring to seal the new toilet to the closet bend. Be sure the new toilet will fit in the same place as the old one. The distance of the center of the closet bend to the wall will determine whether the new toilet will fit. This distance is called "rough-in."

Fig. 10-17. Deluxe water-saver toilet. Courtesy U. S. Brass Co.

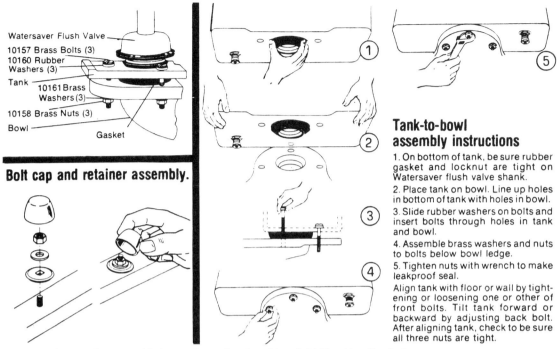

Watersaver Flush Valve
10157 Brass Bolts (3)
10160 Rubber Washers (3)
Tank
10161 Brass Washers (3)
10158 Brass Nuts (3)
Bowl
Gasket

Bolt cap and retainer assembly.

Tank-to-bowl assembly instructions

1. On bottom of tank, be sure rubber gasket and locknut are tight on Watersaver flush valve shank.

2. Place tank on bowl. Line up holes in bottom of tank with holes in bowl.

3. Slide rubber washers on bolts and insert bolts through holes in tank and bowl.

4. Assemble brass washers and nuts to bolts below bowl ledge.

5. Tighten nuts with wrench to make leakproof seal.

Align tank with floor or wall by tightening or loosening one or other of front bolts. Tilt tank forward or backward by adjusting back bolt. After aligning tank, check to be sure all three nuts are tight.

Fig. 10-18. China toilet assembly instructions. Courtesy Mansfield Plumbing Products.

Rough-ins are standard at 10, 12, and 14 inches. Older toilets with wall-hung tanks might have a greater rough-in, but this will not affect the installation of the toilet with a tank mounted on the bowl. If you are replacing this type of toilet, remove the tank for ease of handling. In the bottom of the tank are two or three flat slotted-head bolts with rubber and steel washers under their heads. These bolts extend through the bowl flange behind the seat bolts. These nuts are square, which is normal; hex would be better, but that is what is supplied. If removing the nuts is difficult and the toilet is to be discarded, get help and remove the toilet as a unit. Replacement bowls are available, but it is better to replace the complete unit so you will get all new operating parts in the tank. A replacement bowl must be of the same make and style or the tank will not fit the new bowl and it will leak at that point. This procedure is shown in Fig. 10-18.

The tank bolt heads must be held by a large screwdriver inside the tank as you remove the nuts. The toilet is held in place by two or four bolts, with their lagscrew ends screwed into the floor. Nuts and washers hold the bowl base to the floor. Remove the white caps over the bolt ends with a putty knife or screwdriver. Pry gently all around. After the nuts are removed, rock the bowl gently and it should come free. Lift the bowl up carefully, making sure nothing falls into the closet bend (the cast iron or plastic fitting just below the floor level). Plug this opening with a rag large enough not to fall down the opening. Clean the floor and closet bend of all sealing materials. In some cases, you might have to reposition the bolts in the floor to meet the base holes in the new toilet bowl.

If everything is ready, remove the rag blocking the opening and check for anything that would interfere with setting the bowl in place. Place the wax ring on the "horn" (the part projecting from the base of the toilet) and lower the bowl carefully over the hold-down bolts. After the bowl is set down on the floor, twist it slightly in a circular motion to seat the wax ring to the horn and closet bend (Fig 10-19). Place the washers and nuts on the hold-down bolts and tighten the nuts.

Caution: Tighten carefully, but not too much because the flange is very easy to break. Tighten the nuts alternately. Place a level across the bowl edge to assure that it is level as you are tightening.

Now pour a pail of water in the bowl to check for leaks at the new connection. Again, do not try to tighten excessively if a leak appears. The wax ring might have slipped, or some other defect might appear after you remove the bowl again. Any damage that you do to the toilet will cancel a warranty on it, so be very careful.

If there are no leaks, you can now attach the tank. Each manufacturer has their own design for attaching the tank to the bowl. There will be a gasket or washer and either two or three bolts for holding the tank in place. If there are directions, follow them. Make sure all gaskets or washers are in place, including those for the hold-down bolts on the inside of the tank. As before, do not tighten these bolts excessively. After assembly, pour water into the tank to check for leaks.

If no leaks appear, you can now connect the water supply to the tank. You might be able to use the old supply tube. Be sure the connection at the ball cock end will fit the ball cock threads and make a tight fit. The supply tube might be too long or too short. If too long, you can cut off the end at the shutoff valve. You will need only the 3/8-inch ferrule that you can get at a hardware or auto parts store.

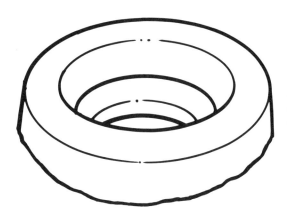

Fig. 10-19. Wax ring for sealing the joint between the water closet bowl and the closet bend (elbow below the floor).

If the tube is too short, you will have to buy a new tube.

This time you will need both the ferrule and the compression nut, both 3/8 inch. The tube will go into the shutoff valve about 1/4 inch, and into the ball cock connection less than this or not at all. With the tube cut to the correct length, insert the end into the shutoff valve after sliding the compression nut and ferrule on the tube (the tube can be a bit short, just so the ferrule is on the tube 1/8 inch from the tube end). You might have to bend the tube slightly to fit it in place, then straighten it out again. This is why the tube length is critical. Do this carefully and you will have no trouble.

After you have checked for leaks and flushed the toilet a few times, the installation is complete except for caulking around the base of the bowl where it meets the floor. Use a silicon-type sealant or caulking. Run a small bead completely around the bowl base.

THE LAVATORY

Lavatories are replaced for various reasons—chipped or stained surfaces on old lavatories, or simply the desire to modernize the bathroom. When replacing a lavatory, decide if you want a complete change—replacing a wall-hung lavatory with a cabinet vanity or installing a new countertop with drawers and storage space underneath—or just replacement with a similar lavatory.

If you plan to install a different style lavatory, decide what you want the final result to be. Wall-hung lavatories have a steel bracket screwed on the wall into a 1-x-6-inch wood support that is installed flush with the finish wall. If the new lavatory will be wall mount, make sure the wood support is solidly fastened to the studs on both ends.

A new metal support bar is furnished because each lavatory support method is different. If screws are not furnished, use No. 12 x 1 1/2-inch flat-head wood screws.

Caution: Wall-hung lavatories *without* support legs under the two front corners are liable to be broken loose from the wall if undue pressure downward is applied to the front edge. Children might climb on the lavatory and it could break away from the wall. Chrome support legs are highly recommended for wall-hung units.

Modern bathrooms are designed with countertops, including storage space underneath. The lavatory for these counters has an integral "self-rim" that rests on the counter surface and is clamped tightly from underneath. A bead of caulking or plumber's putty is spread on the underside of rim before the lavatory is set in place. Formed clamps with setscrews are hooked to flanges on the underside of the rim and squeeze the rim tightly against the counter surface.

If the new lavatory is larger than the hole in the counter, the hole will have to be enlarged. To do this, use a power jigsaw with a fine-tooth blade. Place masking tape on the jigsaw faceplate to prevent scratching the counter surface when sawing. Before starting, lay the lavatory face down on the counter and mark around the rim edge in pencil. Then remove the lavatory and draw a line parallel to and *inside* the first line, 3/8 to 1/2 inch from the first line. The minimum width must be 3/8 inch, more is better if it does not interfere with the lavatory bowl. Check all around the edge of the lavatory by placing the rim on the edge of the counter at points around the circumference of the lavatory. It will be difficult to enlarge the hole in the counter by only 1/8 inch, so make this check before sawing the hole larger.

Now that you have decided on the type of lavatory you want, start to remove the old one. Close both stop valves in the hot and cold supply lines. In most cases, the 3/8-inch lines from the valves to underneath the faucet will need a basin wrench (Fig. 10-20). This is a wrench with a reversible head on one end and a sliding handle on the other end, made especially for these situations. After the stop valves are

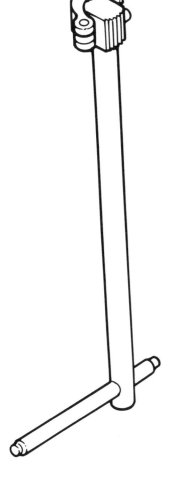

Fig. 10-20. Basin wrench. Used to tighten or loosen nuts and pipe connections underneath lavatories and sinks.

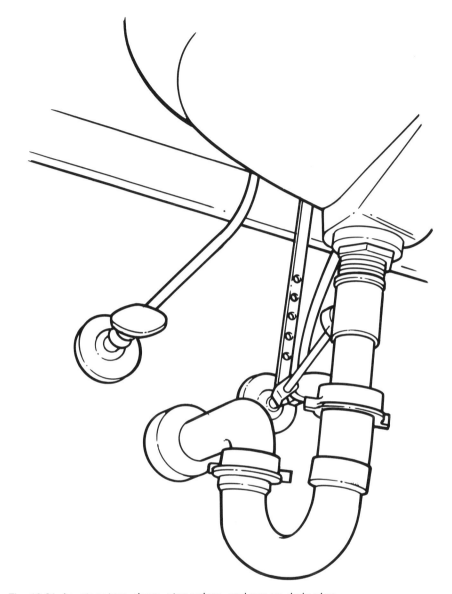

Fig. 10-21. Lavatory trap, risers, stop valves, and pop-up drain plug.

closed, open both faucets to drain the water out.

Remove the **P** trap by loosening the collar nuts on each end. Save the gaskets that might fall out as you remove the trap. You will need a basin or pail because there will be water in the trap. At the lower end of the pop-up lift rod is a clevis bar with a formed end that provides for a set screw to clamp the lift rod that passes through the clevis bar end. This allows for adjustment of the lift rod. Loosen the screw and you can remove the lift rod (Refer to Fig. 8-21). Also loosen and remove the retaining nut where the pivot rod enters the drain tail-piece so you can remove the pivot rod (Figs. 10-21 through 10-23). Loosen the nuts holding the supply pipes to the base of each faucet, then loosen and unscrew the holding nuts that hold the faucet to the lavatory. Loosen and remove the clamps holding the lavatory to the counter. There can be as many as 10 or 12. If the lavatory is still "stuck" to the counter by the putty or caulking, pull up on the lavatory by sticking your fingers in the faucet holes. Be careful of sharp hole edges; it is best to use gloves. Use a putty knife if necessary to loosen the rim from the countertop.

After removing the old lavatory, clean the surface of the counter where the putty or caulking was placed. If the new lavatory is larger than the old one, mark the edge as described before. If it fits, install as is. Install the faucet assembly now while the lavatory is upside down. Be sure to clean the base of the faucet of all old putty or caulking. All single-lever faucet assemblies furnish a rubber gasket for installation under the faucet base rather than having you use putty or

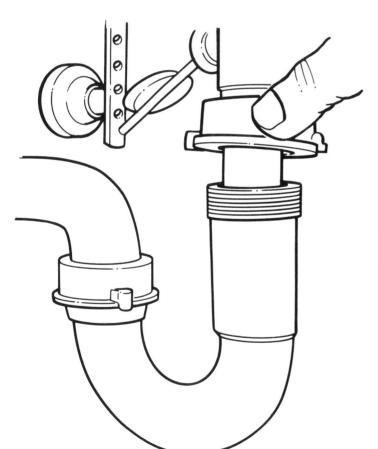

Fig. 10-22. Removing the lavatory trap. This trap is plastic.

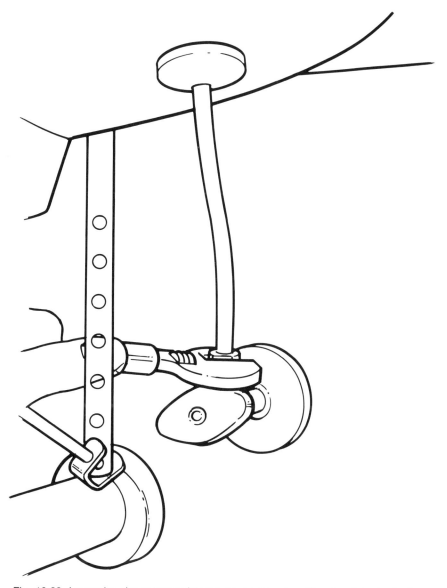

Fig. 10-23. Loosening the compression nut on a stop valve. The riser tube is plastic.

caulking there. Figures 10-24 and 10-25 illustrate square and oval lavatories; Fig. 10-26 illustrates a single-lever lavatory faucet.

A new single-lever faucet handle that tilts and turns works better than one that pulls up (out). Single-lever faucets can be purchased
with many different types of supply tubes—long or short, extra flexible with corrugated surface (refer to Fig. 5-10), or plain soft copper.
Purchase an assembly with tubes long enough to extend to and be

Fig. 10-24. Square vanity top lavatory. Courtesy U. S. Brass Co.

Fig. 10-25. Oval vanity lavatory. Courtesy U. S. Brass Co.

Fig. 10-26. Single-lever faucet for vanity. Courtesy U. S. Brass Co.

connected to the stop valve outlet and be connected with compression nuts and ferrules. If the length you need is not available, additional 3/8-inch OD copper tubing and 3/8-inch compression unions (couplings) are available at most hardware stores. In this way, you can extend the short lines on the faucet assembly that you have.

As to which brand of faucet to buy, well-known brands are the

Fig. 10-27. Single-lever faucet for kitchen sink, with swing spout and spray. Courtesy U. S. Brass Co.

Fig. 10-28. Double laundry tray shut-off valve assembly. Because this is very convenient to operate, a person is more apt to turn off the valve and thus may avoid a burst hose.

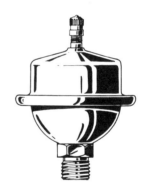

Fig. 10-29. Water hammer arrestor, which eliminates the "bang" when an automatic valve closes quickly. This might help avoid a leak from a poorly soldered fitting.

best, and you can buy the repair kit at the same store. The larger manufacturers will continue to furnish repair kits for many years to come (Fig. 10-27).

For your automatic washer hoses there is single-lever dual connection valve on the market that makes it easy to shut off the water to both the hot and cold lines to the washer. The ease of operation makes it simple to close the valve assembly and eliminate the possibility of the hoses bursting and causing water damage (Fig. 10-28).

Figure 10-29 illustrates a water hammer arrestor that is installed in each of the automatic washer water lines. This will eliminate the "bang" when electrically operated valves in the machine close rapidly.

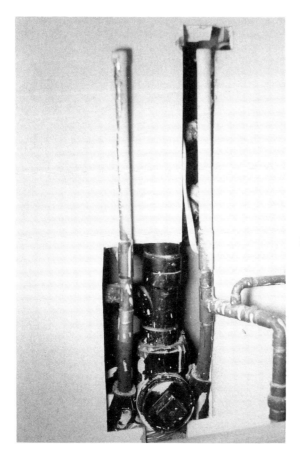

Fig. 10-30. Cleanout in plastic riser vent and drain line. Note the copper water lines and the hammer arrestors.

A water hammer arrestor made on the job is shown in Fig. 10-30. Two are on each of the drain vent lines, extending about 12 inches above the drywall opening.

OUTSIDE WATER CONNECTIONS

Outside sill cocks are subject to freezing in cold climates, therefore each line that goes to a sill cock will have a stop and waste valve. This special valve has a drain opening on the side closed off by a cap that resembles a tire valve cap. In the late fall this inside valve is closed, the outside sill cock opened, and the cap is removed from the drain opening on the valve. The sill cock is left open until spring, and is not damaged by freezing temperatures.

There is a special non-freeze sill cock available. This valve has a shank about 14 inches long which extends inside. The outside looks the same as a standard sill cock (Fig. 10-31). The valve seat and valve washer are at the far inside end of the shank, so each time the sill cock is closed all the water is drained out from the seat-washer location to the outside faucet section. This sill cock can be used all winter

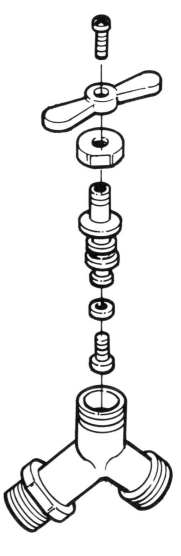

Fig. 10-31. Exploded view of sill cock (hose faucet).

because shut-off and drainage are accomplished after each use.

Note: This special sill cock does *not* have a removable seat, and because a seat dresser will not reach the seat, there is the question of the value of this type of sill cock over the standard type having the inside stop and waste valve. The stop and waste valve and the outside sill cock both do have removable seats. It takes only a few minutes to close the stop and waste valve and open the sill cock in the fall, then reverse the procedure in the spring.

A new item on the market is an insulating cover for the outside sill cock. This cover completely surrounds the sill cock and is attached to the house wall using adhesive.

11

Major Appliance
Installation and Repair

Major appliances used in the average home represent an expensive investment. Most are electrically operated and many have hot and cold water and drain connections. Each manufacturer's product, while achieving the same result, is designed and operates differently than any other brand. No parts of one brand are interchangeable with another brand. The only exceptions might be the hoses from the hot and cold water supplies, the drain hose (the discharge hose from the washer into the laundry tray), and the electrical cord.

Some appliances simply plug into an electrical outlet directly, while others are hard-wired (wired permanently and cannot be disconnected except by removing a fuse or tripping a circuit breaker). Every manufacturer can furnish a repair and parts manual, giving detailed instructions on repair and replacement of parts for under $10. Write to the address given on the machine.

THE DISHWASHER

Dishwashers have become a permanent part of the kitchen in a great many homes. For large families, they are a great labor saver.

If you are installing a new dishwasher in a present kitchen, you will have to decide on the best location. Sometimes, depending on the size of the kitchen, there will be only one possible location with enough space for installation. Most dishwashers require an area 24 inches wide, 24 inches deep, and 34 1/2 inches high as the minimum size opening, although a few brands of dishwashers might be slightly smaller.

There is usually a base pan that you should install according to instructions. Plumbing connections can be made to the hot water line feeding the kitchen sink, and to the sink drain line using a tee-type tail piece from the sink drain. Garbage disposals have a connection built in to the disposal body. *Note:* The disposal connection is blanked off. Knock this blank out before making the connection, also remove this blank from inside the disposal top section. Remove the rubber guard. Pull the plug on the disposal, reach inside and retrieve the blank. A flashlight will help to find it. The tee-type sink tail piece, is available in plastic or brass and replaces the present tail piece.

The drain line from the dishwasher should be 5/8-inch OD (outside diameter), 1/2-inch nominal size, and should extend out from the base at least 6 inches. The discharge outlet is usually 3/4-inch or 1/2-inch female iron pipe. If you have a flaring tool you can buy a 5/8-inch flare nut and a 5/8-inch flare × 3/8- or 1/2-inch male half union to make the connection. You can also use compression fittings instead of flare type. Some machines might have a hose leading out, but the instruction sheet will explain your specific machine.

Note: It is recommended that an "air gap" be used. This is installed above the countertop near the backsplash. It will eliminate back siphoning and will meet the Plumbing Code requirements. This is an add-on item, and must be purchased separately or ordered with the dishwasher. You might have enough length of hose for the drain line to go to the air gap and back down to the disposal or drain tail piece connection, if not, hose can be purchased from an appliance parts store. This store will also stock the air gap device. *Caution:* If no air gap is used, the drain hose must go up above the dishwasher top and then down to the drain connection to prevent back siphoning.

The water supply can be taken from the HOT water line feeding the sink faucet or from the basement. The connection to the water line should be taken from the feed line, not from the 3/8-inch riser to the faucet. On copper lines, a tee can be soldered in the feed line. If possible, get a 1/2-inch copper × 1/2-inch copper × 1/2-inch female pipe thread tee. Screw a valve into the tee branch (side opening) and continue the line to the dishwasher with copper, using either flare or compression fittings. This line must be 1/2-inch OD copper.

The water line shutoff valve must be away from the dishwasher location so that in case of a leak the valve will be accessible for closing quickly. Water for the dishwasher must be a minimum of 140 degrees F. for the dishwasher to do its job properly. Flow must be at least 10 quarts per minute and not less than 15 psig. Instead of soldering a tee in the hot water line, you can buy a saddle tee. To use this fitting (shut the water off first), drill a hole 1/4 inch in the pipe;

clamp the tee, rubber washer, and back-up plate on the pipe; and insert the two screws. Tighten the screws, install a shutoff valve in the opening, close the valve, and open the water valve feeding the hot water line. Check for leaks. If none are found, run the line to the dishwasher connection. In either case, be sure to test for leaks at all joints.

Electrical wiring to the dishwasher should have its own circuit, using No. 14-2 Romex with ground, and be fused at 15 amps. If the garbage disposal is to be on the same circuit, use No. 12-2 Romex with ground and fuse at 20 amps. Most distribution panels have additional space for another circuit breaker, and some panels, using fuses, might have unused circuits. In this case, the extra wiring is simple to do. Books are available that explain how to run a new, separate circuit to the dishwasher. One such book is TAB book No. 1587, *Mastering Household Electrical Wiring*. Wiring should be done according to the National Electrical Code.

Position the machine in front of the opening. Protect the floor covering with a pad, cardboard, or plywood. Follow the directions, making sure all the connections are properly hooked up. Sometimes the spring tension on the door must be adjusted. There will be a diagram showing you how to do this.

Refer to Table 11-1 for troubleshooting the dishwasher.

The Effect of Water and/or
Detergent on Cleaning Ability of Dishwasher

Minerals in water, especially calcium and magnesium in appreciable quantities will cause spotting and filming of dishes and glassware, and can discolor metals. Water hardness ranges from 0 to 4 grains hardness per gallon, which is soft—to 8 to 12 grains hardness per gallon, which is hard. Over 12 grains per gallon is considered very hard.

Hard water film can build up on the racks, walls, spray head, and the heating element of the dishwasher, which will cause many problems. For water less than 10 grains per gallon, the spotting and filming can be controlled by the amount of detergent used. For the higher hardness figures, the detergent cup should be *filled*, and under some circumstances, more detergent than the full cup should be added to the main wash cycle.

For hardness over 12 grains per gallon (very hard water), a water softener is needed to remove the calcium and magnesium. It might also be that a presently installed water softener is not functioning properly and is not removing these minerals. This method might help you remove hard water film from glassware and the dishwasher itself: Allow the dishwasher to fill up for the main wash cycle, then place two cups of vinegar in the water and let the machine complete its cycle. Place *only* glassware in the dishwasher for this cleaning operation.

When using any dishwasher, be sure to follow the directions exactly. Use newly purchased detergent made for automatic dishwashers only. Nationally advertised brands are usually satisfactory, but it might be necessary to change brands to get good results. The amount of detergent to use is usually specified in the instructions. Too much will cause sudsing and too little will not clean well.

Occasionally, etching will occur on soft glassware. This is caused by an alkaline compound. Etching cannot be removed because the surface of the glass has been destroyed. If you see a white film, try to scratch it with a pin. If this film can be scratched, it can be removed by washing with vinegar. Conditions that promote etching:

- Extremely hot water (it should be no hotter than 140 degrees F.)
- Using too much detergent for water hardness
- Soft water (0-4 grains hardness per gallon) softener
- Mineral content of the water
- Soft glassware.

On older dishwashers, the starting contacts inside the motor casing might have accumulated oily lint or fuzz. This can prevent the contact points from closing so as to make contact. In this case, the motor must be removed. Remove the motor end bell where the wires go into the motor and clean the contact points by passing a business card between the closed points a number of times until no more greasy black marks show on the card. Remove the end bell by taking off the through bolts and holding both end bells to the center casting. The end bell to be removed is the one having the external wires going to a terminal plate. The contacts are on a fiber plate; these will be in the open (separated) position when the end bell is removed from the motor. *Caution:* There will be wires from the end bell going into the center section of the motor, so be careful not to pull on them when removing the bell.

Both of the end bells must be replaced in the identical position as before they were removed. Before removing the through bolts, mark the end bells, using a center punch to make a dimple on the bell and center casting opposite each other. On the other end bell, make 2 dimples on it and the center casting. This provides the information for realignment of the bells. Re-assemble the motor, being careful to not pinch any wires, and note that no wires interfere with the rotor turning freely. Replace the motor in the cabinet.

Many electrical components can be tested by putting a voltage tester across their terminals when the device (relay or solenoid) is energized. If there is current at these two terminals and the device does not operate, it might be defective. Also, on some dishwashers the starting contacts for the motor are on an external relay. These contacts will also accumulate greasy or soapy dust on them and must be cleaned. This work is easy because the motor does not have to

Table 11-1. Troubleshooting the Dishwasher.

Trouble	Cause and Solution
1. Dishes do not come clean:	— Low water temperature, water should be at least 140° F. — Not enough or old detergent. — Improper loading, refer to instructions. — Spray arm not turning, might be blocked by a dish. — Dishwasher not filling full, water pressure might be low.
2. Dishes are not dry:	— Water temperature too low, must be 140° F. — Improper loading, do not stack dishes close together. — Wetting agent disperser might be empty, fill if necessary.
3. Spotting and filming on glasses and dishes:	— Not enough or too much detergent. — Water not at 140° F or more. — Water is very hard, try another brand of detergent. — Place a bowl with 2 cups of vinegar on bottom rack, *after* wash and rinse cycle but *before* drying period. Close dishwasher and run through regular cycle. — Low water pressure which does not allow dishwasher to fill properly.
4. Bronzing of silverplate:	— Silver plate has worn thin, silver should be replated.
5. Smudges on stainless steel:	— Food allowed to stand on stainless steel, rinse pans and let stand.
6. Dark spots on silverware:	— Concentrated detergent has been spilled on silverware.
7. Aluminum has darkened:	— Combination of hot water and detergent, change detergent and scour with a soap-filled steel wool pad.
8. Colored aluminum fades:	— Is not dishwasher safe.
9. Dishes and dishwasher are turning yellow:	— Iron or manganese in the water. Install an iron filter in line to dishwasher.

10. Dishwasher will not operate:
   - Is door closed tightly?
   - Is cycle set to start of action?
   - Is cord plugged in (on portable)?
   - Is fuse blown or breaker tripped?
   - Does house have electrical power?
   - Motor may be off on overload, it will start again by itself.

11. Runs with door open:
   - Door switch defective, replace.

12. Does not complete all cycles:
   - Bad timer switch, replace.

13. Stays on one portion of cycle:
   - Motor has open circuit, replace.
   - Wire disconnected, repair.
   - Damaged switch, replace.

14. Will not fill:
   - Water valve closed, open it.
   - Fill valve defective or wire disconnected, check or replace valve.

15. Does not fill completely:
   - Low water pressure, must be at least 20 psig.

16. Fill valve stays open:
   - Defective valve, replace valve.
   - Dirt under diaphragm, clean valve.

17. Water siphons out after fill for either wash or rinse. NOTE: Installation of air gap solves both problems and should be installed to conform to Plumbing Code. (It is normal for a small amount of water to remain in tub).
   - No loop in drain line. If no air gap is used, drain line must rise up to top of washer and then go down to drain. Drain line connected after sink trap. Move to above sink trap, get "dishwasher tail piece."

18. Will not drain:
   - Pump discharge opening plugged, clean or replace casting.
   - Impeller vanes broken off, replace impeller and other broken parts of pump.

19. Does not drain completely:
   - Drain line is too small, line must be 1/2-inch ID

20. Will not heat water hot enough:
   - Bad heating element. Check continuity and replace element if bad.
   - Open circuit or defective thermostat. Check circuit and thermostat, and replace thermostat, if bad. Repair circuit if defective.

be removed to reach the contacts. Use the business card method here as well.

The electrically operated timer that runs the dishwasher through its cycle might have a bad motor or burned contact points that will have to be replaced. A handy item to have when disconnecting wires from a device are terminal (wire) identifying numbers. These come on a card and are peeled off and wrapped around the wire insulation near the bared end or terminal and identify the wire. Single numbers are used to identify the terminal for that wire. These number sets (1-25) are available at electrical wholesalers.

The rotating spray arm in the dishwasher might split and reduce the spray action. If the split is on the opposite side of the spray holes, this could slow the rotation of the arm. The arm must rotate at 25 to 45 rpm for proper washing action.

On models with an electric heating element, it is possible for the element to fail because the element wire has broken inside the metal covering. You can test this element by using an ohmmeter. With the current to the dishwasher OFF, put the test probes on the terminals of the heating element (one probe on each terminal). A reading about center scale shows the element to be good. No movement of the needle shows a broken element. Because each brand of dishwasher uses a different element, you will have to go to their service and parts department for a replacement.

When checking any electrical component, be sure the current to the dishwasher is OFF. There is usually a wiring diagram furnished with the machine, glued to a panel or included in the manual furnished. A complete repair manual can also be purchased from the manufacturer.

GARBAGE DISPOSALS

Because many municipalities have enacted ordinances requiring garbage disposals in new homes, many homes, new and old, have these devices. Disposals come in two styles, the batch type and the continuous feed type.

The batch type disposal has a locking cover that must be inserted in the top to close the hopper. The cover is then turned and locked. Early models had two interlock switches, one in the water line that would turn the disposal on only when water was flowing out of the faucet, and another switch activated by locking the cover in place. This was for safety and to provide lubrication as the waste was carried away through the drain pipe. Later the water flow interlock was eliminated because most people turn on the water when using the disposal.

The continuous feed type has been most popular, and 90 percent of the disposals are of this type. Sometimes water will spray out when this disposal is started, but only for a few seconds. This type can be fed continuously as long as you have waste to put in it. This style does have a cover (stopper), if you want to use it. Watery garbage will need the cover in place, but the disposal does need water to operate and to flush away the waste.

Certain items such as corn husks and large beef or pork bones should be disposed in the trash. Corn husks are stringy and might wedge between the cutter bar and the wall and stop the unit. Sometimes the only way to remove these husks is to remove the complete unit from under the sink and dismantle the top section. Alternatively, the rubber gasket with the pie-shaped slits all around can be removed after unplugging the disposal, or removing the fuse, or tripping the circuit breaker. If you have small hands you can also try to dig out the corn husk strands. The large bones can overload the disposal and cause damage to the shredder.

Some disposals are made so that the motor can be reversed to free the shredder. If not, the remedy is to use a **Z** shaped Allen wrench that is furnished with many disposals. With the power OFF, as before, insert this tool in the bottom of the disposal. Rotate the wrench back and forth and if you are lucky, this might free the shredder. If the disposal stops because of an overload, there is usually a red button on the bottom to push to reset the overload switch. Use a mirror to locate this button because it is recessed and hard to find by feel.

The appendix has illustrations of representative disposals, parts lists, and exploded views. Disposals come in various sizes to match the size of the jobs it must do. The better ones have heavy insulation to quiet the noise of operation. It is now common practice to include a cord with the disposal for plugging into a wall outlet with a switch adjacent to the sink to control the disposal operation. Even in this case, if you need to put your hand into the disposal top or need to un-stick the shredder with the tool, pull the plug out of the outlet rather than just turning the switch off (Figs. 11-1 and 11-2).

In a double bowl sink, and the garbage disposal is in one bowl and discharges into a common trap and drain line through a tee (Fig. 11-3). This directional tee must have a baffle to direct the flow downward to prevent the disposal discharge from backing up into the other bowl. A separate trap for each sink bowl is a better arrangement so there is no chance that the disposal discharges into the other bowl. It is always recommended that a large quantity of water be run into the disposal when it is being operated.

If you are connecting the dishwater water discharge from its pump to the disposal dishwasher connection and there is only one sink bowl, be sure to knock out the plug blocking this opening. Use a screwdriver and a small hammer to knock the plug inwards. The plug piece will then be in the top part of the disposal. You must pick it out by hand. *Caution:* Turn the power OFF or unplug the disposal before reaching inside!

Fig. 11-1. Garbage disposal. Courtesy In-Sink-Erator Co.

Use a flashlight to find out where this plug is lying because you cannot see when your hand is inside. Remove the rubber ring at the top of the disposal at sink level before starting, to give more room. Because this part is not steel or iron, a magnet will not work.

THE AUTOMATIC WASHER

In newer homes, there is usually a space provided for the automatic washer and dryer, either in a utility/furnace room or in the basement. In the sunbelt, the washer and dryer might be located in the carport

Fig. 11-2. Dishwasher water discharge connection. Plug must be knocked out before hose is attached.

or garage. This is advisable *only* if the temperature does not go below 32 degrees F. In small apartments, the washer and dryer can be stacked one above the other. These are special models, both with front openings. Most washers, however, are top opening.

In the older home that has never used an automatic washer, there might not be the hot and cold shutoff valves necessary to connect the hoses from the washer to the hot and cold supply lines. In this case, clamp a saddle tee to both hot and cold water lines to the laundry tray about 6 inches from the faucet/swing spout assembly. These saddle tees are available at nearly all hardware stores. The package will state the size pipe that the tee will fit.

The pipes to the present faucets are 1/2-inch copper tubing or galvanized iron pipe. The saddle tee without the rubber gasket is clamped on the pipe, and a 1/4-inch hole is drilled through the threaded opening where the shutoff will be screwed in. This procedure is usually described on the package. *Note:* Shut the water OFF and drain the lines by opening the valve below before starting to drill.

A 5/16-inch hole will give greater water flow *if* the directions

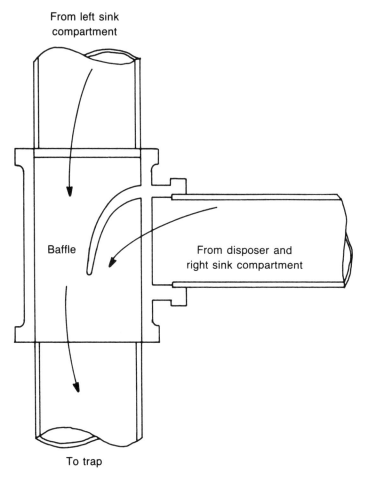

From left sink
compartment

Baffle

From disposer and
right sink compartment

To trap

Fig. 11-3. Directional tee, which is needed when only one trap is used. It directs dishwasher discharge down into drain and not back up into the other sink bowl.

recommend this. The type of water shutoff valves to use here are called "boiler drain cocks." The inlet will be 1/2-inch male pipe threads (mpt) and the outlet hose thread. This will mate with the female pipe thread in the saddle tee. Use Teflon or pipe thread compound on the male threads (Figs. 11-4 through 11-11).

The proposed location of the washer will determine which way the faucet hose end will face, and in turn which side of the vertical water pipes to drill the hole and to face the saddle tee. Another method is to install standard copper tees with the run 1/2-inch copper and the branch (the side opening) 1/2-inch female pipe thread—if the line is copper. If the lines are 1/2-inch galvanized iron pipe, use 1/2-inch "all around" galvanized tees, with short pipe nipples below them. You will then need to remove the vertical pipes (risers) and have them cut and threaded to fit the shorter space, due to the tees and short nipples installed in each riser.

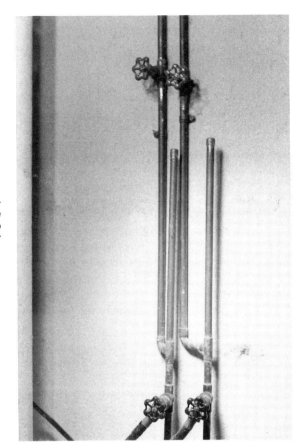

Fig. 11-4. Washing machine shutoff valves and the two water hammer arrestors in place. These arrestors are made on the job from 3/4-inch copper or iron pipe. Above are two shutoff valves for allowing repairs to be made on the other valves.

The drain hose must be connected to the washer. This connection is at the back of the cabinet near the bottom. Use the hose clamp furnished. Connect the hot and cold hoses to the washer mixing valve. If there are strainer washers furnished (a hose washer with a cone-shaped brass strainer in the center), the cone of the washer should

Fig. 11-5. Close-up of the automatic washer hose shutoff valves.

Fig. 11-6. A saddle tee ready for installation.

face toward the water supply, not the washer. Tighten these connections hand tight, then use pliers to tighten a half to one turn more.

Move the washer into place. After the washer is in place, level it using the four leveling legs. A recessed rubber washer fits the head of the leg. Use a spirit level to make the washer level, both front to back and side to side. The washer *must not* rock. Test this by trying to push on the front top, and on the sides at the top. If the washer moves when the top is pushed, re-adjust the legs so that all four rest firmly on the floor, or the washer might "walk" when in spin.

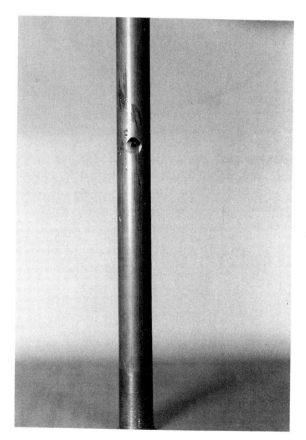

Fig. 11-7. A hole 1/4-inch drilled in a 1/2-inch (nominal) copper pipe to take the saddle valve.

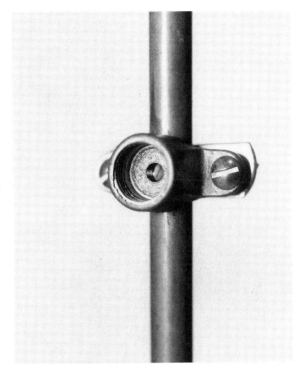

Fig. 11-8. The saddle valve installed on the copper pipe.

Fig. 11-9. Teflon pipe thread tape. Tape roll is shown on the container.

Fig. 11-10. The application of the Teflon tape. The tape end must be held as it is wrapped since the tape has no adhesive.

Fig. 11-11. The completed automatic washer hose connection.

Note: On some wood floors supported on joists, a square of 3/4-inch plywood, sized to fit underneath the washer, but not extending beyond the cabinet dimensions, is placed underneath the washer. This prevents the washer from vibrating in the spin cycle because of a weak floor.

If you have a laundry tray, the curved end of the drain hose can be hooked over the rear corner of the tub. If there is no laundry tray, a standpipe must be provided for the drain hose end to discharge into. The standpipe must be 30 inches high from the floor. Because the hose must be fairly straight, it might have to be cut in the middle and spliced, using a coupling to make it shorter. This is because both ends are formed: one end is a molded end and the other end is a molded elbow. Connect the two water supply hoses to the faucets provided. Be sure the hot water supply goes to the washer connection marked "HOT" and the cold water supply goes to "COLD."

The washer must be plugged into a 120-volt, 60-hertz, 3-wire grounded receptacle. If this type of circuit is not available, one must be provided. Do not use an adapter that allows the three-prong plug on the washer to be plugged into a 2-wire receptacle. If you are familiar with electrical wiring, you can install such a receptacle. If not, hire a licensed electrician to install one. This is the only *safe* method of operating the washing machine.

A grounding wire could be installed between the frame of the washer and a nearby cold water pipe, if this pipe is continuous all the way back to the water meter. Buy a grounding clamp at a hardware store and clamp it to the water pipe, then run a No. 12 bare copper wire between the clamp and the washer frame. Loosen a screw on the frame and loop the wire under this screw, then tighten the screw. Refer to Table 11-2 for troubleshooting the automatic washer.

Any electrical component such as a switch or pressure or water level control can be tested to see if it makes contact by moving any lever or button that can be actuated by your fingers. After you have pulled the electrical plug from the wall receptacle, you can work on any electrical or mechanical part with complete safety. If you cannot actuate a control in place in the washer, remove the control by unplugging the two wires and either removing the control or disconnecting the arm that actuates the control when the washer is operating.

Testing is accomplished by using a *continuity tester*. This tester is used only when the electrical power is OFF (the plug is pulled). Some testers look like a screwdriver. A test lead extends out from the handle with a test clip on the end to clamp to a terminal. The screwdriver tip is touched to the other terminal. If the control is making contact, the lamp inside the handle lights up. If the control contacts are open, the lamp stays out. If you operate the control, the lamp will go on and off as you move the lever, or otherwise actuate the control. This tester sells for about $3 to $4 in electronics stores. An ohmmeter will indicate open or closed contacts, but this tool costs more.

Each brand of automatic washer and each different model of the same brand will differ in its components and wiring arrangement from any other washer. If you want to do your own repair and maintenance, the best advice is to purchase a repair manual for the model that you own.

Many controls have more then two wires attached to them. If three or more wires are attached to a control, each needs to be labeled. Stick-on labels are available at electrical wholesalers just for this purpose. Sometimes the control terminals are labeled by embossed numbers or letters on the plastic cover or metal part. Before removing any wire, record carefully in a notebook which (numbered) wire goes to which terminal.

Printed wiring diagrams are usually glued on the back panel of the washer. This is the diagram *only*, and will not give any other information. This is why you should buy and use a repair manual.

Laundry Trays

Laundry trays (tubs) are used with washing machines, both manual and automatic. When used with a wringer-type washer, the tray will

Table 11-2. Troubleshooting the Automatic Washer.

Problem	Cause	Solution
1. Does not run	No power	Check fuse or breaker
	Bad cord on washer	Replace cord
	Defective timer	Replace timer .
2. Washer does not fill	Faucets closed	Open faucets
	Hoses kinked	Straighten hoses and arrange so they do not kink
	Plugged inlet screens on hoses	Remove screens and clean
	Bad water level	Check switch. May have wire loose or off
	Loose wires in harness	Check all connections
3. Drive motor will not run	See No. 1 problem	
	Motor off on overload	Motor may start again after cooling off
	Internal starting switch contacts dirty	Disassemble motor and clean contacts by passing business card between closed contacts
4. Washer will not agitate	Broken drive belt or loose drive belt	Tighten or replace drive belt
	Loose pulleys	Tighten pulleys on shaft. Use allen wrench on set screw to tighten
5. Water will not drain from washer	Hose kinked	Move hose to straighten
	Too much suds	Add cold water to washer. Check amount of detergent used
6. Tub will not spin	Broken or loose belt	Replace or tighten belt
	See No. 4 problems	
	Lid not closed	
7. Leaks water	Loose hoses	Tighten connections
	Tub leaks	Tighten screws holding tub to base
8. Washer will not stop	Timer defective	Replace timer
9. Washer shakes	Shipping blocks have not been removed	Remove blocks
	Load unbalanced	Rearrange clothes more evenly in tub
10. Water will not shut off	Defective water level switch	Replace switch
	Defective timer	Replace timer
11. Timer does not advance	Defective water timer	Check timer and timer motor
12. Clothes do not spin dry	Water not being removed from washer	Check pump and drain hose. Clean pump, straighten drain hose
13. Lint on clothes	Dirty or plugged filter	Remove and clean filter
	Wrong clothes mixture	Separate clothes by type
	Overloaded tub	Load less clothes each time

have two compartments, each filled with water, thus providing two water rinses. Older wringer washers drained on to the floor near a floor drain. Newer wringer washers had a pump that would discharge into one compartment of the laundry tray. These older two-compartment laundry trays were made of cement or soapstone and were very heavy.

Modern homes have the single-compartment fiberglass-plastic laundry tray. This saves space, and modern automatic washing machines need only a place to discharge their water, as all operations are carried on in the washer itself. Some small apartments have only a standpipe for the discharge of the washer, again to save space. This is a 2-inch pipe attached to a trap and extending about as high as the top of the automatic washer.

Faucets on laundry trays are of the swing spout style, although for the single compartment the swing spout serves no real purpose in that case. See Fig. 11-12 for a modern laundry tray and faucet assembly. A view under the laundry tray (Fig. 11-13) shows the trap, and shutoff valves to the faucet, and the valves to shut off the automatic washer hoses when not in use. This is a precaution to prevent the hoses from bursting and causing a flood, which would be a disaster—especially if the machine is on the first floor and the hose bursts when no one is home. Always close these two valves when the machine is not in use. A close-up view of the swing spout laundry tray faucet is shown in Fig. 11-14. The body of the faucet is plastic; only the valve seats and the swing spout are metal.

FLOOR DRAINS AND RELATED ITEMS

Every basement and laundry room must have a drain in the floor according to the Plumbing Code. Floor drains do not have to be vented if they are within 25 feet of a vented drainage pipe. The floor drain

Fig. 11-12. Laundry tray with chrome swing spout. Notice the automatic washer water discharge at right corner.

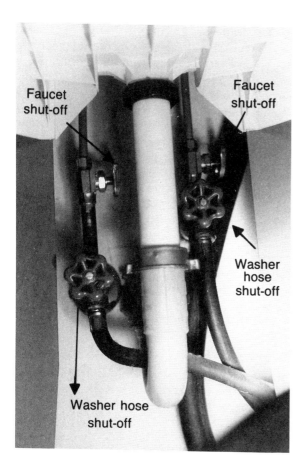

Faucet shut-off

Faucet shut-off

Washer hose shut-off

Washer hose shut-off

Fig. 11-13. View underneath laundry tray. Shows the shut-off valves for tray faucets. Below are the shutoffs for the automatic washer hoses.

must have the following features:

- Drain outlet must be 2-inch nominal pipe
- Cover must be removable
- Free area of cover holes must equal the 2-inch pipe in area

Fig. 11-14. Close-up view of the swing spout faucet on the laundry tray. Only the spout and seats are metal; the rest is plastic.

Fig. 11-15. Laundry room/furnace room floor drain. Plastic line is from the humidifier (winter) and the condensate pan of the air conditioner (summer).

● Floor drain traps must be "deep seal"—a 3-inch trap seal the distance from the top of the lowest part of the trap to the bottom of the discharge pipe. A standard trap has a 2-inch seal.

● Floor drains installed below ground level (basements) must have a backwater valve. This is a check valve to prevent drain lines from backing up during heavy rains.

A typical floor drain is shown in Fig. 11-15. The plastic line shown leading to the floor drain is a combination humidifier overflow/air conditioner condensate line.

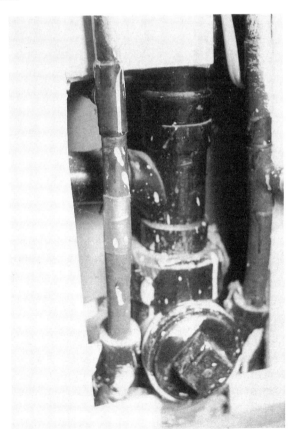

Fig. 11-16. Close-up of cleanout plug. The sewer line can be rodded from this point to the outside sewer.

Fig. 11-17. A saddle valve installed to provide water to the furnace humidifier. The valve is clamped onto the copper line, then the valve stem is screwed down and pierces the copper line. When the valve is opened, water flows to a humidifier or refrigerator icemaker.

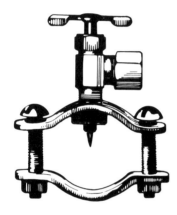

Fig. 11-18. Close-up view of a saddle-type needle valve. Courtesy Plumb Shop.

Figure 11-16 illustrates a cleanout in a vent stack. This installation is all plastic; notice the drain line from the left that is from the laundry tray. The cleanout plug is also plastic. In Fig. 11-17, notice the self-piercing needle valve. This feeds the humidifier installed in the hot air furnace, an add-on installed after the furnace was installed. Figure 11-18 shows a close-up of this valve. These valves work satisfactorily but tend to clog up from the minerals in the water. The humidifier also accumulates a lime coating and must be cleaned each fall before the heating season. Both plates or the pad on the wheel can be cleaned with white vinegar undiluted.

WET BARS

The wet bar (barsink) is installed the same as a lavatory or kitchen sink. There should be hot and cold faucets, a drain, and a vent. Most wet bars are installed in basements to serve a small bar adjacent to a recreation room. The bar sink is usually below the bar countertop and may be up to 14 × 18 × 6 inches deep. The faucet is the two-handle style having a "high rise" solid spout. This makes it easy to wash or fill glasses and utensils without hitting them against the spout

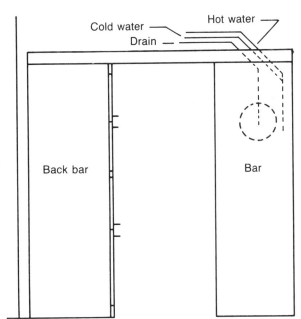

Fig. 11-19. Piping layout for a wet bar. (Plan view)

Cold water — Hot water —
Drain —

Back bar

Bar

or sink edge. The sink is generally stainless steel for ease of cleaning. Either a chrome-plated or plastic 1 1/4-inch trap is used. Because the sink is under the bar top, the water lines and drain line must lead right or left to be connected to the plumbing lines. A connection can be made to the laundry tray piping.

Be sure to plan the sink piping before building a bar so that you can correlate the bar design with the sink location and the routing of the piping (Figs. 11-19 and 11-20). The trap can be 1 1/4 inch because the dfu is only 1. The water lines and drain lines can be plastic, and plastic is easy to work with. Fittings are now available to attach copper or galvanized pipe to plastic. These are made by Genova, called Uncopper, and by Plumb Shop, called Poly-Lock.

Any drain line can be opened to connect a line from the bar sink drain. Galvanized lines can be cut and a wye inserted. You can use a pipe cutter or a hacksaw if the cutter will not swing because of close quarters. Some tool rental shops might have a three-wheel cutter. This

Fig. 11-20. Piping layout for a wet bar. (Elevation)

Back bar

Bar

Bar sink

215

will work with only a 30-degree swing. Plastic pipe should be sawed with a hacksaw (keep the cut exactly at 90 degrees to the pipe for a leak-proof joint). Use a plastic wye as with the galvanized connection. Plan for a slope of 1/4 inch per running foot of the drain line. The hot and cold water lines are connected using the same methods as for the drain line. These lines will be galvanized, copper, or plastic. It is wise to install a shutoff valve in the water lines for convenience in servicing the sink faucets.

SWIMMING POOLS

Many homes now have swimming pools in their backyards. The most common home pool is the "recirculating" type. A pool like this has a pump, filter, and a chlorine feeder to keep the water clean, clear, and free of bacteria and organic matter. As you may already know, this requires constant maintenance. This is not difficult, but it must be done regularly.

Caution: Local laws and ordinances are very strict regarding swimming pools, because of the danger of small children falling into the pool and drowning. Building codes require that the pool be fenced in and the gate in the fence be kept locked at all times when the pool is not being used. Some ordinances state that an adult must be present when children are using the pool. Any type of fencing may be used. It must be at least 4 feet high (the higher the better), with a self-latching and self-locking gate.

There are two general types of pools, the in-ground pool and the above-ground. The in-ground pool has evolved somewhat from the all-masonry type with the interior surfaced having a smooth finish such as Gunite, to the type consisting of a vinyl liner supported by the earth sides of the excavation. Either type will have a concrete surface around the pool and a rim holding the pool edge in place.

In-ground pools have at the very lowest part of the bottom, a main drain to empty the pool. Formerly, this drain had a flat grating for a cover. It was subsequently discovered that children could sit on this drain and be held by the suction and drowned. Now the drain is in the form of a dome that cannot be completely covered. This dome-type drain is now required for new construction by the building inspection department of nearly every municipality.

Every pool must have a *vacuum fitting* for connection of a *skimmer* for removing surface debris. *Recirculating piping* (also known as return piping or pool inlet piping) is connected to the discharge side of the pump, after the filter and heater. This returns water to the pool after filtering and heating. *Backwash piping* is a discharge line to lead pool waste water to a disposal site.

The water to fill the pool must meet the quality standards equal to domestic water supply standards. If a pool is filled from a garden hose, the hose faucet *must* have a vacuum breaker installed to pre-

Fig. 11-21. A vacuum breaker for attaching to a sill cock.

vent a cross-connection that would contaminate the domestic water supply. When a pool must be emptied or backwashed, this water must be disposed of in accordance with local ordinances. It can be properly disposed of on the property where the pool is located. One way is by using a drainage field similar to a septic tank drainage field. It is wise to contact the local authorities regarding the best and approved disposal method (Figs 11-21 and 11-22).

Recirculation inlets are required for each 350 square feet of pool water surface or fraction. A minimum of two outlets are required,

Fig. 11-22. The vacuum breaker attached to a sill cock. A setscrew holds the device to the faucet to discourage removal.

217

spaced at least 10 feet apart. The flow from these outlets must not exceed 10 feet per second (fps), and the suction line must not exceed 5 fps when going through the sand filter. A valve must be installed on the main drain line, and located outside the pool walls so that it is accessible. Between the main drain valve and the pump, a hair and lint strainer must be installed to prevent the pump from becoming clogged with debris.

Water filters are of two types: the pressure sand filter and the diatomite filter. The sand filter (sometimes called sand and gravel filter) must contain at least 19 inches of sharp silica sand, screened and graded, on a bed of silica gravel. There should be free space above the sand to allow backwash to clean the sand. The sand will swell by one half to fill this space not so much that it is pushed out the overflow openings. Pressure gauges must be in both the inlet and outlet pipes and the backwash line must have a sight glass installed in order to show when the water runs clear. This filter should have a filtration rate of not more than 5 gallons per minute per square foot of filtering area.

The diatomite-type filter must have a filtration rate of 2 gallons per minute per square foot of filter area. The filtering medium is called diatomaceous earth, a fine siliceous earth composed of the sharp-edged skeletons of diatoms (microscopic algae). This performs the same function as the sharp silica sand medium. The filter needs a treatment periodically, in order to coat the filter medium. Some styles have removable filter elements that can be replaced rather than backwashed.

Each 600 square feet of pool surface or fraction must have a skimmer device. These skimmers must be built into the pool wall a maximum of 10 inches below the water level. A vacuum connection, similar to a household vacuum cleaner, has to be provided for a portable skimmer. In this way leaves and debris on the bottom can be removed easily. Other skimmers are a screen in a round frame, having a long handle—these are easiest to use for debris floating on the water surface.

ABS or PVC Schedule 40 plastic are approved for all lines that are part of the pool plumbing. Figure 11-23 gives a piping connections diagram. Long radius pipe elbows should be used on pool or spa suction piping, especially below grade. All suction piping should be 2-inch nominal. Where dissimilar metals have to be joined, a dielectric union or coupling must be used to prevent corrosion. All piping must be supported and made secure, tested at 40 psig, and made leakproof before concealing the lines.

Pool heaters and boilers must comply with ASME and AGA standards. Oil burners and electric heaters must be listed by Underwriters Laboratories. A 70-percent thermal efficiency is the minimum allowed. Both an operating temperature control and a high limit control should

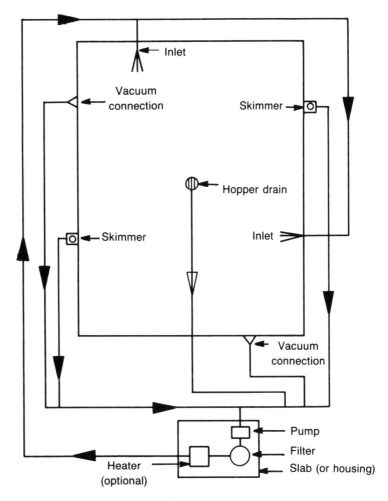

Fig. 11-23. In-ground pool filtration system.

be on the heater or boiler. The maximum temperature allowed is 110 degrees F. The heater or boiler must have two valves so that the heater can be isolated from the rest of the system and a bypass installed around the heater or boiler. This bypass has a valve installed. To take the heater out of the system for repair and replacement, close the valves at the heater—one on the incoming line and one on the outgoing line—then open the valve in the bypass line (this valve is always closed when the heater is operating). In this manner, the pool circulating and filter system can still operate while the heater is being serviced. *Note:* Unions must be provided between each heater valve and the heater so that the heater can be removed for repairs, if necessary.

Spas are, in effect, a small swimming pool, except that people are seated and not exercising as in a pool. All the auxiliary equipment used with a swimming pool is needed for a spa, but will have a smaller capacity. The spa water temperature must be no higher than 104 degrees F.

Caution: Persons with a medical problem such as heart disease or high blood pressure must be careful when using a spa. Maximum temperature should be 100 degrees F., and maximum recommended time spent in the water is 20 minutes. It is required that a sign stating the maximum temperature be posted prominently on or close to the spa. A spa cannot exceed 3250 gallons of water.

Winterizing pools and spas must be done in climates where the temperature goes below freezing. The pool or spa—including any equipment such as the filter, hair and lint strainer, pump, and heater—can be drained. You must be positive that no water is left in *any* of the equipment. It might be necessary to rent an air compressor to blow out any residual water in the lines.

Private pools must have a pool filter of sufficient rating in gallons per hour (gph) to "turnover" the total water in the pool in 8 hours. Therefore, a pool of 8,000 gallons will need a filter rated at 1,000 gph. This filter capacity might seem excessive, but it enables the filter to go longer periods before cleaning becomes necessary. The filtering equipment will also have a larger pump for better operation.

The pump for the filtering system must be the self-priming type; the non-self-priming type will not pump if there is air in the system. The head against which the pump must operate should be 45 to 60 feet (20 to 26 psig). Most pools need to have the pipe runs and connections of at least the 1/4-inch size. This enables the pump to operate more efficiently because there are less restriction in the suction and discharge lines.

WHIRLPOOLS AND SAUNAS

Whirlpool baths resemble a standard bathtub in appearance and shape. They can be similar to a bathtub in style, in that they can be recessed, sunk into the floor, or mounted on a pedestal. The whirlpool differs from a bathtub in that it has four or more combination air/water jet openings to give the water message. Whirlpool tub shapes vary from oval, to round, to rectangular. The oval bath measures 71 3/4 inches long × 36 inches wide × 21 3/4 inches deep. The nearly round bath measures 60 inches × 72 inches × 19 1/2 inches deep. Most, but not all, will fit in a 60-inch-long recess. Some shapes are quite elaborate, having been styled architecturally. Some have built-in seats and hand rails (grab rails). Some tubs are as deep as 32 inches.

All whirlpools come with the pump, motor, and piping preinstalled, ready to be connected to the plumbing and electrical supplies. A 3/4-hp pump and motor supply 70 to 80 gallons per minute (gpm) of circulation through the jet openings. The water jets are directional and can be rotated to direct the jets as desired. An airflow regu-

Fig. 11-24. The Centari fiberglass whirlpool bath, Model 6582. Courtesy Universal-Rundle Bath Products.

lator allows adjustment of the air to water ratio as needed.

Some models have a toiletry ledge sloped back for reclining, and arm rests. Faucets are either mounted on the ledge at one end and provide the 1-inch air gap, or are wall-mounted as in a standard bathtub. Nearly all are of gelcoated fiberglass and have a high-gloss finish for ease of cleaning.

Universal-Rundle Bath Products manufactures a whirlpool bathing system, the Centari, an extra-long, acrylic-faced fiberglass whirlpool featuring a high, reclining back, molded armrests, and side toiletry shelves. This reversible unit comes complete with a polished chrome drain. The HyFlow whirlpool system has six fully adjustable jets and a single air control. Model No. 6582 measures 72 inches long by 37 inches wide by 17 inches deep.

The Centari Whirlpool/Spa is shown in Fig. 11-24. Notice the type of faucets used. The tub is sunk in the floor and the faucets are also at floor level. The spout is designed to maintain the 1-inch air gap required by the Plumbing Code.

Caution: As with spas, persons with heart conditions or high blood pressure should make sure the water is no hotter than 100 degrees F. and must not remain in the water longer than 20 minutes. This warning *must* be posted on the equipment as a printed sign, large enough to be seen easily by the user.

Permits and Inspections

Because of the technical nature of any mechanical work, it is necessary to apply for permits *before* any work is started. Many inspection departments are very strict, and might require that the work be removed if no permit has been obtained. This will cause a great deal of difficulty; but the law is the law. Figures 12-1 and 12-2 illustrate a Plumbing Permit and a Home Owner Affidavit.

When you apply for your permit and sign the affidavit, it is a good time to talk your project over with the department. Do this before starting any work, buying any material, or tearing out any old work. The department's advice is usually very helpful and the people there will be glad to advise you before you start.

On the "Homeowners Permit" you must state that you, the homeowner, will do the work yourself and not contract someone else to do it for you. The permit usually costs about $10.

The plumbing inspector will require that you show in detail the installation and work you will be doing. Talk with the inspector before buying any materials because certain materials and fittings might not be approved by the inspection department. If this is a complete system the plans must show the complete water, sewer, and drainage lines as they will be installed in the dwelling. Be sure to show all cleanouts, the pitch used (1/4 inch per foot), and the connection to the public sewer and water lines, or to the septic system and well system.

CITY OF TROY
PERMIT INSPECTION DEPARTMENT
524-3344
PLUMBING PERMIT Permit No. _____

Date Issued _____ Lic. No. _____.

Licensed Plumber _____Telephone No. _____
is hereby granted permission, when properly signed, numbered, and validated, to
install plumbing equipment as listed below at the following address:

Lot No. _____ Subdivision

House No. _____ Street

BLDG.　[ ] New　[ ] Add'n　[ ] Existing　[ ] Res.　[ ] Comm.　[ ] Ind.

TYPE	NO.	FEE	
Stacks, Conductors			
Sink			
Bath			
Water Closet			
Lavatory			
Tank and Heater			
Laundry Tray			
Water Distribution Systems			
Floor Drain Trap			
Pump and Water Lift			
Fountain (drinking)			
Sump			
Grease Trap			
Urinal			— TREASURER'S VALIDATION OF FEE PAID —
Hose Bibbs			
Shower Trap			
Dishwashing Machine			
Humidifier			
Garbage Unit			
Washing Machine			
Crock, to Iron			
Inside Drains			
Special Fixtures			
* Transfer of Permits			
* Special Inspection			
TOTAL FEE			

[ ] Ready for Inspection　[ ] Will Call

FOR INSPECTION CALL 689-5744 (12:00 - 7:00 P.M.)

_____　_____
signature of contractor　　　　signature of issuing clerk

Fig. 12-1. Permit for installation of plumbing. Courtesy City of Troy, Michigan.

CITY OF TROY

500 W. Big Beaver | 524-3344

HOME OWNER AFFIDAVIT

LOCATION _____ DATE _____

As the bona fide owner of the above mentioned property which is a single residence, and which is, or will be on completion my place of residence and no part of which is used for rental or commercial purposes nor is now contemplated for such purpose, I hereby make application for an owner's permit to install _____ as listed on the permit application.

I certify that I am familiar with the provisions of the applicable Ordinance and the rules governing the type of installation which is contemplated at the above mentioned location and hereby agree to make the installation in conformance with the Ordinance.

In making this application, I realize I am assuming the responsibility of a licensed contractor for the installation of the work mentioned in the permit application and for putting the equipment in operation. I further agree that I shall neither hire any other person for the purpose of installing any portion of the _____ or related equipment at the above premises, nor sub-contract to any other person, firm or corporation the installation of any portion of the above equipment.

I agree to notify the Inspection Department within seventy-two (72) hours after the installation is completed and is ready for service so that the Department may make its required inspection. I further agree to keep all parts of the installation exposed until the installation is accepted as being in compliance with Ordinance requirements.

I further agree to correct within two weeks time any violations on the work installed and to provide access to the premises between the hours of 8 a.m. and 5 p.m. Monday through Friday for the necessary inspection or inspection. Failure to correct violations or to provide access will subject the permit to cancellation in which case a licensed contractor must be employed to complete the work.

APPLICATION: ☐ ACCEPTABLE ☐ NOT ACCEPTABLE

_____
Department Representative

If not acceptable, list reason _____

Subscribed and sworn to before me this

_____ day of _____, 19____.

Notary Public _____ County, Michigan.

My commission expires _____

_____
Owner

_____
Present Address

_____
Telephone Number

Fig. 12-2. Home Owner Affidavit that the home owner will do all the work. Courtesy City of Troy, Michigan.

There are many areas in the country that prohibit the installation of plumbing except by a licensed plumber. Again, check with your plumbing inspector before starting any major work. Minor repairs such as faucet replacements may be done by you.

If you have obtained the permit, you may now start your installation. After you have finished the rough-in work, call for a "first inspection" by notifying the Inspection Department 48 hours before the inspection is wanted. Some Departments might specify a longer or shorter lead time for the inspection call.

The inspector will go over the installation with you and point out any violations of the Code, and make suggestions to improve your work, if necessary. If this is a completely new system the inspector will have told you that you must make a pressure test on all the lines—sewer, drain/vent, and water. All water lines that extend out from the wall for lavatories, sinks, etc., must be capped. Outdoor hose bibs will have the bib closed, as will any other valves that are already in place.

The water system must be tested at 150 psi. This pressure must hold for 24 hours to get approval for use. The sewer/drainage system is tested at only 5 psi, also for 24 hours. All openings in this system can be plugged with special inflatable rubber plugs, which are available from rental shops. A goodsized hand tire pump or a small air compressor can be used to build the required pressure. Either system requires a lot of pumping the water system for the high pressure and the sewer for the large volume needed. You might also be able to rent special pumps.

Different governing bodies have different local codes, depending on the areas of the country (southern versus the northern states), regarding freeze protection and other local ordinances. These requirements are sometimes based on custom and local practices, but they must be followed to get the approval of the inspection department. This is why plastic pipe and fittings do not have approval in all areas.

Most public libraries have copies of previous National Plumbing Codes. The Code is updated and issued every three years; try to get the latest issue. Very few changes from issue to issue will affect household plumbing. Ask at the inspection department if there are any changes that will affect what you will be doing. As noted before, most inspectors will help you to make a good and safe installation. The inspector will check carefully for cross connections and siphon conditions. You might have made some prohibited connection without realizing it.

If you read the Plumbing Code, you might find that many of the sections are hard to understand. In this case the local inspector will again prove helpful.

THE NATIONAL PLUMBING CODE

All information given in this book is based on the National Plumbing code, 1984 Issue, published by the Building Officials & Code Administration International, Inc., Country Club Hills, Illinois. Tables 4-1 through 4-8 are excerpted from the 1984 issue of the Plumbing Code.

Copies of the Plumbing Code may be purchased from Building Officials and Code Administrators International, Inc., 5041 West Flossmoor Road, Country Club Hills, IL 60477-5795. Write in advance for the current price.

Appendix:
Manufacturers' Information

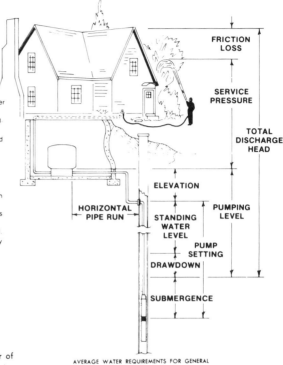

NOTE: "**Top of Well**" also means "**pitless adapter level**".

"**Service inlet**" also means "**storage tank inlet**".

Standing or Static Water Level - distance from top of well to natural water level when pump is not operating.

Drawdown distance - distance water level drops while pump is operating.

Drawdown level - standing water level plus drawdown.

Submergence - distance submersible pump intake screen is installed below drawdown level.

Elevation - vertical distance between top of well and service inlet.

Pump Setting - distance from top of well to pump inlet screen.

Pumping Level - distance from drawdown level to service inlet.

Service Pressure - pressure (in PSI) at service inlet.

Friction Loss - loss of pressure due to friction of water flowing through pipe and fittings.

Total Discharge Head - discharge head (in feet) delivered when pump is operating at desired capacity.

Horizontal Pipe Run - horizontal distance between service inlet and well.

NOTE: PSI can be converted to equivalent feet of head by multiplying by 2.31.

HOW TO SELECT THE CORRECT PUMPING EQUIPMENT

The answer to four basic questions will help select the proper pump.

1. *WHAT IS THE SIZE OF THE WELL?* The inside diameter of the well must be known so that the proper size pump, injector, cylinder or drop pipe and foot valve can be determined.

2. *WHAT IS THE PUMPING LEVEL?* The vertical distance in feet from the pump to the water level while the pump is operating. If the pump is installed away from the well and is on higher ground, this elevation must also be included. Most wells draw down while being pumped so this must not be confused with the standing water level.

3. *WHAT SHOULD BE THE AVERAGE DISCHARGE PRESSURE?* Usual average discharge pressure is 40 lbs.—halfway between the 30 lbs. to 50 lb. switch setting of most water systems. When the tank is installed away from the pump at a higher level, or when house or yard fixtures are above the pump and tank, a greater pressure is needed and a larger pump must be used.

4. *WHAT CAPACITY IS REQUIRED?* The discharge capacity of the pump in gallons per hour that is needed for satisfactory service. The pump should have enough capacity so that it can deliver the total water requirement in 2 hours of continuous operation. See table of water requirements at right.

AVERAGE WATER REQUIREMENTS FOR GENERAL
SERVICE AROUND THE HOME AND FARM

Each person per day, for all purposes	50 gal.
Each horse, dry cow or beef animal	12 gal.
Each milking cow	35 gal.
Each hog per day	4 gal.
Each sheep per day	2 gal.
Each 100 chickens per day	4 gal.

AVERAGE AMOUNT OF WATER REQUIRED BY
VARIOUS HOME AND YARD FIXTURES

Drinking fountain, continuously flowing	50 to 100 gal. per day
Each shower bath	Up to 60 gal.
To fill bathtub	30 gal.
To flush toilet	6 gal.
To fill lavatory	2 gal.
To sprinkle ¼" of water on each 1000 square feet of lawn	160 gal.
Dish Washing Machine — per load	3 gal.
Automatic washer — per load	Up to 50 gal.
Regeneration of Domestic Water Softener	50-100 gal.

AVERAGE FLOW RATE REQUIREMENTS BY
VARIOUS FIXTURES

(g.p.m. equals gal. per minute; g.p.h. equals gal. per hour)

Shower	4 to 6 g.p.m.
Bathtub	4 to 8 g.p.m.
Toilet	4 to 5 g.p.m.
Lavatory	1 to 3 g.p.m.
Kitchen sink	2 to 3 g.p.m.
½" hose and nozzle	200 g.p.h.
¾" hose and nozzle	300 g.p.h.
Lawn sprinkler	120 g.p.h.

WATER EQUIPMENT DIVISION
STA-RITE INDUSTRIES, INC., DELAVAN, WISCONSIN

S1685

EFFECTIVE	SUPERSEDES
Feb. 1983	Feb. 1970

TROUBLE SHOOTING GUIDE — JET PUMPS

PUMP WON'T START OR RUN

CAUSE OF TROUBLE	HOW TO CHECK	HOW TO CORRECT
1. Blown fuse.	Check to see if fuse is OK.	If blown, replace with fuse of proper size.
2. Low line voltage.	Use voltmeter to check pressure switch or terminals nearest pump.	If voltage under recommended minimum, check size of wiring from main switch on property. If OK, contact power company.
3. Loose, broken, or incorrect wiring.	Check wiring circuit against diagram. See that all connections are tight and that no short circuits exist because of worn insulation, crossed wire, etc.	Rewire any incorrect circuits. Tighten connections, replace defective wires.
4. Defective motor.	Check to see that switch is closed.	Repair or take to motor service station.
5. Defective pressure switch.	Check switch setting. Examine switch contacts for dirt or excessive wear.	Adjust switch settings. Clean contacts with emory cloth if dirty.
6. Tubing to pressure switch plugged.	Remove tubing and blow through it.	Clean or replace if plugged.
7. Impeller or seal.	Turn off power, then use screwdriver to try to turn impeller or motor.	If impeller won't turn, remove housing and locate source of binding.
8. Defective start capacitor.	Use an ohmmeter to check resistance across capacitor. Needle should jump when contact is made. No movement means an open capacitor; no resistance means capacitor is shorted.	Replace capacitor or take motor to service station.
9. Motor shorted out.	If fuse blows when pump is started (and external wiring is OK) motor is shorted.	Replace motor.

MOTOR OVERHEATS AND OVERLOAD TRIPS OUT

CAUSE OF TROUBLE	HOW TO CHECK	HOW TO CORRECT
1. Incorrect line voltage.	Use voltmeter to check at pressure switch or terminals nearest pump.	If voltage under recommended minimum, check size of wiring from main switch on property. If OK, contact power company.
2. Motor wired incorrectly.	Check motor wiring diagram.	Reconnect for proper voltage as per wiring diagram.
3. Inadequate ventilation.	Check air temperature where pump is located. If over 100°F., overload may be tripping on external heat.	Provide adequate ventilation or move pump.
4. Prolonged low pressure delivery.	Continuous operation at very low pressure places heavy overload on pump. This can cause overload protection to trip.	Install globe valve on discharge line and throttle to increase pressure.

TROUBLE SHOOTING GUIDE — JET PUMPS

PUMP STARTS AND STOPS TOO OFTEN

CAUSE OF TROUBLE	HOW TO CHECK	HOW TO CORRECT
1. Leak in pressure tank.	Apply soapy water to entire surface above water line. If bubbles appear, air is leaking from tank.	Repair leaks or replace tank.
2. Defective air volume control.	This will lead to a waterlogged tank. Make sure control is operating properly. If not, remove and examine for plugging.	Clean or replace defective control.
3. Faulty pressure switch.	Check switch setting. Examine switch contacts for dirt or excessive wear.	Adjust switch settings. Clean contacts with emory cloth if dirty.
4. Leak on discharge side of system.	Make sure all fixtures in plumbing system are shut off. Then check all units (especially ballcocks) for leaks. Listen for noise of water running.	Repair leaks as necessary.
5. Leak on suction side of system.	On shallow well units, install pressure gauge on suction side. On deep well systems, attach a pressure gauge to the pump. Close the discharge line valve. Then, using a bicycle pump or air compressor, apply about 30 psi pressure to the system. If the system will not hold this pressure when the compressor is shut off, there is a leak on the suction side.	Make sure above ground connections are tight. Then repeat test. If necessary, pull piping and repair leak.
6. Leak in foot valve.	Pull piping and examine foot valve.	Repair or replace defective valve.

PUMP WON'T SHUT OFF

CAUSE OF TROUBLE	HOW TO CHECK	HOW TO CORRECT
1. Wrong pressure switch setting or setting "drift".	Lower switch setting. If pump shuts off, this was the trouble.	Adjust switch to proper setting.
2. Defective pressure switch.	Arcing may have caused switch contacts to "weld" together in closed position. Examine points and other parts of switch for defects.	Replace switch if defective.
3. Tubing to pressure switch plugged.	Remove tubing and blow through it.	Clean or replace if plugged.
4. Loss of prime.	When no water is delivered, check prime of pump and well piping.	Reprime if necessary.
5. Low well level.	Check well depth against pump performance table to make sure pump and ejector are properly sized.	If undersized, replace pump or ejector.
6. Plugged ejector.	Remove ejector and inspect.	Clean and reinstall if dirty.

TROUBLE SHOOTING GUIDE — JET PUMPS

PUMP OPERATES BUT DELIVERS LITTLE OR NO WATER		
CAUSE OF TROUBLE	**HOW TO CHECK**	**HOW TO CORRECT**
1. Low line voltage.	Use voltmeter to check at pressure switch or terminals nearest pump.	If voltage under recommended minimum, check size of wiring from main switch on property. If OK, contact power company.
2. System incompletely primed.	When no water is delivered, check prime of pump and well piping.	Reprime if necessary.
3. Air lock in suction line.	Check horizontal piping between well and pump. If it does not pitch upward from well to pump, an air lock may form.	Rearrange piping to eliminate air lock.
4. Undersized piping.	If system delivery is low, the discharge piping and/or plumbing lines may be undersized. Refigure friction loss.	Replace undersized piping or install pump with higher capacity.
5. Leak in air volume control or tubing.	Disconnect air volume control tubing at pump and plug hole. If capacity increases, a leak exists in the tubing of control.	Tighten all fittings and replace control if necessary.
6. Pressure regulating valve stuck or incorrectly set. (Deep well only.)	Check valve setting. Inspect valve for defects.	Reset, clean, or replace valve as needed.
7. Leak on suction side of system.	On shallow well units, install pressure gauge on suction side. On deep well systems, attach a pressure gauge to the pump. Close the discharge line valve. Then, using a bicycle pump or air compressor, apply about 30 psi pressure to the system. If the system will not hold this pressure when the compressor is shut off, there is a leak on the suction side.	Make sure above ground connections are tight. Then repeat test. If necessary, pull piping and repair leak.
8. Low well level.	Check well depth against pump performance table to make sure pump and ejector are properly sized.	If undersized, replace pump or ejector.
9. Wrong pump-ejector combination.	Check pump and ejector models against manufacturer's performance tables.	Replace ejector if wrong model is being used.
10. Low well capacity.	Shut off pump and allow well to recover. Restart pump and note whether delivery drops after continuous operation.	If well is "weak," lower ejector (deep well pumps), use a tail pipe (deep well pumps), or switch from shallow well to deep well equipment.
11. Plugged ejector.	Remove ejector and inspect.	Clean and reinstall if dirty.
12. Defective or plugged foot valve and/or strainer.	Pull foot valve and inspect. Partial clogging will reduce delivery. Complete clogging will result in no water flow. A defective foot valve may cause pump to lose prime, resulting in no delivery.	Clean, repair, or replace as needed.
13. Worn or defective pump parts or plugged impeller.	Low delivery may result from wear on impeller or other pump parts. Disassemble and inspect.	Replace worn parts or entire pump. Clean parts if required.

TROUBLE SHOOTING GUIDE — SUBMERSIBLE PUMPS

FUSES BLOW OR CIRCUIT BREAKER TRIPS WHEN MOTOR IS STARTED		
CAUSE OF TROUBLE	**HOW TO CHECK**	**HOW TO CORRECT**
1. Incorrect line voltage	Check the line voltage terminals in the control box (or connection box in the case of the 2-wire models) with a voltmeter. Make sure that the voltage is within the minimum-maximum range prescribed by the manufacturer.	If the voltage is incorrect, contact the power company to have it corrected.
2. Defective control box: a. Defective wiring.	Check out all motor and powerline wiring in the control box, following the wiring diagram found inside the box. See that all connections are tight and that no short circuits exist because of worn insulation, crossed wires, etc.	Rewire any incorrect circuits. Tighten loose connections. Replace worn wires.
b. Incorrect components	Check all control box components to see that they are the type and size specified for the pump in the manufacturers' literature. In previous service work, the wrong components may have been installed.	Replace any incorrect component with the size and type recommended by the manufacturer.
c. Defective starting capacitor (skip for 2-wire models).	Using an ohmmeter, determine the resistance across the starting capacitor. When contact is made, the ohmmeter needle should jump at once, then move up more slowly. No movement indicates an open capacitor (or defective relay points); no resistance means that the capacitor is shorted.	Replace defective starting capacitor.
d. Defective relay (skip for 2-wire models).	Using an ohmmeter, check the relay coil. Its resistance should be as shown in the manufacturer's literature. Recheck ohmmeter reading across starting capacitor. With a good capacitor, no movement of the needle indicates defective relay points.	If coil resistance is incorrect or points defective, replace relay.
3. Defective pressure switch.	Check the voltage across the pressure switch points. If less than the line voltage determined in "1" above, the switch points are causing low voltage by making imperfect contact.	Clean points with a mild abrasive cloth or replace pressure switch.
4. Pump in crooked well.	If wedged into a crooked well, the motor and pump may become misaligned, resulting in a locked rotor.	If the pump does not rotate freely, it must be pulled and the well straightened.
5. Defective motor winding or cable: a. Shorted or open motor winding.	Check the resistance of the motor winding by using an ohmmeter on the proper terminals in the control box (see manufacturer's wiring diagram). The resistance should match the ohms specified in the manufacturer's data sheet. If too low, the motor winding may be shorted; if the ohmmeter needle doesn't move, indicating high or infinite resistance, there is an open circuit in the motor winding.	If the motor winding is defective — shorted or open — the pump must be pulled and the motor repaired.
b. Grounded cable or winding.	Ground one lead of the ohmmeter onto the drop pipe or shell casing, then touch the other lead to each motor wire terminal. If the ohmmeter needle moves appreciably when this is done, there is a ground in either the cable or the motor winding.	Pull the pump and inspect the cable for damage. Replace damaged cable. If cable checks OK, the motor winding is grounded.
6. Pump sand locked.	Make pump run backwards by interchanging main and start winding (black and red) motor leads at control box.	Pull pump, disassemble and clean. Before replacing, make sure that sand has settled in well. If well is chronically sandy, a submersible should not be used.

TROUBLE SHOOTING GUIDE — SUBMERSIBLE PUMPS

PUMP OPERATES BUT DELIVERS LITTLE OR NO WATER		
CAUSE OF TROUBLE	**HOW TO CHECK**	**HOW TO CORRECT**
1. Pump may be air locked.	Stop and start pump several times, waiting about one minute between cycles. If pump then resumes normal delivery, air lock was the trouble.	If this test fails to correct the trouble, proceed as below.
2. Water level in well too low.	Well production may be too low for pump capacity. Restrict flow of pump output, wait for well to recover, and start pump.	If partial restriction corrects trouble, leave valve or cock at restricted setting. Otherwise, lower pump in well if depth is sufficient. Do not lower if sand clogging might occur.
3. Discharge line check valve installed backward.	Examine check valve on discharge line to make sure that arrow indicating direction of flow points in right direction.	Reverse valve is necessary.
4. Leak in drop pipe.	Raise pipe and examine for leaks.	Replace damaged section of drop pipe.
5. Pump check valve jammed by drop pipe.	When pump is pulled after completing "4" above, examine connection of drop pipe to pump outlet. If threaded section of drop pipe has been screwed in too far, it may be jamming the pump's check valve in the closed position.	Unscrew drop pipe and cut off portion of threads.
6. Pump intake screen blocked.	The intake screen on the pump may be blocked by sand or mud. Examine.	Clean screen, and when reinstalling pump, make sure that it is located several feet above the well bottom—preferably 10 feet or more.
7. Pump parts worn.	The presence of abrasives in the water may result in excessive wear on the impeller, casing, and other close-clearance parts. Before pulling pump, reduce setting on pressure switch to see if pump shuts off. If it does, worn parts are probably at fault.	Pull pump and replace worn components.
8. Motor shaft loose.	Coupling between motor and pump shaft may have worked loose. Inspect for this after pulling pump and looking for worn components, as in "7" above.	Tighten all connections, set-screws, etc.

TROUBLE SHOOTING GUIDE — SUBMERSIBLE PUMPS

PUMP STARTS TOO FREQUENTLY		
CAUSE OF TROUBLE	**HOW TO CHECK**	**HOW TO CORRECT**
1. Pressure switch defective or out of adjustment.	Check setting on pressure switch and examine for defects.	Reduce pressure setting or replace switch.
2. Leak in pressure tank above water level.	Apply soap solution to entire surface of tank and look for bubbles indicating air escaping.	Repair or replace tank.
3. Leak in plumbing system.	Examine service line to house and distribution branches for leaks.	Repair leaks.
4. Discharge line check valve leaking.	Remove and examine.	Replace if defective.
5. Air volume control plugged.	Remove and inspect air volume control.	Clean or replace.
6. Snifter valve plugged.	Remove and inspect snifter valve.	Clean or replace.

MOTOR DOES NOT START, BUT FUSES DON'T BLOW		
CAUSE OF TROUBLE	**HOW TO CHECK**	**HOW TO CORRECT**
1. Overload protection out.	Check fuses or circuit breaker to see that they are operable.	If fuses are blown, replace. If breaker is tripped, reset.
2. No power.	Check power supply to control box (or overload protection box) by placing a voltmeter across incoming power lines. Voltage should approximate nominal line voltage.	If no power is reaching box, contact power company for service.
3. Defective control box.	Examine wiring in control box to make sure all contacts are tight. With a voltmeter, check voltage at motor wire terminals. If no voltage is shown at terminals, wiring is defective in control box.	Correct faulty wiring or tighten loose contacts.
4. Defective pressure switch.	With a voltmeter, check voltage across pressure switch while the switch is closed. If the voltage drop is equal to the line voltage, the switch is not making contact.	Clean points or replace switch.

TROUBLE SHOOTING GUIDE — SUBMERSIBLE PUMPS

FUSES BLOW WHEN MOTOR IS RUNNING		
CAUSE OF TROUBLE	**HOW TO CHECK**	**HOW TO CORRECT**
1. Incorrect voltage.	Check line voltage terminals in the control box (or connection box in the case of 2-wire models) with a voltmeter. Make sure that the voltage is within the minimum-maximum range prescribed by the manufacturer.	If voltage is incorrect, contact power company for service.
2. Overheated overload protection box.	If sunlight or other source of heat has made box too hot, circuit breakers may trip or fuses blow. If box is hot to the touch, this may be the problem.	Ventilate or shade box, or remove from source of heat.
3. Defective control box components (skip this for 2-wire models).	Using an ohmmeter, determine the resistance across the running capacitor. When contact is made, the ohmmeter needle should jump at once, then move up more slowly. No movement indicates an open capacitor (or defective relay points); no resistance means that the capacitor is shorted. Using an ohmmeter, check the relay coil. Its resistance should be as shown in the manufacturer's literature. Recheck ohmmeter reading across running capacitor. With a good capacitor, no movement of the needle indicates relay points.	Replace defective components.
4. Defective motor winding or cable.	Check the resistance of the motor winding by using an ohmmeter on the proper terminals in the control box (see manufacturer's wiring diagram). The resistance should match the ohms specified in the manufacturer's data sheet. If too low, the motor winding may be shorted; if the ohmmeter needle doesn't move, indicating high or infinite resistance, there is an open circuit in the motor winding. Ground one lead of the ohmmeter onto the drop pipe or shell casing, then touch the other lead to each motor wire terminal. If the ohmmeter needle moves appreciably when this is done, there is a ground in either the cable or the motor winding.	If neither cable or winding is defective—shorted, grounded, or open—pump must be pulled and serviced.
5. Pump becomes sand-locked.	If the fuses blow while the pump is operating, sand or grit may have become wedged in the impeller, causing the rotor to lock. To check this, pull the pump.	Pull pump, disassemble, and clean. Before replacing, make sure that sand has settled in well. If well is chronically sandy, a submersible should not be used.

TROUBLE SHOOTING GUIDE — SUBMERSIBLE PUMPS

PUMP WON'T SHUT OFF

CAUSE OF TROUBLE	HOW TO CHECK	HOW TO CORRECT
1. Defective pressure switch.	Arcing may have caused pressure switch points to "weld" in closed position. Examine points and other parts of switch for defects.	Clean points or replace switch.
2. Water level in well too low.	Well production may be too low for pump capacity. Restrict flow of pump output, wait for well to recover, and start pump.	If partial restriction corrects trouble, leave valve or cock at restricted setting. Otherwise, lower pump in well if depth is sufficient. Do not lower if sand clogging might occur.
3. Leak in drop line.	Raise pipe and examine for leaks.	Replace damaged section of drop pipe.
4. Pump parts worn.	The presence of abrasives in the water may result in excessive wear on the impeller, casing, and other close-clearance parts. Before pulling pump, reduce setting on pressure switch to see if pump shuts off. If it does, worn parts are probably at fault.	Pull pump and replace worn components.

INSTRUCTIONS ON INSTALLATION
and SERVICE INFORMATION of the

DRYMASTER SUMPLESS PUMP™

manufactured by **DRYMASTER PUMP CO.**

15580 TELEGRAPH ROAD, DETROIT, MICHIGAN 48239

NOTICE TO INSTALLER: Please read and follow all instructions herein, in addition to brochure attached. Then leave both for owner's use, as well as the Warranty Registration Card.

NOTICE TO OWNER: Please read completely. If any information is not clear, call your installing contractor now. He will be happy to assist you.

MODELS AVAILABLE

- DM-4 fits onto top of 4" S/D plastic pipe as shown.
- If a cast iron pipe or crock pipe riser is desired, properly align and connect 4" S/D plastic pipe to it, allowing at least 4" of plastic pipe above the floor.

  NOTE: The DM-4 is designed for depth as shown in instructions. If a longer unit is desired, order a number DM-4-12, which denotes 12" longer than regular (therefore changing the measurement on the drawing from 21" to 33").

INSTALLATION

- Drymaster Sumpless Pumps are packed ready for easy installation. When unpacking, examine for possible damage and report immediately to seller. Care should be taken not to chip or scratch the corrosion-resistant epoxy coating.

- Install as shown on drawing. Please Note: Voltage over or under in excess of 10% can be detrimental to motor and controls.

- If a larger reservoir of water is desired than shown, the last 10 to 15 feet of seepage line may be lowered to desired amount, and a longer drymaster must be ordered to fit. (Model #DM-4-12).

- If the seepage line is higher than shown (21") merely raise Drymaster, using clamp to tighten at correct position. Nothing else to adjust. Note: The diaphragm which operates

the built-in motor switch is spring-loaded with an adjustable nut on the top of the housing. This nut adjusts the water pressure at which the switch operates and is preset at the factory. If it becomes necessary to change this adjustment it can be done with an Allen set screw wrench. This will prevent tampering.

- If the Drymaster is installed at the same time as seepage line is installed, remove any sand and debris in bottom of reservoir prior to installing riser above tee. If the Drymaster is installed at a later time, if there is any sand or debris, which is infrequent, it is easily removed by using a post hole auger.

- Discharge piping should be installed in a manner to keep the Drymaster plumb.

- Eliminate noise transmission by installing appropriate rigid plastic tubing so as not to touch floor joists, etc.

- Built-in brass and neoprene check valve — No need to install additional check valve in discharge pipe.

- Once Dryamster is inserted into riser do not turn motor or Drymaster because of possibly twisting the air tube.

- Designed for domestic seepage water removal; not for septic tank use.

- Odor-tite in all respects.

- Refer to descriptive brochure attached for additional information.

- Protect pump from freezing.

- Once installed, merely plug in service cord — Drymaster is ready to go! Use grounding pin (supplied) for your safety and install wiring in accordance with all national and local electrical codes.

- Run water into seepage line until pump goes on. Shut water off. Let pump run, pumping water out, until it shuts off by itself.

(continued on other side)

Copyright 1972
Drymaster Pump Co.
Detroit, Michigan
Form No. 57011

SERVICE INFORMATION

For best results, keep reservoir and pump clean. It is recommended to periodically clean any debris from the riser. This is accomplished merely by lifting entire unit out of riser and turning unit over so that the debris cup will empty out into receptical, and reinstalling. Usually this need be done once or twice in the first months after a new installation. Thereafter, it would be wise to check, but probably every six months would be sufficient. After cleaning, flush with water.

Use manual turn-on switch at any time you want to test the unit. This proves motor is operating, but if you want to be positive water is being pumped, run water into seepage line until pump goes on. Shut water, Let pump run, pumping water out, until it shuts off by itself. If a motor problem develops bring to motor manufacturer's closest office (address list enclosed). If pump operates infrequently, due to abnormally dry conditions, water may rise and fill air tube, preventing automatic starting. Merely remove entire unit and allow water to drain out of air tube.

CAUTION
Pump will not function properly unless there is 3" of space between the bottom of the pump and the bottom of the reservoir (cemented cap).

ROUGH-IN AND INSTALL, FOLLOWING DIRECTIONS AS SHOWN BELOW

WATER DISCHARGED AS PER CODE

BASEMENT WALL

DRYMASTER SUMPLESS PUMP
DM-4
INSTALL AS PER DRAWING
ROUGH-IN PLASTIC RISER 4" ABOVE FINISH FLOOR LEVEL, AND BE SURE TO REMOVE ALL ROUGH EDGES FROM PIPE BEFORE INSTALLATION.

AIR TUBE
DO NOT CEMENT CAP, TIGHTEN 4 SCREWS FOR ODOR PROTECTION

4"

BASEMENT FLOOR

21"

PLASTIC 4" RISER
MUST BE VERTICALLY INSTALLED

SEEPAGE LINE

17" MINIMUM

DEBRIS CUP

PUMP

4" CEMENTED CAP

CAUTION! ALWAYS DISCONNECT THE ELECTRICAL PLUG BEFORE HANDLING THE DRYMASTER.

IF PUMP DOES NOT RUN

- Check electric fuse. If blown, replace with 15 AMP. Reg. fuse. (or reset breaker).
- Possible indication that the unit is locked. Remove dust cover over the end of the motor shaft and by using a screw driver check to see if motor is free by turning screw driver several times clockwise and counter-clockwise.
- Remove pump from riser and check over carefully for foreign objects inside reservoir and pump.

- Clean as follows: Clean screen on bottom of pump — use brush, making sure that all the holes are open. If further cleaning is required, remove screen by loosening two screws on the side; then pry off cover on bottom of pump carefully with screw driver. Remove pump assembly by pulling assembly from its enclosure. Clean all passageways. Clean debris cup. Then replace.

IF PUMP RUNS, BUT DOES NOT PUMP WATER

- Pump will not discharge water if the head, which is the vertical distance from pump to discharge outlet, is more than 23 feet.
- Check for debris and clean if necessary (see above).

- Be sure that the check valve is not stuck. Clean out discharge line for possible icing conditions.
- If pump is pumping water but is in low volume, check to see if debris cup, pump, screen, or bottom of reservoir is plugged with sand or debris. Clean as described above.

DRYMASTER PUMP CO.
15580 TELEGRAPH ROAD, DETROIT, MICHIGAN 48239
313-255-3930

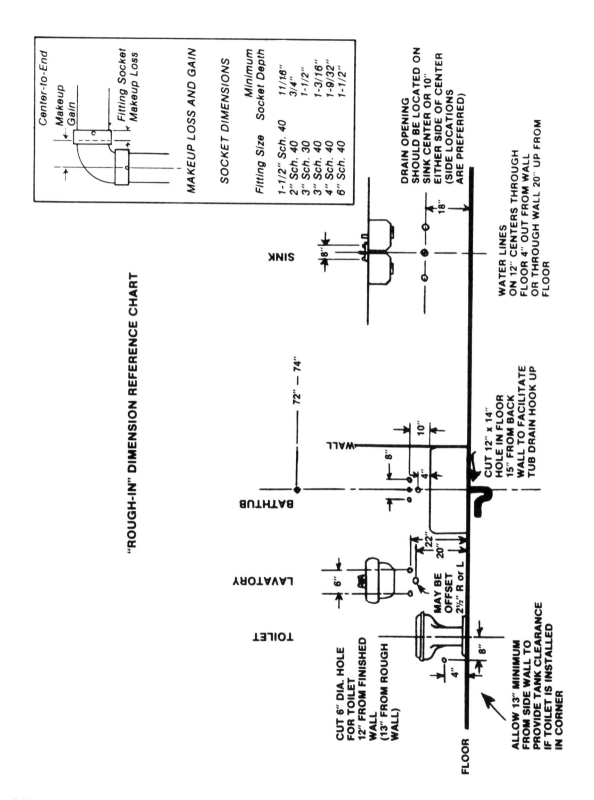

"ROUGH-IN" DIMENSION REFERENCE CHART

MAKEUP LOSS AND GAIN

Center-to-End
Makeup Gain
Fitting Socket Makeup Loss

SOCKET DIMENSIONS

Fitting Size	Minimum Socket Depth
1-1/2" Sch. 40	11/16"
2" Sch. 40	3/4"
3" Sch. 30	1-1/2"
3" Sch. 40	1-3/16"
4" Sch. 40	1-9/32"
6" Sch. 40	1-1/2"

SINK

8"

DRAIN OPENING
SHOULD BE LOCATED ON
SINK CENTER OR 10"
EITHER SIDE OF CENTER
(SIDE LOCATIONS
ARE PREFERED)

18"

WATER LINES
ON 12" CENTERS THROUGH
FLOOR 4" OUT FROM WALL
OR THROUGH WALL 20" UP FROM
FLOOR

72" — 74"

WALL

BATHTUB

10"

8"

4"

CUT 12" x 14"
HOLE IN FLOOR
15" FROM BACK
WALL TO FACILITATE
TUB DRAIN HOOK UP

LAVATORY

6"

22"

20"

MAY BE
OFFSET
2½" R or L

TOILET

8"

4"

CUT 6" DIA. HOLE
FOR TOILET
12" FROM FINISHED
WALL
(13" FROM ROUGH
WALL)

FLOOR

ALLOW 13" MINIMUM
FROM SIDE WALL TO
PROVIDE TANK CLEARANCE
IF TOILET IS INSTALLED
IN CORNER

240

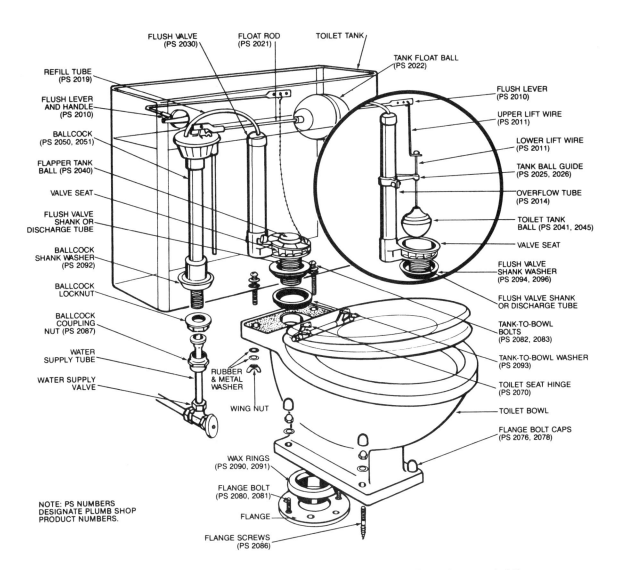

FLUSH VALVE
(PS 2030)

FLOAT ROD
(PS 2021)

TOILET TANK

TANK FLOAT BALL
(PS 2022)

REFILL TUBE
(PS 2019)

FLUSH LEVER
AND HANDLE
(PS 2010)

BALLCOCK
(PS 2050, 2051)

FLAPPER TANK
BALL (PS 2040)

VALVE SEAT

FLUSH VALVE
SHANK OR
DISCHARGE TUBE

BALLCOCK
SHANK WASHER
(PS 2092)

BALLCOCK
LOCKNUT

BALLCOCK
COUPLING
NUT (PS 2087)

WATER
SUPPLY TUBE

WATER SUPPLY
VALVE

RUBBER
& METAL
WASHER

WING NUT

FLUSH LEVER
(PS 2010)

UPPER LIFT WIRE
(PS 2011)

LOWER LIFT WIRE
(PS 2011)

TANK BALL GUIDE
(PS 2025, 2026)

OVERFLOW TUBE
(PS 2014)

TOILET TANK
BALL (PS 2041, 2045)

VALVE SEAT

FLUSH VALVE
SHANK WASHER
(PS 2094, 2096)

FLUSH VALVE SHANK
OR DISCHARGE TUBE

TANK-TO-BOWL
BOLTS
(PS 2082, 2083)

TANK-TO-BOWL WASHER
(PS 2093)

TOILET SEAT HINGE
(PS 2070)

TOILET BOWL

FLANGE BOLT CAPS
(PS 2076, 2078)

WAX RINGS
(PS 2090, 2091)

FLANGE BOLT
(PS 2080, 2081)

FLANGE

FLANGE SCREWS
(PS 2086)

NOTE: PS NUMBERS
DESIGNATE PLUMB SHOP
PRODUCT NUMBERS.

Plumb Shop also offers a complete line of ballcock repair kits.

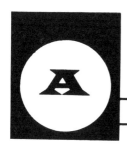

ADVANCE CONCRETE PRODUCTS CO.

975 NORTH MILFORD ROAD • HIGHLAND, MICHIGAN 48031 • PHONE: 887-4173 OR 474-6539

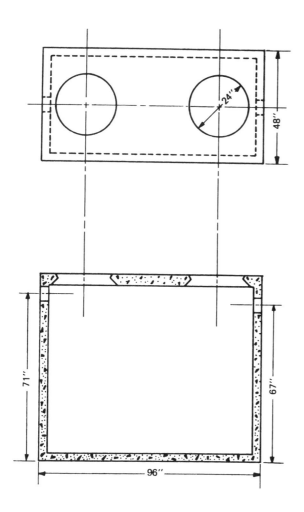

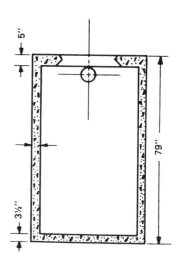

1,000 Gallon Regular Septic Tank

To be used where normal conditions exist.

Approximate Weight 8,000 lbs.

ADVANCE CONCRETE PRODUCTS CO.

975 NORTH MILFORD ROAD • HIGHLAND, MICHIGAN 48031 • PHONE: 887-4173 OR 474-6539

1-800-824-8351

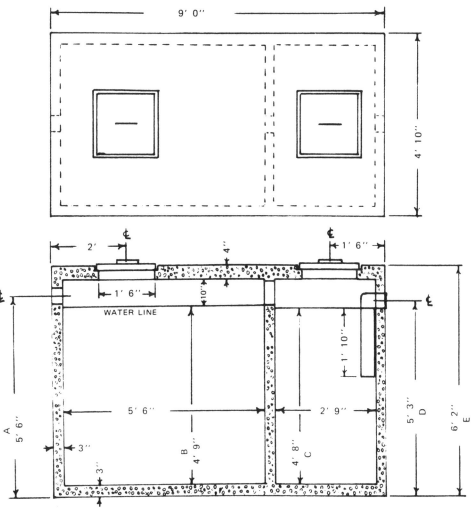

1250 Gallon Double Compartment Septic Tank — Shown

1000 Gallon Double Compartment Septic Tank — A Dimension 4 Ft. 7 In.
                                              B Dimension 3 Ft. 10 In.
                                              C Dimension 3 Ft. 9 In.
                                              D Dimension 4 Ft. 2 In.
                                              E Dimension 5 Ft. 3 In.

ADVANCE CONCRETE PRODUCTS CO.

975 NORTH MILFORD ROAD • HIGHLAND, MICHIGAN 48031 • PHONE: 887-4173 OR 474-6539

1-800-824-8351

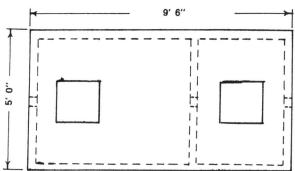

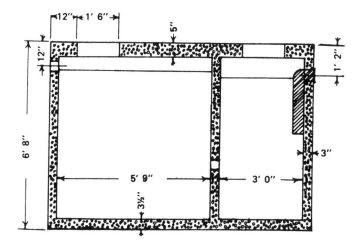

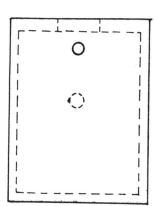

1,500 Gallon Double Compartment Septic Tank (A Double Protection System)

Recommended for Homes with Garbage Disposals

Assists in increasing life of Drain Field by reducing chances of sludge entering Field

Approximate Weight: 12,400 lbs.

244

KITCHEN FAUCETS

MOEN SINGLE HANDLE (LEVER) KITCHEN DECK
Models 7300, 7305 and 7310

CHATEAU SINGLE HANDLE (LEVER) KITCHEN DECK
Models 7531-A, 7533-A, 7536-A, and 7538-A

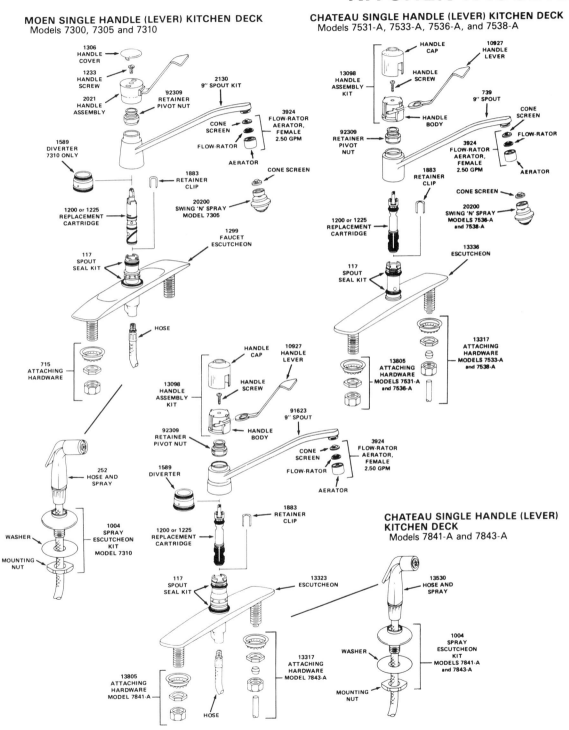

1306 HANDLE COVER

1233 HANDLE SCREW

2021 HANDLE ASSEMBLY

2130 9'' SPOUT KIT

92309 RETAINER PIVOT NUT

CONE SCREEN

FLOW-RATOR

AERATOR

3924 FLOW-RATOR AERATOR, FEMALE 2.50 GPM

1589 DIVERTER 7310 ONLY

1883 RETAINER CLIP

CONE SCREEN

1200 or 1225 REPLACEMENT CARTRIDGE

20200 SWING 'N' SPRAY MODEL 7305

1299 FAUCET ESCUTCHEON

117 SPOUT SEAL KIT

HOSE

715 ATTACHING HARDWARE

252 HOSE AND SPRAY

WASHER

1004 SPRAY ESCUTCHEON KIT MODEL 7310

MOUNTING NUT

HANDLE CAP

10927 HANDLE LEVER

13098 HANDLE ASSEMBLY KIT

HANDLE SCREW

92309 RETAINER PIVOT NUT

HANDLE BODY

91623 9'' SPOUT

CONE SCREEN

FLOW-RATOR

AERATOR

3924 FLOW-RATOR AERATOR, FEMALE 2.50 GPM

1589 DIVERTER

1883 RETAINER CLIP

1200 or 1225 REPLACEMENT CARTRIDGE

117 SPOUT SEAL KIT

13323 ESCUTCHEON

13805 ATTACHING HARDWARE MODEL 7841-A

13317 ATTACHING HARDWARE MODEL 7843-A

HOSE

HANDLE CAP

10927 HANDLE LEVER

13098 HANDLE ASSEMBLY KIT

HANDLE SCREW

HANDLE BODY

739 9'' SPOUT

CONE SCREEN

FLOW-RATOR

AERATOR

3924 FLOW-RATOR AERATOR, FEMALE 2.50 GPM

92309 RETAINER PIVOT NUT

1883 RETAINER CLIP

CONE SCREEN

20200 SWING 'N' SPRAY MODELS 7536-A and 7538-A

1200 or 1225 REPLACEMENT CARTRIDGE

13336 ESCUTCHEON

117 SPOUT SEAL KIT

13805 ATTACHING HARDWARE MODELS 7531-A and 7536-A

13317 ATTACHING HARDWARE MODELS 7533-A and 7538-A

CHATEAU SINGLE HANDLE (LEVER) KITCHEN DECK
Models 7841-A and 7843-A

13530 HOSE AND SPRAY

WASHER

1004 SPRAY ESCUTCHEON KIT MODELS 7841-A and 7843-A

MOUNTING NUT

BAR SINK FAUCETS

CHATEAU SINGLE HANDLE (LEVER) BAR SINK
Model 4901

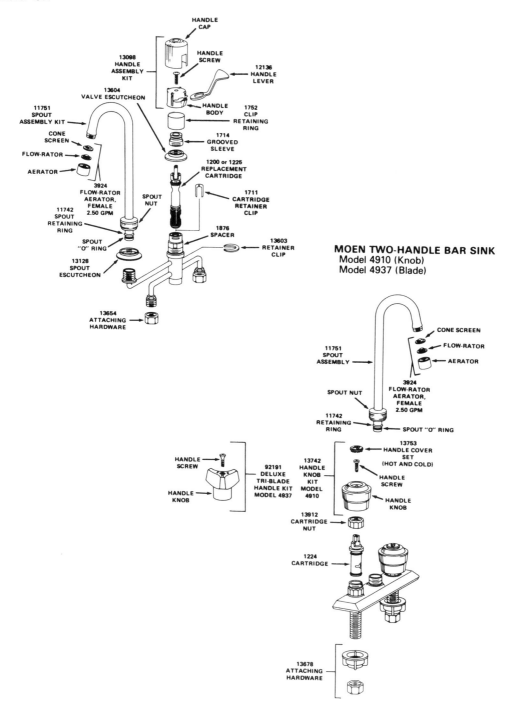

MOEN TWO-HANDLE BAR SINK
Model 4910 (Knob)
Model 4937 (Blade)

246

LAVATORY FAUCETS

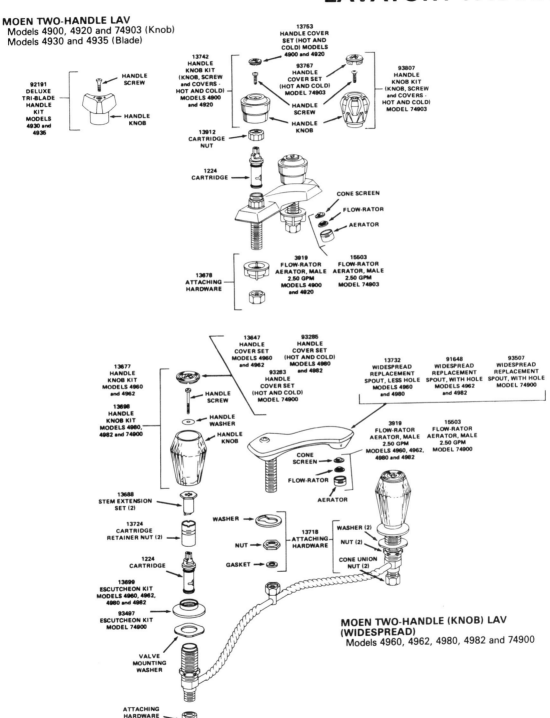

MOEN TWO-HANDLE LAV
Models 4900, 4920 and 74903 (Knob)
Models 4930 and 4935 (Blade)

92191
DELUXE
TRI-BLADE
HANDLE
KIT
MODELS
4930 and
4935

HANDLE
SCREW

HANDLE
KNOB

13742
HANDLE
KNOB KIT
(KNOB, SCREW
and COVERS -
HOT AND COLD)
MODELS 4900
and 4920

13753
HANDLE COVER
SET (HOT AND
COLD) MODELS
4900 and 4920

93767
HANDLE
COVER SET
(HOT AND COLD)
MODEL 74903

93807
HANDLE
KNOB KIT
(KNOB, SCREW
and COVERS -
HOT AND COLD)
MODEL 74903

HANDLE
SCREW

HANDLE
KNOB

13912
CARTRIDGE
NUT

1224
CARTRIDGE

CONE SCREEN

FLOW-RATOR

AERATOR

13678
ATTACHING
HARDWARE

3919
FLOW-RATOR
AERATOR, MALE
2.50 GPM
MODELS 4900
and 4920

15503
FLOW-RATOR
AERATOR, MALE
2.50 GPM
MODEL 74903

13647
HANDLE
COVER SET
MODELS 4960
and 4962

93285
HANDLE
COVER SET
(HOT AND COLD)
MODELS 4980
and 4982

93283
HANDLE
COVER SET
(HOT AND COLD)
MODEL 74900

13732
WIDESPREAD
REPLACEMENT
SPOUT, LESS HOLE
MODELS 4960
and 4980

91648
WIDESPREAD
REPLACEMENT
SPOUT, WITH HOLE
MODELS 4962
and 4982

93507
WIDESPREAD
REPLACEMENT
SPOUT, WITH HOLE
MODEL 74900

13677
HANDLE
KNOB KIT
MODELS 4960
and 4962

13698
HANDLE
KNOB KIT
MODELS 4980,
4982 and 74900

HANDLE
SCREW

HANDLE
WASHER

HANDLE
KNOB

3919
FLOW-RATOR
AERATOR, MALE
2.50 GPM
MODELS 4960, 4962,
4980 and 4982

15503
FLOW-RATOR
AERATOR, MALE
2.50 GPM
MODEL 74900

CONE
SCREEN

FLOW-RATOR

AERATOR

13688
STEM EXTENSION
SET (2)

13724
CARTRIDGE
RETAINER NUT (2)

1224
CARTRIDGE

13699
ESCUTCHEON KIT
MODELS 4960, 4962,
4980 and 4982

93497
ESCUTCHEON KIT
MODEL 74900

WASHER

NUT

GASKET

13718
ATTACHING
HARDWARE

WASHER (2)

NUT (2)

CONE UNION
NUT (2)

VALVE
MOUNTING
WASHER

ATTACHING
HARDWARE

**MOEN TWO-HANDLE (KNOB) LAV
(WIDESPREAD)**
Models 4960, 4962, 4980, 4982 and 74900

TUB/SHOWER VALVES

MOEN SINGLE-HANDLE (KNOB) TUB/SHOWER
Models 2200, 2205, 2210, 2215, 2220, 2225, 2230, 2235, 2250, 2270, 2275, 72246, 72248, 72252, 72253, 72254, 72255, 72256 and 72258

MOEN SINGLE-HANDLE (KNOB) TUB/SHOWER WITH PUSH BUTTON DIVERTER
Models 2400, 2415, 2417, 2420, 2435, 2450 and 2470

1922
CHECK STOPS
(IPS-CC SUPPLY)
MODELS 2270,
2275 and 2470

883
RETAINER
CLIP

10089
STOP TUBE
2200 and
2400 SERIES

15536
STOP TUBE
MODELS 72246, 72248,
72252 and 72253

15579
STOP TUBE
MODELS 72254
and 72255

14092
STOP TUBE
MODELS 72256
and 72258

1200 or 1225
REPLACEMENT
CARTRIDGE

512
CHECK STOPS
(IPS-IPS SUPPLY)
MODELS 2250
and 2450

10510
ADJUSTABLE
TEMPERATURE
LIMIT STOP

1394
PUSHBUTTON
DIVERTER
ASSEMBLY
(LONG)
2400 SERIES

13106
ESCUTCHEON
2200 SERIES

13107
ESCUTCHEON
2400 SERIES

15528
ESCUTCHEON
SCREWS (2)
2200 and 2400 SERIES

15572
HANDLE
ATTACHING KIT
(HANDLE SCREW
and HANDLE WASHER)

15541
ESCUTCHEON
MODELS 72246
and 72248

15345
ESCUTCHEON
MODELS 72256
and 72258

15539
ESCUTCHEON
MODELS 72252
and 72253

15589
ESCUTCHEON
MODELS 72254
and 72255

15529
ESCUTCHEON
SCREWS (2)
MODELS 72246,
and 72248

14093
ESCUTCHEON
SCREWS (2)
MODELS 72256
and 72258

13094
HANDLE
ASSEMBLY KIT
2200 and 2400 SERIES

13127
HANDLE
ASSEMBLY
KIT
MODELS 72246, 72248,
72252 and 72253

15508
HANDLE
ASSEMBLY KIT
MODELS 72254, 72255,
72256 and 72258

15529
ESCUTCHEON
SCREWS (2)
MODELS 72252
and 72253

15399
ESCUTCHEON
SCREWS (2)
MODELS 72254
and 72255

15043
BEZEL CAP
72200 SERIES

15506
BEZEL CAP
2200 and
2400 SERIES

MOEN SINGLE-HANDLE (LEVER) TUB/SHOWER
Models 72240, 72241, 72242, 72243, 72244, 72245, 72250 and 72251

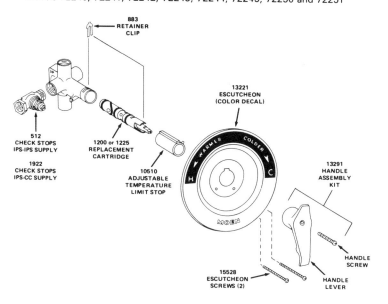

883
RETAINER
CLIP

512
CHECK STOPS
IPS-IPS SUPPLY

1922
CHECK STOPS
IPS-CC SUPPLY

1200 or 1225
REPLACEMENT
CARTRIDGE

10510
ADJUSTABLE
TEMPERATURE
LIMIT STOP

13221
ESCUTCHEON
(COLOR DECAL)

13291
HANDLE
ASSEMBLY
KIT

HANDLE
SCREW

HANDLE
LEVER

15528
ESCUTCHEON
SCREWS (2)

248

LAVATORY AND TUB WASTES

LAVATORY WASTE ASSEMBLY
Model 10790 — Chrome
Model 11730 — Antique Goldtone Brocade
Model 11760 — Antique Brass
Model 15560 — Gold Brocade
— Satin Brass

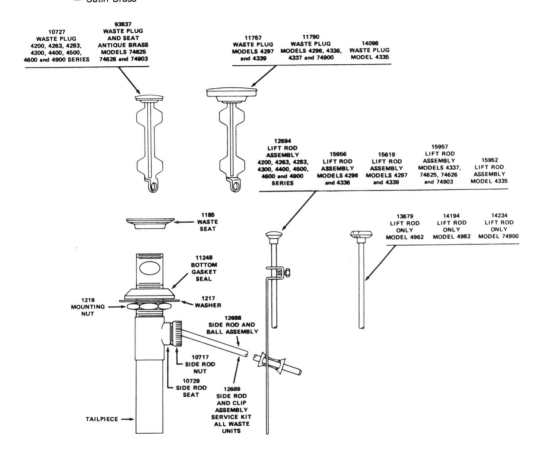

10727
WASTE PLUG
4200, 4263, 4283,
4300, 4400, 4500,
4600 and 4900 SERIES

93837
WASTE PLUG
AND SEAT
ANTIQUE BRASS
MODELS 74625
74626 and 74903

11757
WASTE PLUG
MODELS 4297
and 4339

11790
WASTE PLUG
MODELS 4296, 4336,
4337 and 74900

14098
WASTE PLUG
MODEL 4335

12694
LIFT ROD
ASSEMBLY
4200, 4263, 4283,
4300, 4400, 4500,
4600 and 4900
SERIES

15956
LIFT ROD
ASSEMBLY
MODELS 4296
and 4336

15619
LIFT ROD
ASSEMBLY
MODELS 4297
and 4339

15957
LIFT ROD
ASSEMBLY
MODELS 4337,
74625, 74626
and 74903

15952
LIFT ROD
ASSEMBLY
MODEL 4335

13679
LIFT ROD
ONLY
MODEL 4962

14194
LIFT ROD
ONLY
MODEL 4982

14234
LIFT ROD
ONLY
MODEL 74900

1185
WASTE
SEAT

11248
BOTTOM
GASKET
SEAL

1219
MOUNTING
NUT

1217
WASHER

12688
SIDE ROD AND
BALL ASSEMBLY

10717
SIDE ROD
NUT

10729
SIDE ROD
SEAT

12689
SIDE ROD
AND CLIP
ASSEMBLY
SERVICE KIT
ALL WASTE
UNITS

TAILPIECE →

TUB WASTE (COMPLETE ASSEMBLY)
Model 15480 — Antique Goldtone Brocade
Model 15485 — Gold Brocade
Model 15490 — Antique Brass
Model 15520 — Satin Brass

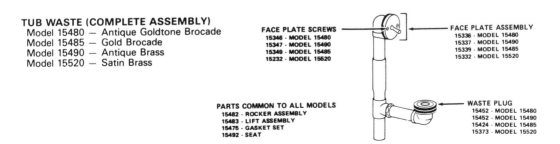

FACE PLATE SCREWS
15346 - MODEL 15480
15347 - MODEL 15490
15349 - MODEL 15485
15232 - MODEL 15520

FACE PLATE ASSEMBLY
15336 - MODEL 15480
15337 - MODEL 15490
15339 - MODEL 15485
15332 - MODEL 15520

PARTS COMMON TO ALL MODELS
15482 - ROCKER ASSEMBLY
15483 - LIFT ASSEMBLY
15475 - GASKET SET
15492 - SEAT

WASTE PLUG
15452 - MODEL 15480
15452 - MODEL 15490
15424 - MODEL 15485
15373 - MODEL 15520

VALLEY FAUCET DIVISION
OF UNITED STATES BRASS CORPORATION
MAINTENANCE INSTRUCTIONS
This faucet has been pre-tested at the factory, however, it is recommended that the owner retain this service sheet for future reference.

INSTRUCTIONS FOR FAUCET DISASSEMBLY

NOTE: Procedure is the same for single handle or lever models except as noted in instructions.

Faucet disassembly can be simplified by completing steps 1 & 2 before turning water supply off.

STEP 1—Loosen set screw at rear of handle and lift off handle. See figure 1.

STEP 2—Loosen bonnet about one turn. (Water pressure will lift control assembly slightly. In case of a tight control assembly, turn water on to a trickle and place thumb over aerator. Pressure build up in the valve will give additional boost to push assembly loose.)

CAUTION: When loosening the bonnet with water supply on, be careful not to unscrew too far. A good check is to observe the gap between the bonnet and the spout hub. This should be about the thickness of a coin. (eg. Nickel)

STEP 3—TURN OFF MAIN WATER SUPPLY LINES BELOW SINK

STEP 4—Remove bonnet completely. See Figure 2.

STEP 5—Lift out control assembly. If necessary, use screwdriver under ears of retainer to ease control assembly from core. See Figure 3.

STEP 6—Remove seals and springs. See Figure 4.

STEP 7—To remove spout lift while turning. To remove O-rings, lift out of grooves and replace. Rings are lubricated for easy assembly, but care must be exercised so as not to cut O-rings. See Figure 5.

RE-ASSEMBLY

STEP 8—Seals R-700, can be easily replaced by slipping the seal and then the spring R-701 on the eraser end of an ordinary pencil, and then pushing seal into the core. Seals should sit upright in core and the face of the seal should be about 1/16 inch above the core and move freely. See Figure 7.

STEP 9—Flat on driver mates with flat in control plate. Figure 8 shows proper relationship of control plate relative to the front of, and the slot in the core. The "V" of the control assembly points to the front of the unit.

STEP 10—Place control assembly into core and push all the way down making sure that the ears of the control assembly are in the slots in the core, and flat on stem is to rear. (On shower models the flat should be to the floor)

STEP 11—Replace bonnet and tighten firmly by hand.

STEP 12—Turn adjusting ring down, using special wrench shown. (See Figure 2) until snug and then back off approximately 1/4 turn.

STEP 13—Replace handle on stem making sure it is all the way down and that set screw is on the flat of the stem. Tighten set screw.

STEP 14—To remove diverter from spout, unscrew aerator, hold hand under spout, slowly turn water on. Water will dislodge diverter.

MAINTENANCE INSTRUCTIONS

1. FAUCET DOES NOT SHUT OFF.
   a) Follow disassembly through step 5. Make sure seals move up and down freely and are in a vertical position. See Figure 7. Seal face should rise about 1/16 inch above core face.
   b) Replace seals if nicked or deformed.
   c) Replace control assembly if control plate is scored or nicked.
   d) Check engagement of control plate and driver as described in Step 9. Make sure handle set screw is to the rear and engages flat on stem.

2. LEAKAGE FROM BENEATH HANDLE.
   a) Follow disassembly through Step 5. Replace control plate O-ring and retainer O-ring. If retainer is scored, replace control assembly.

3. LEAKAGE FROM TOP/BOTTOM OF SPOUT HUB.
   a) Follow disassembly steps 1, 3, 4 and 7. Replace O-ring, seals on core. Do not remove lubricant from seals or O-rings.

4. DECREASE IN FLOW OF WATER WITH USAGE, OR IMPROPER FUNCTION OF SPRAY ON SOME MODELS.
   a) Unscrew aerator and (if spray model) remove diverter. See Step 14. Flush parts and reassemble.
   b) On spray models unscrew nozzle from spray head, flush and re-assemble.

FIG. 2

FIG. 3

FIG. 4

FIG. 5

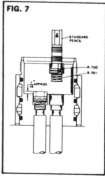
FIG. 7

STANDARD PENCIL
R-700
R-701
APPROX

FIG. 8

FLAT IN CONTROL PLATE SHOULD BE IN POSITION SHOWN
SLOT IN CORE
R-153 CONTROL PLATE
FRONT OF UNIT (DECK OR LAVATORY) DOWN (SHOWER)

POP-UP INSTALLATION GUIDE

NON-METALLIC POP-UP

IMPORTANT– THE WHITE GASKET IS SUPPLIED WITH EACH POP-UP TO SEAL UNDER THE FLANGE. HOWEVER, IF YOU ENCOUNTER A SINK WITH AN UNUSUALLY ROUGH SURFACE, IT MAY BE REQUIRED TO USE PUTTY IN ADDITION TO THE GASKET OR IN PLACE OF IT.

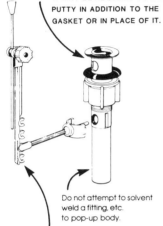

Do not attempt to solvent weld a fitting, etc. to pop-up body.

Pivot rod can be removed–from strap assembly and snapped into upper or lower connecting "C" for added adjustability.

IMPORTANT–Stopper can be installed either removable or non-removable.

REMOVABLE STOPPER INSTALLATION
Install complete pop-up assembly without stopper. Drop stopper into pop-up so that bottom ledge of stopper rests on pivot rod.

NON-REMOVABLE STOPPER INSTALLATION
Before installing pivot rod and strap assembly insert stopper into pop-up. Assemble pivot–strap assembly to pop-up body so that pivot rod goes through lower opening of stopper.

WHEN PERFORMING ROUTINE MAINTENANCE USE ONLY GENUINE DELTA REPLACEMENT PARTS.

INSTALLATION STEPS

METAL POP-UP

STRAP MAY BE BENT if necessary to connect properly with horizontal ball lift rod.

IMPORTANT–Lay ring of putty beneath pop-up flange before installing.

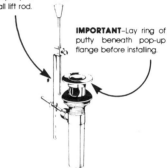

IMPORTANT–Stopper can be installed either removable or non-removable.

REMOVABLE STOPPER INSTALLATION
Install entire pop-up assembly without stopper in unit. Drop stopper in so bottom "U" bail goes to either side of horizontal ball rod.

NON-REMOVABLE STOPPER INSTALLATION
Install stopper "U" bail toward back. Insert ball rod through bail.

DELTA FAUCET COMPANY

Route 46 West
P.O. Box 47
Greensburg, Indiana 47240

251

Price Pfister has carefully engineered this Valve to provide a long trouble-free service life under normal usage. This Valve has been factory-engineered, tested and is ready for installation.

INSTALLATION INSTRUCTIONS

Read installation instructions thoroughly to familiarize yourself with the parts and their names.

I TO ROUGH-IN VALVE BODY (1)

1. Recommended VALVE CENTER LINE dimensions from SUPPLY INLET to FINISHED WALL to be:
   "Verve" and "Marquis" Trim 2 1/2"
   "All Brass" Trim 2 5/8"
   NOTE: STEM PROTECTORS not to be removed until FINISHED WALL is completed and ready for Handle Trim.

II SUPPLY CONNECTIONS

1. COLD on right side, and HOT on left side.
   NOTE: Usable with either TOP or BOTTOM SUPPLY CONNECTIONS.

III TO TRIM VALVE

1. Remove STEM PROTECTORS.
2. Screw Escutcheon Nipples (2) into bushings (3) fingertight.
3. "Verve" and "Marquis" Trim.
   a. Screw Flanges (4) onto Escutcheon Nipples (2) snug against wall.
4. "All Brass" Trim
   a) Place Flanges (5) onto Escutcheon Nipples (2) and thread Sleeves (6) onto Escutcheon Nipples (2) until Flanges (5) are snug against wall.
5. Install Handle components on valve stems.
   a) "Verve" Trim
   Attach Handles (7) onto valve stems with Screws (8). With valves in closed position, snap Plug Buttons (9) into Handles (7); "C" on right side and Arrow in the center pointing "down".
   b) "Marquis" Trim
   Attach Handle Insert (10) and Handle (11) onto valve stem with Screw (12). With valves in closed position, snap Plug Buttons (13) into Handles (11); "H" on left side and "Arrow" in the center pointing down.
   c) "All Brass" Trim
   Attach Handles (14) onto valve stems with Screws (15). With valves in closed position, snap Plug Buttons (16) into Handles (14); "H" on left side, "C" on right side and "Price Pfister" Button in the center.
   NOTE: For top inlet supply connections, center diverter stem to be in open position when handle is attached.

IV FLUSH VALVE BY RUNNING BOTH HOT AND COLD WATER IN FULL OPEN POSITION

VERVE MARQUIS BRASS TRIM
8" Three Valve Diverter Units
CATALOG NO'S 01 SERIES

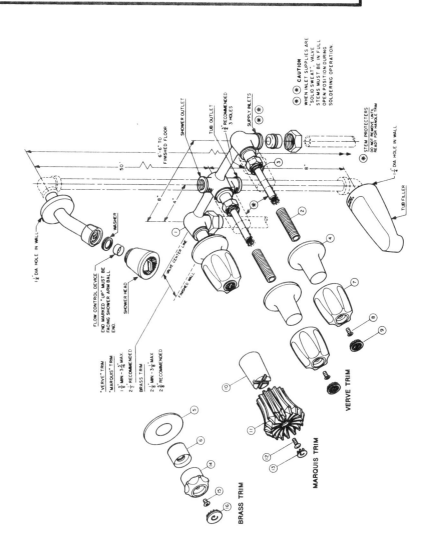

"VERVE" TRIM
1 1/8" MIN - 3 1/2" MAX.
2 1/2" RECOMMENDED

BRASS TRIM
2 1/8" MIN - 3 1/2" MAX.
2 1/4" RECOMMENDED

SHOWER OUTLET
TUB OUTLET
RECOMMENDED 3 HOLES
SUPPLY INLETS
SHOWER HEAD
FLOW CONTROL DEVICE END MARKED "UP" MUST BE FACING SHOWER ARM BALL END.
WASHER
MAIN CENTER LINE
FINISHED WALL
1 1/4" DIA HOLE IN WALL
6'-6" TO FINISHED FLOOR
5'-0"
8"
4"
8"
TUB FILLER
1" DIA HOLE IN WALL
STEM PROTECTERS DO NOT REMOVE UNTIL READY FOR HANDLE TRIM

CAUTION
WHEN INLET SUPPLIES ARE "SOLID SWEAT", VALVE STEMS MUST BE IN FULL OPEN POSITION DURING SOLDERING OPERATION.

MARQUIS TRIM
VERVE TRIM
BRASS TRIM

Glossary

adapter—A pipe or tubing fitting designed to enable one form or type of tubing or pipe to be connected to another to make a leak-proof joint.

angle valve—A water or gas valve designed to allow a pipe to enter from the bottom of the valve (opposite the handle) and another pipe to leave from the side of the valve (at right angles to the handle).

anti-syphon valve—A valve that will not allow water to flow or be drawn backwards into a clean water system in the event that a vacuum forms in the system.

back vent—A vent line installed directly behind a fixture. It may vent to the atmosphere or into another main vent line.

ball cock—A faucet type device controlled by a hollow ball floating on water in a water closet tank that stops the flow of water when the tank is full.

basket strainer—The lift-out strainer in a kitchen sink that can be turned or pushed down to stop up the sink drain so it holds water.

bell (hub)—The large end on clay or cast-iron soil pipe, into which the plain end of another soil pipe is inserted.

branch—Any part of a piping system that is not a main line.

building sanitary drain—A drain that carries sewage only.

building sewer—The sewer line from the building to the public sewer or private disposal system.

building supply line—The water line directly after the water meter that supplies water to the fixtures.

bypass—A connecting line between the inlet and outlet of a device such as a water softener. This consists of two tees, one in the inlet and one in the outlet. The side openings of both tees are connected together by pipe nipples and a shutoff valve. Below this assembly are valves just above the top of the device. When these are closed the device can be serviced.

check valve—A special valve having a flapper plate hinged and lying against a slanting seat. Water or gas thus can flow in only one direction, by pushing on the flapper. Reverse flow is stopped by the closing of the flapper against the seat.

cleanout—An access to the sewer lines installed at convenient locations, usually at a change in direction of the line, for the purpose of cleaning the sewer line.

common seal trap—The standard trap sold in hardwares and home centers.

compression faucet—A standard faucet in which the washer is compressed down upon the seat by a stem having threads and a handle on the top of the stem.

corporation stop—A valve in the water line as it leaves the street water main.

curb cock or **curb stop**—A valve located near the curb or sidewalk to turn the water off when conditions warrant it—such as when water leaks underground between the cock and the dwelling, or when water bills are not paid.

drum trap—A cylindrical cast body with inlet and outlet, used formerly on bathtubs.

dwv—Copper tubing or galvanized iron pipe used for drainage, waste, and vent. Copper tubing for this purpose is similar to other copper tubing but the wall is thinner as no pressure exists.

female thread—An internal thread on pipe or fitting ends.

finish work—The installation of plumbing fixtures and trim after building construction is nearly complete.

fittings—Plumbing materials such as elbows, tees, adapters, bushings, reducers, and unions.

fixture drain—The pipe leaving the fixture trap and connecting to a main drain.

floor drain—A flush drain usually in basements and laundry rooms to receive any water from the floor.

flood level rim—The top edge of a tub or fixture from which water would overflow.

flush valve—The rubber ball or flapper that is raised when the flush lever of a water closet is pushed down.

gate valve—A water valve that is closed by a flat piece of metal sliding down in grooves inside the valve body. This metal piece is the "gate."

globe valve—Similar to a compression faucet except both ends have female threads for pipe.

grade/pitch—The slant or slope of a length of pipe so that one end is lower than the other. Usually used for drain and sewer lines.

horizontal drain (branch)—A drain running horizontally from a fixture and connecting to another horizontal drain and then into a vertical drain line to the sewer.

hub—*See* bell.

lavatory—Sink used in a bathroom for washing hands and face.

male thread—An external thread on a pipe end or fitting end.

offset—A change in direction of a pipe line to one side and then a change back to the original direction but parallel to the original direction (as a "jog in a road").

plug—A solid metal piece having male threads, used to stop a flow of liquid or gas from a valve or other female fitting.

plumbing fixture—Plumbing ware, such as lavatory, bathtub, water closet, or laundry tray.

pressure reducing valve—A device to reduce excessive pressure of the water supply to a dwelling. Usually set at 40 psi.

psi—Pounds per square inch.

P trap—*See* common seal trap.

relief valve—Any device for relieving excessive pressure in a vessel or pipe. *Also see* temperature and pressure relief valve.

riser—A vertical water supply pipe.

rough-in—The installation of pipes for water, drainage, and vents necessary for proper operation of the system. Also included are the necessary supports for the pipework.

sill cock—A hose faucet on the outside of a dwelling.

soil pipe—When soil pipe is assembled it forms the sewer line from the house to the sewer main in the street.

stack cleanout—A tee in a vertical sewer line having the side outlet plugged (usually 4-inch) with a plug. This is used to clear the line using a sewer "snake."

stop and waste valve—A valve in the line to an outside sill cock to shut off the water in winter. A small cap on the side of the valve is removed after the valve is closed to drain the sill cock and line between it and the stop and waste.

stop box—Cast-iron pipe leading down to location of curb stop (valve to shut off water to dwelling). A long rod is used to operate this valve. A cast-iron cover closes the top opening.

storm sewer—A sewer system carrying only surface water from rains and storms. No sewage is carried.

syphonage—A condition whereby contaminated water or other liquids are sucked into a clean water system. When the clean water system is drained for any reason a vacuum is formed in the system, and contaminated liquids are drawn in.

temperature and pressure relief valve—This device is used on gas and electric water heaters to prevent an explosion in the event the fuel control fails to shut off. This valve will open and discharge water to relieve this dangerous condition.

water closet—Toilet bowl and tank.

water hammer—A banging of water pipes when an automatic valve closes suddenly.

water heater—An appliance to heat water using gas, electricity, or sometimes oil. It works automatically.

water meter—A recording device to register the amount of water used in a dwelling. May be manual or automatic.

water softener—A special device to soften domestic water by removing the minerals that cause hardness.

vacuum—A condition in which the pressure in a vessel or piping system is less than atmospheric pressure.

valve—A device to close a line carrying water or gas.

Index

Edited by Cherie R. Blazer

Other Bestsellers From TAB

☐ **DREAM HOMES: 66 PLANS TO MAKE YOUR DREAMS COME TRUE—Jerold L. Axelrod, Architect**

If you are planning on—or just dreaming of—building a new home, you will find this book completely fascinating. Compiled by a well-known architect whose home designs have been featured regularly in the syndicated "House of the Week" and *Home* magazine, this beautifully bound volume presents one of the finest collections of luxury home designs ever assembled in a single volume! 88 pp., 201 illus., 20 pp. of full-color illus. 8 1/2" × 11".

Paper $16.95   **Hard $29.95**
Book No. 2829

☐ **MAJOR HOME APPLIANCES: A Common Sense Repair Manual—Rains**

Prolong the life and efficiency of your major appliances . . . save hundreds of dollars in appliance servicing and repair costs . . . eliminate the inconvenience of having an appliance quit just when you need it most *and* the frustration of having to wait days, even weeks, until you can get a serviceman in to repair it! With the help and advice of service professional Darell L. Rains, even the most inexperienced home handyman can easily keep any major appliances working at top efficiency year after year. 160 pp., 387 illus., 7" × 10".

Paper $14.95   **Hard $21.95**
Book No. 2747

☐ **THE COMPLETE BOOK OF BATHROOMS—Ramsey and Self**

Simple redecorating tricks . . . remodeling advice . . . plumbing techniques . . . it's all here. Find literally hundreds of photographs, drawings, and floorplans to help you decide exactly what kind of remodeling project you'd like to undertake; plus, step-by-step directions for accomplishing your remodeling goals. It's all designed to save you time and money on your bathroom renovations! 368 pp., 474 illus. 7" × 10".

Paper $15.95   **Hard $24.95**
Book No. 2708

☐ **ALL ABOUT LAMPS: CONSTRUCTION, REPAIR AND RESTORATION—Coggins**

You'll find step-by-step directions for making a wall lamp or a hanging lamp from wood, novelty lamps from PVC plumbing pipe, and designer lamps from acrylic or polyester resins. Shade projects range from needlepoint and fabric models to globes, balls, and tubular forms. There are suggestions for advanced projects, using salvaged and low-cost materials, and more! 192 pp., 196 illus. 7" × 10".

Paper $16.95   **Hard $24.95**
Book No. 2658

☐ **HOW TO PLAN, CONTRACT AND BUILD YOUR OWN HOME—Richard M. Scutella and Dave Heberle, Illustrations by Jay Marcinowski**

After consulting the expert information, instruction, and advice in this guide, you'll have the basic understanding of house construction that you need to get involved in all the planning and construction particulars and pre-construction choices entailed in building your home. Best of all, by learning how to make these decisions yourself, you can make choices to *your* advantage . . . not the builders. 440 pp., illustrated.

Paper $14.95   **Hard $19.95**
Book No. 2806

☐ **THE BUILDING PLAN BOOK: Complete Plans for 21 Affordable Homes—Ernie Bryant**

Here, in one impressive, well-illustrated volume, are complete building plans for a total of 21 custom-designed homes offering a full range of styles and features—efficiency dwellings, ranches, capes, two-story homes, split-levels, even duplexes. It's a collection of practical, good looking home designs that not only offer comfort, convenience, and charm but can also be built at a reasonable cost. 352 pp., 316 illus., 8 1/2" × 11".

Paper $14.95   **Hard $24.95**
Book No. 2714

☐ **THE ILLUSTRATED DICTIONARY OF BUILDING MATERIALS AND TECHNIQUES—Paul Bianchina**

Here's a one-stop reference for do-it-yourselfers and professionals that gives you clear, straightforward definitions for all of the tools, terms, materials, and techniques used by builders, contractors, architects, and other building professionals. It includes almost 4,000 terms and abbreviations from the simple to the complex, from slang to the latest technical information. 272 pp., 172 illus.

Paper $14.95   **Hard $22.95**
Book No. 2681

☐ **UPHOLSTERY TECHNIQUES ILLUSTRATED—Gheen**

Here's an easy-to-follow, step-by-step guide to modern upholstery techniques that covers everything from stripping off old covers and padding to restoring and installing new foundations, stuffing, cushions, and covers. All the most up-to-date pro techniques are included along with lots of time- and money-saving "tricks-of-the-trade" not usually shared by professional upholsterers. 352 pp., 549 illus., 7" × 10".

Paper $16.95   **Book No. 2602**

Other Bestsellers From TAB